*my thoughts on*

# VICTORIOUS
# CONFESSIONS

30TH ANNIVERSARY EDITION

*my thoughts on*

# VICTORIOUS CONFESSIONS

PASTOR BRIDGET **HILLIARD**

My Thoughts on Victorious Confessions: 30th Anniversary Edition
Copyright © 2015 by Bridget E. Hilliard
ISBN 13: 978-1-881357-07-0


Published by New Spectrum Media Concepts
15814 Champions Forest Drive #75
Spring, TX 77379
mynsmc@gmail.com

Visit our Website at www.newlight.org

Printed in the United States of America

# Contents

# Dedication

To my husband, best friend and pastor, Bishop I.V. Hilliard, I dedicate this book to you because you first modeled for me the power of confession. We have seen our words become a reality.

To my children and grandchildren, I dedicate this book to you as a guide to always speak life over yourselves and your future. I agree with every good word you have spoken over your life.

To the church like no other, New Light Church, I dedicate this book to you because you have had a front row seat in seeing what God can do with people who will trust Him at the not knowing level. The best is truly yet to come.

To all of the spiritual children that God has brought into my life, I dedicate this book to you as a source of strength and wisdom as you walk through life. God's Word will never fail you.

Finally, I dedicate this 30th Anniversary Edition to a new generation of believers who will trust God enough to speak His Word regardless of their circumstances.

# Introduction

*"For assuredly, I say to you, whoever says to this mountain, 'Be removed and be cast into the sea,' and does not doubt in his heart, but believes that those things he says will be done, he will have whatever he says." (Mark 11:23 NKJ)*

Your words matter. We will always have what we say. This was a powerful truth that I learned years ago and it has revolutionized my life. When I first started seeing results from speaking God's Word, I wrote the first edition of this book. Now, 30 years later, I have seen God do exponentially more— not only in my life but also in the lives of others. It has been my joy to see so many people embrace this simple, yet powerful, faith component.

I wrote this book to show how Faith Confession works. I have seen confession change me from the inside out and I have seen it change situations and circumstances around me. God's Word really does work! I still have a passion to see other people win in life by changing what comes out of their mouths.

The right words out of your mouth can change your whole life for the better! I know this is true and the thousands who have joined me in confessing God's Word are witnesses. To show you how effective confession is, I have included testimonies of people just like you who developed the discipline to speak God's Word over their lives. I want you to see God's Word work in your life as well.

A faith confession is a statement that you choose to make in agreement with God's Word regardless of your situation. When you speak, you are either releasing faith or doubt. You will face internal resistance when you begin to confess God's Word. However, you cannot stop making your faith confessions. If you stay the course, and overcome all the internal and external resistance, you will see God's Word produce for you just like it has for so many others and me. The confessions that you are reading have been tested and proven to work.

Each faith confession has the Biblical reference documented so that you will know that your faith rests in God's Word and not in human wisdom. I have also included testimonies of real people who have used these confessions and the amazing manifestations that took place when they committed to confess God's Word over their lives. The same thing will happen for you. Whatever has been a barrier to your success and winning in life will be overcome through daily faith confessions.

I wrote this book to help you. Please don't let it sit on a shelf. Use it as a daily tool to keep you in faith and raise your level of expectation. Your faith will produce what you require in life. Don't settle for sickness, lack, or poverty. Expect that God can turn even the worst situation in your favor. Then release your faith by speaking God's Word. Your circumstances will change and you will discover that God designed you to win!

You will win with your words!

# Faith Confession Changed My Life

My relationship with God started at a very early age. We were taught the importance of giving our lives to Jesus and I made that decision as a little girl. Before I get too far into my story, I want to make certain that you have made the most important decision in your life, and that is to give your heart to Jesus. Jesus is God's best for your life! You can never win in life without Him. Here is a simple confession that will bring you the assurance of salvation.

## SALVATION CONFESSION

Father, in the Name of Jesus, I believe Your Word that says if I ask You to save me You will. Jesus, take the throne of my heart and be my Lord. I believe Jesus died and rose from the dead just for me, therefore I accept Jesus as my Lord and Savior. Father, fill me with Your Spirit so I can live a life pleasing to You. Thank You Father for saving me in Jesus' Name. Amen.

If that was the first time you made a confession like this, I really want to hear from you. At the end of the book, is my address. Please write to me and let me know that you are a part of the family of God!

Even though I was a Christian, I did not have an experience with the Holy Spirit. It was in 1982 when the Word of God personally impacted my life. I was in Los Angeles, California during a difficult time in my life. But God had a plan. I was led to attend an evening service on September 2, 1982. I clearly heard a teaching on the baptism with the Holy Spirit and my life was forever changed. That night, I was filled with the Holy Spirit with the evidence of speaking in tongues.

I want you to know that this experience, the baptism with the Holy Spirit, is available to you right now if you are a believer. Here is a confession for you to invite the Spirit of God into your life.

# CONFESSION TO BE FILLED WITH THE SPIRIT

Father, Your Word declares that after salvation I can ask You for the Holy Spirit and You would fill me with Your power to live a victorious life. I receive the power of the Holy Spirit right now and, I yield my mind, my thoughts and my tongue to You. I know that You will not overtake me and make me speak. I have to speak. So, I thank You, Father, for filling me with the Holy Spirit and I speak in tongues as the Spirit gives utterance. I decree that out of my belly flows rivers of living water as I pray in the spirit daily. Thank You, Father, that You understand what I am saying and, as I pray in the spirit, I build myself up on my most holy faith in Jesus' Name.

After I was filled with God's spirit, I was given a little booklet to help me learn more about this wonderful experience. In that book, I found a Scripture that literally changed my life forever. I had no idea about the awesome things that would happen as a result of reading that book on my plane ride back home.

The Scripture was I John 5:14-15, *"And this is the confidence that we have in Him, that, if we ask any thing according to His will, He heareth us: And if we know that He hear us, we know we have the petitions we desired of Him."* I centered in on the words, *"If we ask anything according to His will, He hears us and we know we have the petitions we desired of Him."*

That word "petition" jumped out at me. I was always taught that the Word of God represented God's will. I also knew that a petition was a written request. I had been taught that to have an effective prayer life, there were very clear Biblical requirements. I knew prayer had to be audible; I had to verbalize my petition. Based on all of this, I had several things to do.

First, I had to find my desire in the Word of God. If my request was not based on the Word then I knew God would not hear it and my prayers would be in vain. Next, I had to speak that desire out of my mouth. Third, I had to have confidence in God and await the manifestation.

As I began to study the Word of God for my specific petitions, I began to grow in my knowledge of the Word of God. I surrounded myself with people who taught the Word in a manner that I could understand. I began to learn a powerful principle as I awaited the manifestation of the prayers I had prayed.

*"For verily I say unto you, that whosoever shall say unto this mountain, Be thou removed, and be thou cast into the sea; and shall not doubt in his heart, but shall believe that those things which he saith shall come to pass; he shall have whatsoever he saith. Therefore I say unto you, what things soever ye desire when ye pray, believe that ye receive them, and ye shall have them." (Mark 11:23-24 KJV)*

It became evident that my words mattered. I realized that what came out of my mouth would impact my situation. I needed to monitor the words I spoke. This was all a part of the faith process that I learned. I believe that once we give our hearts to Jesus, faith is the most important topic that we should learn. Without faith in God's Word, we will never see real manifestation of our prayers.

Once I found the promise in God's Word concerning my circumstance, I asked God in faith for it. Then, I knew I needed to release my faith by the words I spoke. This is called a faith confession. I choose as an act of my will to speak in accordance with the Word of God. My words would create a blessed future or a bleak future. I desired better for my life and I knew God's Word would produce it.

*"Thou art snared with the words of thy mouth…" Proverbs 6:2 (KJV)*

God revealed to me that I was ensnared by the words I spoke. I was my own worst enemy.

*"Death and life are in the power of the tongue…" Proverbs 18:21a (KJV)*

Even though I had confidence in God and His Word, God was expecting me to operate by the Spiritual law of faith. I needed to learn to discipline myself to speak only God's Word over my life and situations rather than speaking my present circumstances or how I felt.

Words are powerful containers; they can carry faith or fear. I had to choose to speak faith-filled words. Faith-filled words would create the blessed life that God had promised me.

*"So then faith cometh by hearing, and hearing by the Word of God."* Romans 10: 17 (KJV)

I would more readily receive God's Word by hearing myself saying it than by hearing someone else say it. Your voice is the most authoritative voice to you. What you hear yourself say causes everything within you to take notice. I later learned that we are *"speaking spirits"* and we operate just like God operated in creation. What He spoke, came to pass. If I possessed the same tenacity to speak God's Word consistently, it would create a new reality.

The principle of confession consumed me and I knew this was the key to my breakthrough. I began to develop faith confessions about every situation of my life. What is a faith confession? A statement has been coined about a faith confession that I believe helped me to grasp exactly what it means to confess God's Word. A faith confession is a statement I choose to make in agreement with the Word of God regardless of my circumstances. I had to begin to put pressure on my mouth and speak what God's Word said regardless of how I felt, what I saw, or what I was going through at the time.

Mark 11:23-24 (KJV) says, *"For verily I say unto you, That whosoever shall say unto this mountain, Be thou removed, and be thou cast into the sea; and shall not doubt in his heart, but shall believe those things which he saith shall come to pass; he shall have whatsoever he saith. Therefore I say unto you, What things soever ye desire, when ye pray, believe that ye receive them, and you shall have them."*

The *"believing you receive"* process starts the moment you pray. According to Colossians 1:16 and Matthew 16:17, there are two arenas: the visible (natural, seen, physical, tangible) and the invisible (spiritual, unseen, intangible). You bring your desire from the spiritual arena (unseen, intangible) into the natural arena (seen, physical, tangible) by the confessions of your mouth.

The Bible says in many places God *"hath"* blessed us. *"Hath"* signifies a past tense designation. (Ephesians 1:3; Colossians

1:13). Therefore, if I pray and believe I receive what I prayed for, I will have it by what I say.

The word "*saith*" in verse 23 is a continuous ad infinitum which means say it and say it and say it and say it continuously. So, if I believe I receive when I pray and continue to say it and say it and say it, regardless of what is happening right now, I will have what I say.

The clearest explanation I have heard on this principle is the example of what occurs when you put an item on layaway at a department store. You don't actually have the item in your hand but you have a receipt; the item is stored in a warehouse with your name on it. But, because you know that you have the receipt, you tell people about your new purchase and how happy you are to own it even though you don't physically have it in your possession.

Hebrews 11:1 says, "*Now faith [the Word of God] is the substance of things hoped for, the evidence of things not seen.*"

When I confess the Word of God for that which I have prayed, it is as if I am making payments on a layaway plan. If I continue to make my payments (confessions), I will have the item so that everyone can see it. The confession of your mouth operates by the same principle. You continue to say what the Word says, and eventually you will have the thing you believed you received when you prayed. It is as if the day you prayed about the desire, and believed you received your desire, the angels in heaven set the desire aside for you in a "spiritual layaway." The Word of God is your evidence (receipt) that the thing you desire is set aside for you. As you make your faith confession, it is as if you are making payments on your desire and it gets closer and closer to the natural realm.

Jesus made statements of faith throughout His earthly ministry. He spoke to a tree that was barren and it dried up from the roots (Mark 11:12-14, 20); He spoke to wind in the midst of a storm and calmed the storm (Mark 4:37-39); and He even told His disciples they could speak to mountains (Mark 11:23).

" *(As it is written, I have made thee a father of many nations,) before him whom he believed, even God, who quickeneth the dead, and calleth those things which be not as though they were. 18 Who against hope believed in hope, that he might become the father of many nations, according to that which was spoken, So shall thy seed be. 19 And being not weak in faith, he considered not his own body now dead, when he was about an hundred years old, neither yet the deadness of Sarah's womb: 20 He staggered not at the promise of God through unbelief; but was strong in faith, giving glory to God;"* (Romans 4:17-20 KJV)

Abram was an elderly man when he received the word from God that he would be a father. Sarai was an elderly woman when her husband Abram told her God wanted to bless her womb to bring forth a child. At the time God spoke to Abram, Sarai was barren, and her womb was dead. Yet, God told them they would have a son. The first thing that God did was change their names. He did this because he wanted them to begin to speak faith-filled words about their situation. You see, Abram's (Abraham) new name now meant "Father of Nations" and Sarai's (Sarah) new name now meant "Mother of Many" (Genesis 17: 5, 15- 16). Although Abram and Sarai had no children, each time they called one another by their new name, it released faith because they were speaking what God's will was for them. So, in my own life I began to ignore my circumstances and began to speak God's Word.

I do need to caution you that unrepented or habitual sin does affect your confessions. I do not want you to miss out on what God has promised you because you have not dealt with persistent sin in your life. So, here is a confession that will bring you to a place of victory as you say it daily. Even if the sin continues, don't stop confessing the Word. The Word will drive that sin out of your life.

# CONFESSION FOR VICTORY OVER SIN

Father, in Jesus' Name, I thank You that I have victory over sin. Sin will not reign in my body and I habitually put my flesh to death. I thank You, Father, that I know how to possess my vessel in sanctification and honor. I thank You that Jesus Christ is Lord over my spirit, soul and body. I flee sin and all acts of immorality, adultery, fornication, lying and all deceitful lust. Jesus, You are Lord over my spirit, soul and body. I give no place, toehold, room or opportunity to the devil to encroach upon my thought life. I cast down imaginations and every high thing that exalts itself against the Word and will of God for my life. I think only those things that are true, honest, pure and of good report about myself and others. I will not be tormented by my past errors and mistakes. I take authority over my thought life and apply the cleansing power of the Blood of Jesus over my emotions and my imagination. I am the righteousness of God and I am in the family of God not because of what

I have done but because of what Jesus has done for me. I thank You Father that Your blood cleanses me, heals me and restores me back in right standing with You. I boldly confess from this day forward that I live a life that pleases You. I declare my body is the temple of the Holy Spirit and I choose to live a holy life. I choose to hear Your voice and the voice of the stranger I choose not follow. I submit myself to Your Word, Father, and Your will for my life and choose to do those things that please You. I make a quality decision to not allow the lust of my flesh to rule over me I submit my thoughts purposes and will to You. I choose to live a holy life because I owe it to God who saved me. I owe it to my family who depends on me. I owe it to my friends who need my example and I owe it to myself because I am free from the bondage of sin I am the righteousness of God in Jesus' Name.

This is so important because I have encountered many who desire God's best but they have allowed sin to get them off track. I don't want this to be your testimony. Once you have gain victory over your habitual sin, then you can have confidence when you declare God's Word.

Now, back to my story.

In 1979 and 1980, my husband, Ira and I went through a very tragic church fight. People who had once proclaimed their love for us turned their backs on us and began to persecute us in ways I had never seen before. We were disrespected in front of our family and our peers. It was a loss of dignity and pride and a very emotional setback for me. I almost became an emotional wreck. I began to lose my hair, I nearly had a breakdown, and I even developed a hatred for the people who had created this ungodly situation.

Even though Ira, being led by God, organized a new church, I did not like church people and had no desire to get close to people again. I would leave the church building as soon as church services were over, take my girls and go sit in the car with all the windows rolled up. I would not talk to anybody because I was so hurt. I spent many days crying and pondering over the things that happened to us. I wanted so badly for everyone to hurt just as I was hurting. I lost all patience with people and I even began to treat Ira meanly and unkindly. I was a wreck, emotionally, spiritually, and physically. I almost got to the point where I thought life was not worth living…until I found 1 Corinthians 10:13 (KJV), "There hath no temptation [trial or test] taken you but such as is common to man: but GOD is faithful, who will not suffer [allow] you to be tempted above that ye are able; but will with the temptation also make a way to escape, that ye may be able to bear it."

*Now look at that verse in the Amplified Version. "For no temptation (no trial regarding as enticing to sin, no matter how it comes or where it leads) has overtaken you or laid hold on you that is not common to man {that is, no temptation or trial has come to you that is beyond human resistance and that is not adjusted and adapted and belonging to human experience, and such as man can bear}. But God is faithful {to His Word and His compassionate nature}, and He [can be trusted] not to let you be tempted and tried and assayed beyond your ability and strength of resistance and power to endure, but with the temptation He will [always] also provide the way out (the means to escape to a landing place), that you may be capable and strong and powerful to bear up under it patiently." (1 Corinthians 10:13)*

After being baptized with the Holy Spirit, I realized I could not enjoy God's best with that excess baggage in my life. I could have remained in the state I was in and been miserable for the rest of my life. I thank God I chose to change. That change was not instantaneous, but it was a gradual change as I began to put pressure on my mouth to change my situation.

Even though the change was gradual, it has been life-changing and I thank God! There are basically two types of changes that can take place in one's life: situational (circumstantial) and behavioral. My circumstances or situations didn't change immediately; however, my behavior changed and my attitude about the circumstances changed immediately. The change in the way I viewed my circumstances eventually caused the circumstances to change. I no longer saw myself struggling with life's situations alone; I now had God's help and God's Word changing the circumstances.

Even though I was so distraught and my thinking was clouded with un-forgiveness and hatred, the Word of God began to penetrate through that cloud and change me. This is what I love about God's Word! It will always work if we apply it. I began to see myself differently as the Word of God began to minister to me. I really don't remember when or how long it took the change to manifest but I can look back on those days now and say, "Thank God! He is faithful."

As part of my personal growth, Scriptures like the ones below became a part of my daily meditation:

*"Who hath believed our report? and to whom is the arm of the Lord revealed? For he shall grow up before him as a tender plant, and as a root out of a dry ground: he hath no form nor comeliness; and when we shall see him, there is no beauty that we should desire him. He is despised and rejected of men; a man of sorrows and acquainted with*

grief: and we hid as it were our faces from him: he was despised and we esteemed him not. Surely he hath borne our griefs and carried our sorrows yet we did esteem him stricken, smitten of God and afflicted. But he was wounded for our transgressions, he was bruised for our iniquities; the chastisement of our peace was upon him and with his stripes we are healed." (Isaiah 53:1-5 KJV)

"The Lord is nigh unto them that are of a broken heart and saveth such as be of a contrite spirit." (Psalms 34:18 KJV)

"For though we walk in the flesh, we do not war after the flesh: For the weapons of our warfare are not carnal, but mighty through God to the pulling down of strongholds; Casting down imaginations and every high thing that exalteth itself against the knowledge of God, and bringing into captivity every thought to the obedience of Christ." (2 Corinthians 10:3-5 KJV)

"No weapon that is formed against thee shall prosper and every tongue that shall rise against thee in judgment thou shalt condemn. This is the heritage of the servants of the Lord, and their righteousness is of me saith the Lord." (Isaiah 54:17 KJV)

"Be careful for nothing but in every thing by prayer and supplication with thanksgiving let your request be made known unto God. And the peace of God, which passeth all understanding, shall keep your hearts and minds through Christ Jesus. Finally brethen, whatsoever things are true, whatsoever things are honest, whatsoever things are just, whatsoever things are pure, whatsoever things are lovely, whatsoever things are of a good report; if there be any virtue, if there be any praise, think on these things." (Philippians 4:6-8 KJV)

"The Lord is my light and my salvation; whom shall I fear? the Lord is the strength of my life; of whom shall I be afraid? When the wicked even mine enemies and my foes, came upon me to eat up my flesh, they stumbled and fell. Though an host shall encamp against me, my heart shall not fear: thou war should rise against me, in this will I be confident. One thing have I desired of the Lord and that will I seek after; that I may dwell in the house of the Lord all the days of my life, to behold the beauty of the Lord, and to enquire in his temple. For in the time of trouble he shall hide me in his pavilion; in the secret of his tabernacle shall he hide me; he shall set me up upon a rock." (Psalms 27:1-5 KJV)

"Peace, I leave with you, my peace I give unto you; not as the world giveth, give I unto you. Let not your heart be troubled, neither let it be afraid." (John 14:27 KJV)

"Let not your heart be troubled: ye believe in God, believe also in me." (John 14:1 KJV)

*"Thou wilt keep him in perfect peace whose mind is stayed on thee; because he trusteth in thee." (Isaiah 26:3 KJV)*

*"He that dwelleth in the secret place of the most High shall abide under the shadow of the Almighty. I will say of the Lord, He is my refuge and my fortress; my God in him will I trust." (Psalms 91:1, 2 KJV)*

*"He healeth the broken in heart, and bindeth up their wounds. (Psalms 147:3 KJV)*

*"Casting all your care upon him; for he careth for you." (1 Peter 5:7 KJV)*

*"Cast not away therefore your confidence, which hath great recompense of reward. For ye have need of patience, that after ye have done the will of God, ye might receive the promise." (Hebrews 10:35–36 KJV)*

*"Being confident of this very thing, that he which hath begun a good work in you will perform it until the day of Jesus Christ." (Philippians 1:6 KJV)*

After meditating on these scriptures daily, I then developed various confessions.

# CONFESSION TO OVERCOME PAST HURTS

Father, in Jesus' Name, I thank You that there is no temptation taken me but such as is common to man You are faithful to not allow me to be tempted, tried or tested above that which I am able and You will with every temptation, reveal to me a way of escape to a safe landing place. Father, I trust You for the wisdom and direction to overcome this trial in my life.

Father, I thank You that even though Your Son was rejected and despised by men, He forgave. I now forgive those (call out their names) who hurt me and I choose to walk in that forgiveness from this day forth.

Father, I thank You that You are the God who heals the brokenhearted and You promised to bind up my wounds. I thank You Father no weapon formed against me shall prosper. I choose to only think on those things that are true, honest, pure and of a good report. I cast the whole of my care on You and I know that You care for me. In the day of trouble, I thank You Father that You hide me in Your pavilion. Because I dwell in the secret place of the most High, I will abide under the shadow of the Almighty. I will say of the Lord that You are my refuge and my fortress; my God in You do I trust.

I thank You Father for the peace of God that passeth all understanding and because I keep my mind on You, You keep me in perfect peace. I now have the peace of God that passeth all understanding.

Father, I thank You that I now have the mind of Christ and as I patiently await the manifestation of Your Word in my life, I thank You Father that You have begun a good work in me, and You will perform it until the day of Jesus Christ.

# MY PRESENT PERSONAL DAILY CONFESSION

Father, I love You with all my whole heart, my body and my soul. I thank You it is because of You that I have been made righteous. I have a right to come boldly to Your throne of grace where I know I find mercy and favor to help me just when I need it. Thank You Father daily You are causing others to go out of their way to give me preferential treatment because Your favor surrounds me as a shield.

Father thank You for allowing me the wonderful privilege of being a capable, intelligent and virtuous wife, I decree the heart of my husband does safely trust in me. I live in daily expectation of Your will coming to pass in my life. I plead the blood of Jesus over my children and my grandchildren. I declare no weapon formed against me and my family prospers. We are redeemed from the curse of the law and no plague comes nigh our dwelling. All of my children and grandchildren are marked for the Kingdom of God.

Father, thank You for New Light Church 'the church like no other' I decree we are a light for the lost and hurting to come and find hope and healing. All our partners and members fulfill their purpose in the earth and You are fulfilling their days with health and prosperity. Father, I declare we are living in our best days and there are no feeble among us. Thank You, Father, that every member and partner experiences abundant provisions and supernatural supply for debt reduction, debt removal, debt relief and debt resourcefulness.

Father, thank You for every person that You have connected me with as a friend, Spiritual mother or as a mentor. I decree that I am an asset in every relationship and I handle all my affairs with integrity. I treat every person with the compassion of Jesus. I chose not to be offended or hold grudges because of past errors, bad choices, betrayal and mistakes because I am forgiven, I chose to forgive others and I do everything as unto You Lord.

Father, in the Name of Jesus, I commit my works, my desires and my eating habits to You! I will not be a slave to food. When I find pleasures as sweet as honey like desserts, candy bars, cakes and pies, I only eat what is sufficient for me. All foods are permissible for me but not all foods are helpful and good for me to eat. I will not allow food to Lord over me because I have made Jesus my Lord. I desire to drink water because I know water is a cleansing agent for my organs. My body is the temple of the Holy Spirit and I choose to glorify You with my body. My body belongs to You and I dedicate my body, presenting all my members and faculties as a living sacrifice, pleasing to You. I am a person of discipline and self-control.

Father, You always cause me to triumph in every situation therefore I always WIN in Jesus name!

I share this confession with you so that you can see as the situations in your life change and as your desires in prayer change, your confession changes. Because God's Word has worked so wonderfully in my life, my daily confessions now are just declaring the will of God in my life, my family members' lives and our church.

# Overcoming Financial Challenges

Once Ira and I received the Word of God in our own personal lives, we felt compelled to share what we learned and experienced with others. Despite the fact that I experienced emotional healing, one of the greatest principles I learned from God's Word was the principle of sowing and reaping.

As a teenager, my parents had taught me to give God a portion of what He blessed me with, so I knew about tithing and giving offerings. Ira had also learned to be a tither in his early adult life. We were committed to give God His part from the start of our relationship together. However, it was not until we learned the Word of God that we discovered it was the will of God for us to receive from God and live a prosperous life.

In many of the churches we had been in, no one ever taught us to receive from God. As a matter of fact, they told us that if you were blessed, you should "watch your back" (be cautious or careful), because something bad was going to happen to you. We were never taught to release our faith for God to bless us for what we had given to Him. The idea of even thinking you could confess the Word of God over your financial seed was almost like hypocrisy. But thank God for the truth of God's Word coming to us.

Armed with this truth, we began to confess God's Word over our financial seeds that we had sown and continued to sow. Today, we are living in the manifested reality of those financial seeds sown and the Word of God being made alive in our lives.

I think back on where we were when we started confessing the Word of God over our finances and it is amazing to me where God has brought us. Today, there is no natural need in our lives that God has not totally supplied, and yet, it all started with us giving our tithes and offerings; even though when we started, the amounts were small. We are blessed now to give about twenty-five percent of our yearly income to the work of God.

Prosperity is definitely God's will for His children who are obedient.

*"If they obey and serve Him, they shall spend their days in prosperity and their years in pleasures." Job 36:11 (KJV)*

*"If ye be willing and obedient, ye shall eat the good of the land."* *(Isaiah 1:19 KJV)*

I encourage you to allow God to use your life as a channel of blessings for the Kingdom of God. You will not regret sowing (giving) into the Kingdom of God because as a channel for God's blessings, you will be like a pipe that supplies water. As the pipe supplies the water, the pipe gets wet. As you become a channel for the Kingdom of God, you will be "BLESSED."

# PROSPERITY CONFESSION OF THE GIVER

Father, in the name of Jesus, I confess Your Word over my finances this day. I have given the tithes of my increase and I claim the windows of Heaven blessing open over my life. Thank You Father, my mind is alert and I hear Your voice and the voice of the stranger I will not follow. Thank You, I receive now doors of opportunity opening for me and my family.

Father, I have given to the poor; therefore, I will never lack. I always have all sufficiency in all things as You are raising up others to use their power and ability and influence to help me. I expect daily for the Spirit of God to speak to men and women concerning giving to me. In the name of Jesus, those whom the Spirit of God designates are free to obey and give to me good measure, pressed down, shaken together and running over.

In Jesus' name, I believe every need is met with heaven's best. I have given for the support of the man and woman of God who teach me the Word. They have sown into my life that which is spiritual; according to Your Word, I have sown into their lives that which is natural. You promised that You would supply all my needs according to Your riches in glory by Christ Jesus. Thank You Father, I live in the best, I wear the best, I drive the best, I eat the best, and I go first class in life.

Father, Your Word says I can decree a thing because of my covenant vow with You for the Kingdom of God in the earth. This is my decree and I thank You for wisdom and insight to bring it to pass. You give me and my family richly all things to enjoy. Satan, I bind your activity in my life and I loose the angels, the ministering spirits, to minister for me and bring the necessary finances so that I may continue to finance the Kingdom of God.

Father, Your Word declares my giving increases the fruits of my righteousness. I thank You Father that I have an abundance of peace, joy, patience, temperance and goodness. The optimum return on my giving is mine because I have given to promote the name of Jesus and the Gospel.

## CONFESSION OVER THE TITHES AND OFFERINGS

Father, I know You have a financial plan for the believer called tithes and offerings. At this moment, I set my heart to tap into Your financial plan for me. Satan will not rob me anymore in my finances. In the name of Jesus, by faith, I am at this moment planting my financial seed into the Kingdom of God's field. I am doing this because I know that this is a Biblical truth, and I set my heart to obey the Word. Father, I also know that it is a Biblical truth that in return for my financial faithfulness, You are supplying all my needs and above my needs.

Because I have tapped into Your financial plan, I believe that You are raising up somebody, somewhere, to use their power, their ability and their influence to help me. In Jesus' name, I hold fast to my confession in Your financial plan. Amen!

## CONFESSION FOR CAREER AND BUSINESS

Father, I have committed my works, my plans, my business, and my ministry to You; I entrust them wholly to You. Your Word says that You are causing my thoughts to become agreeable with Your will, so that my career, my business, and my plans are established and succeed. In Jesus name, my eyes are open to receive your vision for my life. My mind is alert to receive creative ideas and inventions. My hands are skilled to perform the work that will bring me success. My ears are tuned to the voice of the Holy Spirit and the voice of the stranger has no power over me.

Father, I have grace to handle the challenges, the obstacles, and the trials and tests of life. I will not fear or be afraid. I thank You for the courage to fulfill my responsibilities, and because of my faith, I am overcoming them all.

Father, I obey Your Word by my pursuit to make an honest living so that I may have to give to those in need. I can do all things through Your power that strengthens me and according to that power, I provide for myself and my own household.

Thank You, Father, for making all grace, all favor abound toward me. You are raising up people to use their power and influence to help me; therefore, I have abundance, I have all sufficiency, and I abound to every good work.

Father, thank You for the ministering spirits that You have assigned to go forth to bring in those across my path to cause my promotion. According to Your Word, I am the light of the world and in Jesus' name, my light is shining before all men that they may see good works, my godly lifestyle, and glorify You, my Heavenly Father. I have the grace and the diligence to seek the knowledge and skill in areas where I am inexperienced. I am faithful and committed to Your Word. Your Word declares that I am positioned for increase, blessings, rewards and abundance. By faith, I see my vision fulfilled. Thank You for the success promised in Your Word.

# CONFESSIONS FOR CAREER AND PROMOTIONS

Father, in Jesus' name, Your Word says promotions don't come from the east, nor the west, nor the south, but God is the judge who puts down one and picks up another. I believe, Father, that according to Your Word, You are elevating me to a higher level of living.

I thank You Father, that You are causing my NAME, my application and my resume to rise to the top, so that those in authority to make decisions concerning my promotion will call me. I thank You Father that I have the wisdom of God in the interview process and You have given me a mouth and a tongue that the enemy cannot gainsay or resist.

I thank You Father, for the creativity and wisdom necessary to fulfill my new assignment. I thank You Father, that You are raising up somebody, somewhere to use their power, their ability and their influence to help me.

I thank You, Father, that this promotion is causing me to prosper so I have more to give to the Kingdom of God. I thank You Father that I live in daily expectation of You opening doors of opportunity for me.

I am often asked to write confessions for our members when they are going into new endeavors. Recently, some young men from our church were drafted to the NFL and I wrote this confession for one of them to excel in his new career.

Jesus Christ is Lord over my spirit, soul and body. I choose to live a victorious overcoming life. I have the wisdom of God in me for every situation and I operate at my maximum and excel in all that I set my hands to do.

I choose not to fear because I cast the whole of my care on You and I know You care for me. I choose not to have anxiety or worry about anything and I am more than a conqueror because I am covered by the blood of Jesus, the angels of the Lord encamp around about me and the power of the Holy Spirit works through me.

I can do all things through Christ who strengthens me. I am confident that He who began a good work in me will perform it until the day of Jesus Christ. I thank You Father for the favor on my life surrounds me as a shield and no weapon formed against me shall prosper. I function at the highest level of my ability at all times proving that I am the head and not the tail. I perform always at a level superior to all my competitors and I am respected for my diligence toward my profession. I thank You Father that you prosper me in all that I set my hands to do and I have the wisdom of God to make the right decisions concerning my finances.

# Overcoming Marital Challenges and Experiencing Happiness in Relationships

I thought I would start this chapter with a testimony from some of the many people I have counseled regarding marital challenges. I have seen tremendous results in the lives of men and women who have applied the principle of faith confession in their marriages. As I thought about it, I realized, no testimony would be more profound than my own on how God's Word changed my marriage.

Many, many years ago as I stated in the previous chapter, Ira and I experienced some very challenging times in our lives. Those challenges caused us to be impatient, verbally abusive and disrespectful to one another. We really had a very bad marriage relationship. Ira hated to come home and I hated to see him come home. It was really, really bad.

Our marriage took a downhill plunge when we went through some challenges with the church, as well as some financial challenges, and then basically we just did not know how to live a married life. I spent many days crying, not knowing what to do. I even came to the point where I decided to leave Ira, with the coaching of my family and friends. I started working and was about to see a lawyer to obtain a divorce.

I thank God that I have always been sensitive to pleasing God with my life and one day while "doing my own thing," the Holy Spirit had Ira call me at work. I agreed to meet Ira at a small Chinese restaurant on Shepherd Drive in Houston, Texas. While eating lunch that day, Ira made the statement, "We could be selfish and go our separate ways, but we are not our own anymore....we belong to God. What we are doing is not pleasing God." We decided that day that we wanted more than anything to please God with our lives. We agreed to get back together and get the necessary information so that we could have God's best in our marriage.

Ira went to two different church growth conferences during a two-week period, in two different cities, and the Holy Spirit arranged for the same minister to be at both meetings! The minister's text at both meetings were God-inspired because it was just what Ira was searching for. Ira tells the story that on his airplane ride to the first meeting, he was talking to God, telling God he knew he wasn't his best preacher, but surely he wasn't his worst preacher. He asked God the question, "Why isn't my church growing?" Ira says his Bible fell open to 1 Peter 3:7, *"Likewise, ye husbands, dwell with your wives according to knowledge, giving honor unto the wife as unto the weaker vessel and as being heirs together of the grace of life, that your prayers be not hindered."*

Ira says he closed his Bible because he didn't want to hear that answer. Well, when he arrived at the first meeting, the first night the minister took his text from 1 Peter 3:7. Ira says he was very uncomfortable in that meeting the entire week and could not wait for the meeting to end. The following week, he went to the next meeting. The same minister showed up with the same text; Ira was finally convinced that God was trying to get a message to him.

After Ira and I met at the Chinese restaurant, I returned home. Later, I was baptized with the Holy Spirit, as I talked about in a previous chapter. I learned the principle of "faith confession." I began to confess God's Word over our marriage, over Ira and myself. As I would do my household chores, like making the bed, ironing shirts, folding clothes and cooking, I would confess God's Word.

Today, we say that we are so close we are each other's best friend for life. God has transformed our lives because we decided to put pressure on our tongues.

*"Behold, we put bits in the horses' mouths, that they may obey us; and we turn about their whole body. Behold also the ships, which though they be so great, and are driven of fierce winds, yet are they turned about with a very small helm, whithersoever the governor listeth." (James 3:3-4 KJV)*

Isn't it amazing that mankind can control all kinds of beasts, animals and objects, yet we have no control over our lives because we won't put a little pressure on our tongues?

I know you are probably thinking to yourself right now, "Sure, I'll put pressure on my mouth, but what about my spouse?" I say to you that if you will begin to work on you, God is committed to work on your spouse.

# SCRIPTURES REGARDING MARRIAGE AND MARRIAGE RELATIONSHIPS

*"Likewise, ye husbands, dwell with your wives according to knowledge, giving honor unto the wife as unto the weaker vessel and*

as being heirs together of the grace of life; that your prayers be not hindered." (1 Peter 3:7 KJV)

"Whoso findeth a wife findeth a good thing, and obtaineth favor of the Lord." (Proverbs 18:22 KJV)

"A capable, intelligent, and virtuous woman–who can find her? She is far more precious than jewels and her value is far above rubies or pearls. The heart of her husband trusts in her confidently and relies on and believes in her securely, so that he has no lack of [honest] gain or need of [dishonest] spoil. She comforts, encourages, and does him good as long as there is life within her. She seeks out wool and flax and works with willing hands [to develop it]. She is like the merchant ships loaded with foodstuffs; she brings her household's food from a far [country]. She rises while it is yet night and gets [spiritual] food for her household and assigns her maids their tasks. She considers a [new] field before she buys or accepts it [expanding prudently and not courting neglect of her present duties by assuming other duties] with her savings [of time and strength] she plants fruitful vines in her vineyard. She girds herself with strength [spiritual, mental, and physical fitness for her God-given task] and makes her arms strong and firm. She tastes and sees that her gain from work [with and for God] is good; her lamp goes not out, but it burns on continually through the night [of trouble, privation, or sorrow, warning away fear, doubt and distrust]. She lays her hand to the spindle and her hands hold the distaff. She opens her hands to the poor; yes, she reaches out her filled hands to the needy [whether in body, mind, or spirit]. She fears not the snow for her family for all her household is double clothed in scarlet. She makes for herself coverlets, cushions, and rugs of tapestry. Her clothing is linen, pure and fine, and of purple [such as that of which the clothing of the priests and the hallowed cloths of the temple were made]. Her husband is known in the gates, when he sits among the elders of the land. She makes fine linen garments and leads others to buy them; she delivers to the merchants girdles [or sashes that free one up for service]. Strength and dignity are her clothing and her position is strong and secure; she rejoices over the future [the latter day or time to come, knowing that she and her family are in readiness for it]. She opens her mouth in skillful and godly wisdom and on her tongue is the law of kindness [giving counsel and instruction]. She looks well to how things go in her household, and the bread of idleness (gossip, discontent, and self-pity) she will not eat. Her children rise up and call her blessed (happy, fortunate, and to be envied); and her husband boasts and praises her, [saying], Many daughters have done virtuously, nobly, and well [with the strength of character that is steadfast in goodness], but you excel them all. Charm and grace are deceptive, and beauty is vain [because it is not lasting], but a woman who reverently and worshipfully fears the Lord, she shall be praised! Give her the fruit of her hands and let her own works praise her in the gates [of the city]!" (Proverbs 31:10–31 AMP)

*"A virtuous women is a crown to her husband; but she that maketh him ashamed is rottenness in his bones." (Proverbs 12:4 KJV)*

*"Let her be as a loving hind and pleasant roe; let her breasts satisfy thee at all times and be thou ravished always with her love." (Proverbs 5:19 KJV)*

*"Let the husband render unto the wife due benevolence: and likewise also the wife unto the husband." (1 Corinthians 7:3 KJV)*

*"The Lord perfects that which concerns me…" (Psalms 138:8 KJV)*

# CONFESSION FOR WIVES

Father, I thank You that I am a capable, intelligent, virtuous woman; the heart of my husband does safely trust in me so he has no need of spoil. I do my husband good all the days of his life. I will respect my husband as a man of God and I will always speak good things about him to others. When I embarrass and speak negatively about my husband, it is rottenness in his bones, so I choose to speak only good things about him and our relationship. I am a good thing that my husband has found and because of me, he has obtained favor of the Lord. My husband dwells with me according to knowledge as he gives honor to me as unto the weaker vessel. My husband loves me as Christ loves the church.

My husband and I have wonderful, intimate times together because my breasts shall satisfy him at all times and he is ravished with my love. We render one to another due benevolence.

My children and husband rise and call me blessed. I live the overcoming life. I live in daily expectation of abundance in my life. I have a sound mind. I live a life of purpose and fulfillment. I am a blessing to my household and the Kingdom of God.

I love my husband and do him good all the days of our lives. God satisfies us with long life and peace. My husband is known in the gates (city, state, nation and abroad) and when he sits with kings and rulers, he gives wise counsel; his gift makes room for him and brings him before great men. Lord, You promised to perfect all that concerns me. In Jesus' name

# WOMEN'S CONFESSION

The following confession is a confession that I have given to every woman in our church who attends our women's fellowship. I instruct them to say it daily and act on what they are saying. We have seen tremendous results.

I am a capable, intelligent, virtuous woman. I live the overcoming life. Health and healing are my covenant right. Prosperity and abundance are the will of God for my life.

God is on my side; therefore, fear has no place in my life; fear shall not torment me. I have the love of God and perfect loves cast out all fear.

I have temperance and self-control and I only eat things needful for my body. I comfort, encourage and do good all the days of my life. Out of my mouth flows the law of kindness; therefore, no corrupt communication will flow out of my mouth.

My husband and children call me blessed. I walk by faith and not by sight. I walk in daily expectation because the wisdom of God is in me today. I am an overcomer. In Jesus' name

# ADDITIONAL CONFESSION FOR WIVES

Father, in the name of Jesus, I embrace the truth of Your Word. I am a virtuous woman and my husband is a mighty man of valor. I set my heart to submit to my own husband as he submits to Your plan for our lives. It is my desire to please my husband and I look to him to protect, provide and nurture my life.

I am spiritually focused, emotionally strong, and a woman of unquestionable character. I will do my husband good all the days of our lives. I am adaptable to my husband's needs and I am the helpmate that God has prepared for him. I will always honor and respect my husband as a man of God. My husband loves and respects me as Christ loves the church.

My husband and I walk hand in hand, striving side by side, united in spirit and purpose, contending with a single mind to do God's perfect will in our lives. I choose to die to those things that are killing our relationship. I gladly drink from the cup that was prepared before we were married. I will gladly bear the cross of our relationship and I will allow my husband to be himself. We are experiencing a new life together where old things are passed away and behold all things are become new. In Jesus' name

## SCRIPTURES:

*1 Corinthians 10:3-6; Proverbs 31:10-31; Judges 6:12; Ephesians 5:22-26; Psalms 119:105; Luke 19:1-8; Genesis 3:16; Hebrews 12:2; Matthew 26:37-42; 2 Corinthians 5:17; Philippians 1:27b*

# FOR MEN ONLY

Ira has an awesome anointing to minister to men. Our church is just about forty percent (40%) men. That is most unusual because in most churches you don't see that many men. I believe men come to our church and stay because they see an example of a real man.

Ira has proven over the years to be a man of utmost character and integrity and real men like to see that. We do not have homosexuals flaunting themselves in our ministry because the men are taught by Ira to love and respect their manhood.

The divorce rate in our church is extremely low. We can just about count on one hand the number of people in our church who have divorced since being there. We teach people to have happy homes and apply the principles of God's Word to their marriages. We see awesome results because people have an example of the Word working in our lives and they have confidence that what God has done for us, He will do for them.

Ira teaches our men that their mouths are offensive weapons against the devil's plans to destroy their lives. On the next pages, you will find the confession that our men are encouraged to confess.

# MEN'S CONFESSION

I am a mighty man of God. I love my wife at all times. I am a patient godly parent. All the blessings of the Lord are mine I seek first the Kingdom of God and His righteousness.

I hold fast to the confession of my faith without wavering because I know that God is faithful to keep His promises. I live the abundant life because Jesus has redeemed me from the curse of the law. I am a world overcomer. I walk in forgiveness and not in strife. I walk in divine health. I believe I receive at the moment I pray the eyes of the Lord are over the righteous and His ears are open unto my prayers. My ears are tuned to the voice of the Holy Spirit and the voice of a stranger I choose not to follow. I am walking worthy of the Lord in every area of my life. I am increasing in the knowledge and wisdom of God daily. In Jesus' name, Amen!

# CONFESSION FOR HUSBANDS

Father, in the name of Jesus, I embrace the truth of Your Word and I commit it to my life. I commit to change whatever needs to be changed in my life in order to bring every thought into captivity to Your Word and will for my life. I am a mighty man of valor and I see my wife as a virtuous woman. I love my wife as Your Son loved the church. The light of Your Word shines on my path. My heart safely trusts my wife. She is good to me and good for me. I place a high value on her preciousness to me. My wife is spiritually focused, emotionally strong, and she has unquestionable character.

Father, in Jesus' name, if there is any damage I have caused my wife through my own deep-rooted, misguided expectations, I commit to make restitution. I will help her develop as a person, and I will let her help me. I will shine on her as the sun shines on the earth. I bring her warmth, nurture, protection and security.

Because of the joy it will bring to both of us, I will gladly drink of the cup that was prepared before we married. I will gladly bear the cross of our relationship, allowing my wife to be herself. I will die to the things that are killing our relationship. We will experience a new creation marriage where old things are passed away and all things are become new. In Jesus' name

## SCRIPTURES:

*1 Corinthians 10:3-6; Psalms 119:105; Judges 6:12; Luke 19:1-8; Proverbs 31:10-31; Hebrews 12:2; Ephesians 5:25-28; Matthew 26:37-42; Genesis 1:16; 2 Corinthians 5:17*

# THE SUCCESSFUL UNMARRIED (SINGLE) STATE

The unmarried state is a wonderful state and we encourage those who are unmarried to see themselves not as being lonely and incomplete, but as complete in God. The confession listed below will allow the unmarried to grow in the Word of God.

# CONFESSION FOR THE UNMARRIED (SINGLE) STATE

Jesus Christ is Lord over my spirit, soul, and body. I am a child of God, loved by my Father. I live the victorious, overcoming life. Every need in my life is met. I choose to walk in the Spirit and the lust of my flesh has no power over me. The Holy Spirit leads and guides me for my steps are ordered by God.

God is preparing the perfect mate for me, and when the Spirit of God causes our paths to cross, I have favor in his/her eyes. I choose to keep myself holy until marriage.

I walk in divine health; sickness and disease have no place in my body because I am covered by the blood of Jesus. I only think those things that are true, honest, pure and of good report. I am committed to be diligent in the things of God, because God is a rewarder of the diligent.

I spend quality time helping others in the Kingdom of God and I am involved in my local church because this is the blessed state. In Jesus' name, I walk by faith and not by sight.

# PARENTING AND CHILD-REARING

One of the most exciting things I have seen since I was saved and filled with the Holy Spirit is God's Word work in the lives of others. As a pastor's wife, I see all kinds of situations and challenges that people face. Also, I have the wonderful opportunity to pray with people through their challenging times. Years ago, a young lady walked into our church looking as if she was homeless: without family, clothing or a place to go. I began talking to the young lady and found out she was an intelligent woman, an educator as a matter of fact, but she was living in such fear and bondage that she would not even take the time to comb her hair.

After this young lady overcame her fear, she had a desire to be a mother. She came to me and asked for help in developing a faith confession so she would get pregnant and have a child. I prayed with her and agreed in prayer with her because I knew it was the will of God for her to conceive. After praying, confessing, and acting on the Word of God, that young lady and her husband did conceive a child who was stillborn. The young couple did not blame God, but realized it had to be human error (something they did wrong) and began to confess the Word again.

Today, they are the proud, busy parents of two normal, healthy children.

This testimony has been replicated many times over in the lives of other members of our church and even other pastors. There is another couple in our church who had been told they could not conceive a child because the wife had no eggs to produce children. Well, that couple learned to confess the Word and act on that confession and are the proud parents of four normal, healthy children.

I know it is the will of God for us to have the desires of our heart and, if children are our desire, God will give them to us.

# SCRIPTURES FOR CHILD-BEARING AND PREGNANCY

*"He makes the barren woman to be a homemaker and a joyful mother of (spiritual) children. Praise the Lord." (Psalms 113:9 AMP)*

*"Your wife shall be like a fruitful vine in the innermost parts of your house; your children shall be like olive plants round about your table. Behold, thus shall the man be blessed who reverently and worshipfully fears the Lord." (Psalms 128:3-4 AMP)*

*"Blessed is the man that feareth the Lord, that delighteth greatly in His commandments. His seed shall be mighty upon the earth and the generation of the upright shall be blessed." (Psalms 112:1-2 KJV)*

*"Children's children are the crown of old men and the glory of children are their fathers." (Proverbs 17:6 KJV)*

*"Behold, children are a heritage from the Lord, the fruit of the womb a reward." (Psalms 127:3 AMP)*

*"For He has strengthened and made hard the bars of your gates, and he has blessed your children within you." (Psalms 147:13 KJV)*

*"And ye shall serve the Lord your God and he shall bless thy bread, and thy water and I will take sickness away from the midst of thee. There shall nothing cast their young nor be barren in thy land the number of thy days I will fulfill." (Exodus 23:25, 26 KJV)*

*"And whatsoever we ask, we receive of Him, because we keep His commandments, and do those things that are pleasing in his sight."* *(1 John 3:22 KJV)*

*"And I will rebuke the devourer for your sakes and he shall not destroy the fruits of your grounds, neither shall your vine cast her fruit before the time in the field, saith the Lord of hosts. And all nations shall call you blessed and ye shall be a delightsome land saith the Lord of hosts." (Malachi 3:11 KJV)*

# CONFESSION FOR CHILD-BEARING AND PREGNANCY

Father, in Jesus' name, I thank You that because I keep Your commandments and do those things that are pleasing to You, I know whatever I ask I receive of You; therefore, Father, according to Your Word, I believe that You make me a joyful mother of children.

I thank You Father that my children are like olive plants around the table. I thank You Father that the fruit of my womb is Your reward and I believe I receive rewards from You.

Father, in Jesus' name, I thank You that I will carry my baby full-term. I am a tither, the devourer is rebuked and my fruit shall not be brought forth for sudden terror or calamity. I will not bring forth my fruit before the time of life. I thank You Father that You make my body strong and You bless the child within me. Your Word says there shall nothing cast their young, neither be barren in the land.

Father, because we honor and reverence You as Lord, I thank You, in the Name of Jesus, that we are blessed with a family, committed to You and Your Word. I thank You Father, for our unborn child; we receive the child as a gift from You. I believe my child is being created in Your image and likeness; therefore, I believe I receive a normal, healthy child with all body parts functioning as You designed them to function.

Father, I thank You I am skillfully and wonderfully made in Your image and likeness. I will have a safe, easy pregnancy and delivery. Pregnancy is Your will for my life; therefore, I accept Your plan for blessing my womb. I believe the Holy Spirit is with me in labor and delivery; therefore, I thank You for protecting me and my child. I thank You Father the Holy Spirit oils my womb and the baby comes forth safely and speedily during delivery.

I thank You Father that our child a blessing from You Father. We have chosen to walk in Your ways, I thank You Father that all nations rise and call us blessed.

# RAISING OBEDIENT CHILDREN

One of the greatest joys in life is becoming a parent. A parent has an awesome responsibility of overseeing an individual in such a manner that the child/children fully develop in all areas. 1 Thessalonians 5:23 teaches us that we are a spirit, have a soul and live in a body. We believe that God perfects our children in every area of his or her being. Parents are responsible to train their children to be capable of handling the challenges of life in a manner that will glorify God.

When a child is born, the doctors and nurses don't give a manual or instruction book for the different stages children will go through. As a parent of three lovely daughters, I have found they each have their very own personality. My husband and I realized very early that we must raise our daughters in the reverence and admonition of God. Over the years, I have had the responsibility of teaching each one of my girls how to confess God's Word over their lives on a daily basis. All of our three girls are grown and I must say I am quite proud of the beautiful examples they are for the Kingdom of God.

I have not only shared the following confessions with my daughters, but I continuously share these confessions with every parent in our local church and the results are tremendous.

The primary thing that a parent should do is be an example and role model for the child so that he or she can see the godly principles lived out in his or her life. I make it a point to always live before my children in such a manner that they see the Word and will of God come to pass in my life.

I have told my children not as a fear tactic, but as godly wisdom, that if they try to go around the guidelines and principles that we have established for them, God will see them and let me know what they are doing.

*"The eyes of the Lord are in every place, beholding the evil and the good." (Proverbs 15:3 KJV)*

I trust that you will take these confessions and use those that apply. Use them for yourself and teach them to your children. Insist that they say these confessions on a daily basis. Because I am the mother of all girls, most of the confessions have been designed for females; however, I have included some confessions for males that have blessed the parents of young men in our church.

This is a powerful chapter and will give you the Spiritual tools to change your family even if your children are adults or if they are currently outside of God's will and in need of deliverance or salvation.

Tina, Ira's daughter from a previous marriage, was given to her mother as the primary custodian for her care. After a few years of our marriage, her mother would no longer allow us to visit or have visitation rights with her. Tina grew up not being allowed to see us and was raised by her mother as a Jehovah witness.

It was not the will of God for that little girl not to know her father as a loving father. Ira is a man of great wisdom and being married to him has taught me some parenting skills I did not have. Ira loved children and we had always from our first serious conversation about marriage talked about raising all our children together. We never allowed our girls to polarize themselves against one another; we also did not allow the mention of the words "step sister" and "step parent." We are all family. I personally have always loved Tina like she was my very own daughter, so we all wanted Tina to be with us.

As family, we daily confessed Tina's deliverance from that situation. The confession is so simple, but it was so profound because Tina is now saved, filled with God's spirit and working in the ministry with us.

The confession came as a result of us finding Proverbs 11:21b which says, "...*but the seed of the righteous is delivered.*"

As a family we confessed daily "Tina is the seed of the righteous and she is delivered." After about ten years of not seeing Tina, in July of 1989, Tina called us and said her mother had allowed her to call and she wanted to see us. Needless to say, we were overjoyed. Through a process of events too lengthy to write in this book, Tina was dismissed from the Jehovah witness faith and came to live with us permanently May of 1990. Our family knows all the things that happened were a result of our consistent confession that "Tina is the seed of the righteous and she is delivered."

You may not have a child who is estranged from you or growing up with a different Spiritual influence from yours perhaps you have a child who is on drugs or living an ungodly life. If you can believe and confess this promise from the Word, you can see your child's deliverance.

# CONFESSION FOR PARENTS

Father, Your Word says children are a blessing from You and the fruit of the womb is Your reward. I appreciate the reward of my children and I thank You that I have the wisdom to raise them in the nurture and admonition of the Lord. My children live a life that glorifies God.

I thank You Father, my children are arrows in my hand and You are revealing to me Your plan and purpose for each of their lives so that I can provide clear direction for them.

I train my children in the way they should go and when they are old, they will not depart from it. I exercise patience and self-control in every situation because greater is He that is in me than He that is in the world.

All of my children are disciples taught of the Lord. Great is their peace and undisturbed composure. My children were not brought forth for sudden terror or calamity, but they are a blessing from You; therefore, in every situation, my seed (my child/children) is delivered because I am in right standing with You.

No weapon formed against my child or this family shall prosper. My children shall be mighty upon the earth and they shall always experience blessings because the generation of the upright shall be blessed. Father, in Jesus' name, I thank You that You daily give me direction on showing my child/children that they are loved, accepted, secure and needed in this family.

My children walk in divine health and no plague comes nigh our dwelling. The angels of the Lord encamp about my children; therefore, their lives are redeemed from destruction.

I thank You Father that my children are the head and not the tail, above only and not beneath. Father, in Jesus' name, our children always bring joy to the household.

The following are scriptures and confessions that our daughters say or have said on a daily basis:

*"And all your [spiritual] children shall be disciples [taught by the Lord and obedient to His will], and great shall be the peace and undisturbed composure of your children." (Isaiah 54:13 AMP)*

*"Forever, O Lord, thy word is settled in heaven. Thy faithfulness is unto all generations: thou hast established the earth, and it abideth." (Psalms 119:89-91 KJV)*

*"The entrance of thy words giveth light; it giveth understanding unto the simple." (Psalms 119:130 KJV)*

*"The Lord is far from the wicked but He hears the prayer of the consistently righteous." (Proverbs 15:29 AMP)*

*"Praise the Lord (Hallelujah), Blessed (Happy, fortunate and to be envied) is the man who delights greatly in his commandments. His seed (offspring/ children) shall be mighty upon the earth; the generation of the upright shall be blessed. Prosperity and welfare are in his house and his righteousness endures forever." (Psalms 112:1-3 AMP)*

*"Blessed are they that keep his testimonies and that seek him with the whole heart. They also do no iniquity; they walk in his ways." (Psalms 119:1-3 AMP)*

# CONFESSION FOR CHILDREN

I am a disciple, taught of the Lord, obedient to God's will with great peace and undisturbed composure. I obey my parents, adults, and my teachers because they have authority over me.

The Word of God is settled in my heart and in the Heavens; I am prospering in all I set my hands to do and lack has no place in my life, because God's faithfulness is unto all generations.

The entrance of the Word brings light, I understand God's Word and live according to His Word. I am righteous; therefore, God hears my prayers. I excel in school and I have favor with my teachers and my peers.

Father, in Jesus' name, I thank You that my dad and mom are righteous. The Word declares their seed shall be mighty upon the earth. I choose to walk upright before God; therefore, I am blessed…wealth and riches are in our house. I am saved and filled with God's spirit. I am blessed because I keep God's commandments. In Jesus' name

Listed below are other confessions our daughters have made:

I am a spirit being, I live in a body, I have a soul. Jesus Christ is Lord of my life and I am submitted to His will. I hear God's voice and I obey and follow His voice, the voice of the stranger (evil one, the devil) has no power over me. I can do all things through Christ who strengthens me.

I have the mind of Christ and hold the thoughts, feelings and purposes of His heart. I am a disciple, taught of the Lord, obedient to God's will, with great peace and undisturbed composure.

I obey and honor my parents because it is the will of God concerning me and God promises to bless me with long life. I choose to keep my room clean at all times for this pleases my parents and God.

I walk in divine health. Germs and diseases have no place in my life. I am covered by the blood of Jesus. Any germ or disease that touches my body dies immediately. God knows every fiber of hair on my head, my hair is growing longer and thicker day by day for my hair is my glory. By Jesus' stripes, I am healed and made whole.

I have the wisdom of God for every situation. Jesus Christ grew in stature and favor with God and man therefore I am growing in stature and favor with God and man. I have favor with all my teachers and my peers. I excel in school because I have the mind of Christ.

I keep myself holy until marriage. I know God is preparing the perfect mate to be in covenant agreement with me. I walk in the Spirit; therefore, the Holy Spirit controls my life and my desires. I always walk uprightly and the generation of the upright shall be blessed I let the Word of God dwell in me richly. The angels of the Lord are encamped about me; therefore, my life is redeemed from destruction. I am a believer and not a doubter. In Jesus' name, I hold fast to my confession of faith. In Jesus' name

## CONFESSIONS FOR SONS

Jesus is Lord over my spirit, my soul and body. Jesus has made unto me wisdom, righteousness, sanctification and redemption, I can do all things through Christ who strengthens me.

The Lord is my Shepherd; I shall not want. I choose not to fret or have anxiety about anything. I have the mind of Christ and hold the thoughts, feelings, and purposes of His heart. I am a disciple, taught of the Lord, obedient to God's will, with great peace and undisturbed composure. I please God in all that I do. I always seek to do that which pleases God; therefore, I obey my parents, for this pleases God.

Just as Jesus grew in stature and favor with God and man, I am growing in statue and favor with God and man.

I keep myself holy until marriage. I walk in the Spirit; therefore, I treat every female as a child of God. I know that her body is the temple where God abides and I choose to protect, honor and respect God's property. I choose to ignore the pressure of my peers to force me to destroy what God has ordained to be holy. I choose to provide protection for young ladies.

I do well in school and I have a quiet, peaceable spirit. I only speak those things that are necessary. I know God has not given me a spirit of fear, but a spirit of power, love, and a sound mind. I walk by faith and not by sight. In Jesus' name

# MISSING CHILD/RUNAWAY CHILD

On April 6, 1991, during a regular Sunday Service as I prayed for the needs of the people, a very attractive lady (Claudette Vernon) came forward. She asked that I pray that her daughter who had been missing for five (5) years would be returned. As I inquired more, I realized she had not seen her child since her fourth birthday when her estranged husband had taken her away. That day, as I began to pray for her, I felt impressed to have her come up after service and I wrote a confession on a piece of paper (I will share it later in this chapter), regarding her daughter's return. I explained to Claudette the need for her to believe God's Word and confess it on a daily basis. Claudette took me at my word and kept that paper, believed what was written, and confessed it daily.

On November 6, 1991, I received a phone call from Claudette stating the authorities thought they had located her child in Weisbaden, Germany. Of course, you know, she booked herself on the first available flight to Germany and I met her at the airport. I was so touched to see that even though she had received the phone call, she was still standing in faith for her daughter's return. Prior to her flight leaving for Germany, she pulled out the paper that I had written for her months before and Claudette told me she had from that first day until then confessed the Word of God.

Well on November 11, 1991, Claudette returned to Houston Intercontinental Airport with her daughter, Erin Vernon.

As I pen this 30th edition of my book Erin Vernon-Hunter is still a member of New Light Church and is currently married and pregnant. Without a doubt I know Erin will share with her child these confessions that changed her life. God is Faithful!!

Prior to my sharing the Scriptures that Claudette stood on during those months, I would like to share the simple confession I wrote for her that Sunday. She was so committed to confess God's Word that she held onto that paper until her child was returned to her. I cannot emphasize it enough God's Word will work for everyone who has the discipline to work it.

# CLAUDETTE'S CONFESSION

Father, In Jesus' name, I believe Your Word that declares the seed of the righteous is delivered. I call Erin's name before You and I believe Your Word that says I can pray to the Lord of the harvest and He can thrust forth laborers into the harvest. I believe You Father for Erin's return and I also believe that Erin's ears are open to the voice of the Lord. Holy Spirit, I depend on You to brood over Erin and bring me to her remembrance. I thank You Father that Erin is free and I thank You she has peace. I set myself in agreement with Pastor Bridget on April 6, 1991. I daily thank You for the manifestation of this prayer in Jesus' Name.

Even though this confession is brief and it may even sound simple, it was effective because Claudette received the Word in her heart, confessed it daily, and believed. The awesome thing about the entire story is when Claudette first saw Erin in Germany, Erin's first words were, "Hi Mama, I have been dreaming you were coming to get me." Isn't God good? Nothing is too hard for God; not even distance.

*"…but the seed of the righteous is delivered." (Proverbs 11:21b KJV)*

*"Pray ye therefore the Lord of the harvest, that he will send forth laborers into his harvest." (Matthew 9:38 KJV)*

*"For he shall give his angels charge over thee to keep thee in all thy ways." (Psalms 91:11 KJV)*

*"Again I say unto you if two of you on earth shall agree on earth as touching anything that they shall ask, it shall be done for them of my Father which is in heaven." (Matthew 18:19 KJV)*

*"…and the sheep follow him: for they know his voice, And a stranger they will not follow, but will flee from him; for they know not the voice of the stranger." (John 10:4b–5 KJV)*

# CONFESSION REGARDING RUNAWAY AND MISSING CHILDREN

Father, I thank You in Jesus' Name that I believe Your Word that declares the seed of the righteous is delivered. I call (child's name) before You and I believe (child's name) is delivered.

I thank You Father, Your Word says You are the Lord of the harvest; therefore, I believe You are sending laborers into the harvest to minister to (child's name). Father, in Jesus' name I believe that (child's name) hears Your voice and obeys Your voice and the stranger's voice (child's name) will not follow.

I thank You Father that the angels go forth and find my child.

I depend on the Holy Spirit to brood over my child and bring me back to my child's remembrance. I believe Father (child's name) is free and I thank You my child has peace. I thank You daily for the manifestation of the prayer.

## CHILDREN OVERCOMING CHALLENGES IN SCHOOL

One of my three daughters that I talked about in a previous chapter was having a serious challenge in school grasping the information from her instructor. One afternoon, we received a phone call from her teacher stating, "If your child's grades don't improve, she will repeat the 6th grade." We knew our daughter would have to make a great adjustment going from elementary school to middle school, but we had no idea it was so critical.

We sat down with our daughter and went through the normal parental reprimand. We applied the rod of correction and talked to her. In fact, we did everything we knew to help her.

One day, as my husband was reprimanding her, the Holy Spirit impressed on him that what he was doing was not working and he needed to change his approach.

Ira did change his approach by telling our daughter to basically start where she was, and not try to make A's, but try to start making D's. From D's, we instructed her to try to make C's, and then on to B's, and A's. We also developed a very simple confession for her so she would be assured God wanted to help her change her situation.

As you probably know, that daughter improved tremendously and graduated from high school in the top 25% of her class. I know the results she experienced were because of the action we took as well as the confession of her mouth.

# SCRIPTURES THAT APPLY TO OVERCOMING CHALLENGES IN SCHOOL

*"For it is God which worketh in you both to will and to do his good pleasure." (Philippians 2:13 KJV)*

*"That the God of our Lord Jesus Christ the Father of glory, may give unto you the spirit of wisdom and revelation in the knowledge of him." (Ephesians 1:17 KJV)*

*"For God has not given us the spirit of fear; but of power, love, and a sound mind." (2 Timothy 1:7 KJV)*

*"If any of you lack wisdom, let him ask of God who giveth all things liberally and upbraideth not; and it shall be given him." (James 1:5 KJV)*

*"And the Lord shall make you the head and not the tail, above only and not beneath…" (Deuteronomy 2:13a KJV)*

*"So shalt thou find favor and good understanding in the sight of God and man." (Proverbs 3:4 KJV)*

*"And God gave Solomon exceptionally much wisdom and understanding and breadth of mind like the sand of the seashore." (1 Kings 4:29 AMP)*

# CONFESSION FOR OVERCOMING CHALLENGES IN SCHOOL

I choose to walk by faith; God is on my side. I choose to have confidence and approach my work without fear. It is God that worketh in me to will and to do His good pleasure.

I have the mind of Christ. I am daily growing in stature and favor with God and my teachers. I have favor with my peers, my teachers and family. The wisdom of God is in me today. Because God is no respecter of persons, I believe just as God gave Solomon exceptional wisdom and understanding, He has also given to me wisdom and understanding, in Jesus' Name.

Your family will always need the protection of God. Rather than worrying about your family's safety and protection, confess

God's Word over your entire family. Here is a confession that produces result.

# FAMILY PROTECTION CONFESSION

Father, in the Name of Jesus, I thank You that Your Word declares that the Name of the Lord is a strong tower and the righteous can run into Your name and find safety. You said in Your Word I can call on Your Name in the time of trouble and You will deliver me; therefore, I call on You, God, as my deliverer and the protector of me and my family. I choose to dwell in the secret place of the Most High, I believe that You are my refuge and my fortress. My family and I are protected by the Blood of Jesus. Therefore, no evil shall befall us and neither shall any plague come nigh our dwelling. My family is delivered from hurt, harm, and danger and no weapon formed against my family or me prospers. I thank You that You give me and my family wisdom to overcome life's situations, and the angels of the Lord are encamped around us and we have peace and protection in every situation. We support the work of God in the earth, we prosper in all that we set our hands to do and we are protected all the days of our lives in Jesus' name, Amen.

From time to time, I will get specific requests to write confessions for children and their aspirations. Here is a confession for your children who are interested in sports and they desire to be successful and play at the highest levels. With a simple modification, you can use it for any of your children's aspirations.

# EXCELLING IN SPORTS CONFESSION

Jesus Christ is Lord over my spirit, soul and body. I choose to live a victorious overcoming life. I have the wisdom of God in me for every situation and I operate at my maximum and excel in all that I set my hands to do.

I choose not to fear because I cast the whole of my care on You and I know that You care for me. I choose not to have anxiety or worry about anything and I am more than a conqueror because I am covered by the Blood of Jesus and the angels of the Lord encamp around about me and the power of the Holy Spirit works through me.

I can do all things through Christ who strengthens me. I am confident that He who began a good work in me will perform it until the day of Jesus Christ. I thank You Father for the favor on my life that surrounds me as a shield and no weapon formed against me shall prosper. I function at the highest level of my ability at all times proving that I am the head and not the tail. I perform always at a level superior to all my competitors and I am respected for my diligence toward my profession. I thank You Father that You prosper me in all that I set my hands to do and I have the wisdom of God to make the right decisions concerning my finances.

I am a child of God who commits to walk in righteousness all the days of my life. I will handle all my affairs in a manner that pleases God, because I owe it to God who saved me, I owe it to my family who depends on me, I owe it to this generation that needs my example, I owe it to my church that has taught me righteousness and I owe it to myself because I am a child of God. In the name of Jesus, I thank You, Father that You perfect all that concerns me.

# Overcoming Worry, Stress and Sleeplessness

During our Worship services, we often make an appeal for people to come forward if they need prayer for sickness or disease in their body; for mental depression, or if they are experiencing an unusual amount of fear.

From time to time, people come forward and they are depressed because things are not going the way they planned and it is causing them to not sleep at night. Not knowing it is the will of God for us to have peace of mind can be frustrating. I have instructed people over the years that God wants them to have sweet rest, to cast the whole of their care upon Him and to have confidence that He cares for them.

Surely, a person hearing this information for the first time would be totally amazed. I will generally see their amazement and pray for them a simple prayer, then I instruct them to come up after service and I give them a confession so they can experience God's best. The will of God for our lives is not automatic. We must know what to do to get God involved in our circumstances. The Bible says in Hosea 4:6 *"My people are destroyed for a lack of knowledge..." (KJV)*.

You know there is an old saying that goes something like this, "what you don't know won't hurt you." Well, when it comes to the principles and promises of God, "what you don't know, will hurt you."

I feel obligated to share this chapter in the book with those persons who are struggling with sleepless nights. It is the will of God for you to enjoy your rest. What you must do is take authority over the powers of darkness (the devil, satan) that would try to interfere with God's perfect will for your life. If you don't know your rights as a believer, I encourage you to find a church that teaches the Word and ask them to pray for your deliverance.

After you have prayed, make the following Scriptures and confessions a part of your daily routine. It is important that you understand that the Word of God is medicine to your flesh (Proverbs 4:22). Just as you would go to the doctor and he would give you a prescription, this is your Word prescription.

# SCRIPTURES FOR OVERCOMING WORRY, STRESS AND SLEEPLESSNESS

*"Be careful (anxious, worried) for nothing;but in every thing by prayer and supplication with thanksgiving let your requests be made known unto God. And the peace of God, which passeth all understanding, shall keep your hearts and minds through Christ Jesus." (Philippians 4:6–7 KJV)*

*"And let the peace of God rule in your hearts, to the which also ye are called in one body; and be ye thankful." (Colossians 3:15 KJV)*

*"Thou wilt keep him in perfect peace, whose mind is stayed on thee: because he trusteth in thee." (Isaiah 26:3 KJV)*

*"I will both lay me down in peace, and sleep: for thou, Lord, only makest me dwell in safety." (Psalms 4:8 KJV)*

*"When thou liest down, thou shalt not be afraid: yea thou shalt lie down, and thy sleep shall be sweet." (Proverbs 3:24 KJV)*

*"It is vain to rise up early, to take rest late, to eat the bread of [anxious] toil for He gives [blessings] to His beloved in sleep." (Psalms 127:2 AMP)*

*"Great peace have they which love thy law: and nothing shall offend them." (Psalms 119:165 KJV)*

# CONFESSION FOR OVERCOMING WORRY AND STRESS

Father, I thank You that I can commit every anxiety, every worry and every care to You. I receive from You the peace of God and that peace rules my heart and my mind. My heart and mind are fixed on You; therefore, I have perfect peace. When I lie down my sleep shall be sweet and I have peace and safety. I am Your beloved and You promised Your beloved sweet rest.

Father, in the name of Jesus, I thank You that I have great peace and because I love the Word, nothing shall offend me.

Father, I thank You that when I lie down I receive blessings from You and I choose to cast every anxious thought on You and I know You care for me.

# CONFESSION FOR SWEET SLEEP

Father, in the Name of Jesus, I thank You for sweet rest. Your Word declares You give Your beloved sweet rest. I am loved by You and I declare when I lay down to sleep that my sleep shall be sweet. I will awaken refreshed and revitalized because You are Lord over my dreams, my thoughts and my heart while I sleep. I am Your child therefore I have great peace and undisturbed composure. I believe according to Your Word that you perfect all that concerns me. I thank You I am perfected and protected by the Blood of Jesus. I choose not to fear because I cast the whole of my care on You and I know that You care for me. I choose not to have anxiety or worry about anything because I know I am covered by the blood of Jesus and the angels of the Lord encamp around about me and my family. Father, thank You that no weapon formed against me shall prosper. I am righteous. I am delivered out of all adversity. I thank You Father that I dwell in the secret place of the most High and I abide under the shadow of the Almighty therefore no plague comes nigh my dwelling. I thank You Father in Jesus' name that I am a child of God and because of Your love for me I am covered and protected by Your blood in Jesus' Name.

# CONFESSION FOR FAVORABLE JUDGMENT IN COURT

Father, in the Name of Jesus, I thank You that You give me a mouth and tongue the enemy cannot gainsay or resist. As I stand before those who are in court, before the judge and those who have authority over me, I decree I am slow to speak and diligent to listen. Thank You Father that the king's heart is in Your hand and You turn it whatsoever way You will. As I stand before the judge, I thank You that You turn his heart in my favor.

Father, Your Word says if I make a vow and pay it I can intercede for those who are not innocent and they will be delivered by the pureness of my hand. Thank You Father as_____ goes before the judge and/

or parole board I intercede on their behalf and I decree supernatural wisdom and favor is _____.

Thank You, Father, that my steps are ordered by You and You protect and perfect all that concerns me, in Jesus' name.

If you are an entrepreneur, there are times when your business may be under attack or there is an economic cycle of recession and you need to rise above it. Your faith can keep your business strong so that you are not gripped with fear, doubt or worry.

# CONFESSION FOR BUSINESS SUCCESS

Father, In the Name of Jesus, I confess Your Word over my business and my finances this day. I am a giver therefore men give to me: good measure, pressed down, shaken together and running over. I am an heir of salvation so angels have been assigned to me. The angels of the Lord listen to the voice of His Word so I give voice to the Word and I decree favor surrounds me like a shield. Angels go forth now and bring forth my prosperity. Holy Spirit, I thank You that You are brooding over people from the north, south, east and west and You are speaking to them about me and my business. I believe You are causing people to be attracted to my business. I do what pleases You, Father God, therefore I prosper in all my endeavors and business transactions. My steps are ordered by You. My path is cleared of all obstructions and I hear the voice of the good Shepherd. I say without a doubt I am blessed, my family is blessed and my business is blessed. I live in the best. I eat the best. I wear the best. I go first class in life. Money I command you come to me! Favor, come to me! Abundance, come to me! Increase, come to me! Prosperity, come to me now, in the Name of Jesus!

# Overcoming Sickness, Disease, Fear and Mental Depression

In most of our services, we make an appeal similar to this, "If you are here today and there is sickness or disease in your body, your body is not functioning like it was created or designed to function, you are experiencing mental depression or perhaps you are experiencing an unusual amount of fear, we would like to pray for you."

Over the years, we have prayed for thousands of people and the results have been phenomenal. I believe it is the will of God for every person to walk and live in divine health. Health and healing is our covenant right as believers.

I will never forget one particular lady that came forward one Sunday for prayer. The lady stated that she had seen Bishop Hilliard on television and had been tremendously blessed by the television program. She was so excited that I wanted to see what her enthusiasm was all about. She later told me the reason she was so excited was because Bishop had taught on healing and she had received a supernatural healing in her body. The lady explained to me that she had arthritis so bad that her children and her husband would have to carry her to the restroom, bathe her, clothe her and feed her. But thank God she heard the Word on healing, believed it, confessed it and acted on it and was now walking with no pain. The reason she came forward for prayer was she did not want to get back in that state again, so she wanted me to agree with her for her total healing. I agreed with her and later that day wrote out a simple confession for her to daily thank God for her healing. Sickness and disease are not the will of God for His children. God does not put sickness and disease on us to teach us a lesson either. There are many references in the Bible where God records Jesus going about healing all the sick. So, if sickness and disease were God's will, why would Jesus work against the will of God? You see, it is not God who put the sickness and disease on you.

This chapter is not designed to teach you a complete lesson on divine healing; however, I will share a few scriptures to encourage you.

# SCRIPTURES FOR OVERCOMING SICKNESS, DISEASE, FEAR AND MENTAL DEPRESSION

*"How God anointed Jesus of Nazareth with the Holy Ghost and with power: who went about doing good, and healing all that were oppressed of the devil; for God was with him." (Acts 10:38 KJV)*

*"When the even was come, they brought unto him many that were possessed with devils: and he cast out the spirits with his word, and healed all that were sick;" (Matthew 8:16 KJV)*

*"And Jesus went about all the cities and villages, teaching in their synagogues, and preaching the gospel of the kingdom, and healing every sickness and disease among the people." (Matthew 9:35 KJV)*

*"Surely he hath borne our griefs, and carried our sorrows: yet we did esteem him stricken, smitten of God and afflicted. But he was wounded for our transgressions, he was bruised for our iniquities: the chastisement of our peace was upon him; and with his stripes we are healed." (Isaiah 53:4-5 KJV)*

*"Who his own self bare our sins in his own body on the tree, that we, being dead to sins, should live unto righteousness: by whose stripes ye were healed." (1 Peter 2:24 KJV)*

*"Be not over much wicked, neither be thou foolish: why shouldest thou die before thy time?" (Ecclesiastes 7:17 KJV)*

*"I shall not die, but live, and declare the works of the Lord." (Psalms 118:17 KJV)*

*"Jesus Christ the same yesterday, today, and forever." (Hebrews 13:8 KJV)*

# CONFESSION FOR OVERCOMING SICKNESS, DISEASE, FEAR AND MENTAL DEPRESSION

Father, in the Name of Jesus, I thank You that Jesus has borne my sickness and infirmities in His own body on the tree and with His stripes I am healed. I thank You Father that sickness and disease have no place in my life…I am redeemed from the curse of the law.

I thank You Father that Jesus Christ is the same yesterday, today, and forever and therefore I believe just as You healed people yesterday, I believe I am healed today in Jesus' name.

I thank You Father that every muscle, every cell, every organ in my body functions as they were designed to function. Father, I thank You that Your Word says, "Why should I die before my time?" Therefore I declare that I will live and not die and declare the works of the Lord.

## OVERCOMING FEAR AND WALKING IN DIVINE HEALTH

In a previous chapter, I promised you I would share in detail about the young lady who came to our church looking like a homeless "bag" lady. This is not an attack on homeless people but just an illustration to help you understand how horrifying this young lady looked.

The young lady walked into our church one night as we were having a prayer service. After the service was over, the young lady went into our bookstore and I just happened to step into the bookstore at that time.

As I walked in, I immediately asked the young lady what was wrong. Her response was shocking. She said, "I am going to die."

After a few minutes of talking to her, I found out that she had been having a health challenge for several years, which had caused some strain on her marriage. Due to the fact that doctors had no idea what was wrong with her, she had been given all types of antidepressants and sleeping pills. The young lady was convinced she was going to die. She was afraid to leave home, and she was afraid to go back home, she was living in constant fear.

Needless to say, that was not the will of God for her. Since our church was not as large as it is now, I took a personal interest in this young lady. I wrote personal confessions for her, prayed for her, and called her when I was available to ensure that she was confessing and believing God's Word. Today, that young lady is totally delivered.

*"For God has not given us a spirit of fear; but of power, and of love, and of a sound mind." (2 Timothy 1:7 KJV)*

*"In God have I put my trust; I will not be afraid what man can do unto me." (Psalms 56:11 KJV)*

*"So that we may boldly say, The Lord is my helper, and I will not fear what man shall do unto me." (Hebrews 13:6 KJV)*

*"The Lord is my light and my salvation; whom shall I fear? the Lord is the strength of my life; of whom shall I be afraid? Though an host should encamp against me, my heart shall not fear; though war should rise against me, in this will I be confident." (Psalms 27:1, 3 KJV)*

*"I shall not die, but live, and declare the works of the Lord." (Psalms 118:17, KJV)*

*"Beloved, I wish above all things that thou mayest prosper and be in health even as thy soul prospereth." (3 John 2 KJV)*

*"Jesus Christ the same yesterday, and today and forever." (Hebrews 13:8 KJV)*

*"For I will restore health unto thee, and I will heal thee of thy wounds, saith the Lord." (Jeremiah 30:17a KJV)*

*"And said, If thou wilt diligently hearken to the voice of the Lord thy God, and wilt do that which is right in his sight, and will give ear to his commandments, and keep all his statutes, I will put none of these diseases upon thee, which I have brought upon the Egyptians: for I am the Lord that healeth thee." (Exodus 15:26 KJV)*

*"He sent his word and healed them, and delivered them from their destructions." (Psalms 107:20 KJV)*

*"Who his own self bare our sins in his body on the tree, that we, being dead to sins, should live unto righteousness: by whose stripes ye were healed." (1 Peter 2:24 KJV)*

*"But he was wounded for our transgressions, he was bruised for our iniquities: the chastisement of our peace was upon him; and with his stripes we are healed." (Isaiah 53:5 KJV)*

*"No weapon that is formed against thee shall prosper." (Isaiah 54:17a KJV)*

# CONFESSION ON OVERCOMING FEAR AND WALKING IN DIVINE HEALTH

I will live and not die and declare the works of the Lord. God has not given me a spirit of fear, but of power, love and a sound mind. I have a calm and well-balanced mind with discipline and self-control. Fear cannot torment me; I choose to walk by faith. No weapon formed against me shall prosper.

Father, Your Word says You sent Your Word and healed them and delivered them from their destruction; therefore, I believe I am healed and delivered from sickness and disease. I walk in divine health; sickness and disease have no place in my body. My mind is alert, my body is strong, and I live an overcoming life. Any germ or disease that touches my body dies immediately because I am covered by the blood of Jesus.

Father, I thank You that Jesus already bore my sickness and infirmities in His own body on the tree and by His stripes I am healed. I thank You Father that no plague comes nigh my dwelling; therefore, no sickness or disease shall overtake me or lay hold on me. I walk in total health and wholeness and by the stripes of Jesus I am healed and made whole.

To close out this chapter, I think it's important to show you how to handle situations when your trust has been broken.

Whenever we deal with people, the potential exists to be betrayed and hurt. When the restoration process has begun, the enemy will usually attack you so that you remain in an offended state. I wrote this confession to help you while the relationship is being restored and to keep your heart free from offense and un-forgiveness.

# CONFESSION TO RESTORE TRUST

Father, in the name of Jesus, I thank You that I am skillfully and wonderfully made and have been equipped to overcome every emotional attack. I cast every care, every worry and all anxiety on You Lord. I am a new creature predestined for greatness. I am a child of God fully accepted by the Father. I bring every thought captive to the Word of God and choose to think only those things that are true, honest, pure and of a good report. I choose not to fear, be frustrated, fatigued or allow falsehoods to discourage me. I plead the blood of Jesus over my conscience and I declare the blood cleanses my conscience of dead works. I set my heart and mind to forgive those who have betrayed me, deceived me and hurt me. I do not hold on to offenses but I choose to forgive. I realize before trust is restored that I must set the terms for restoration of the relationship. I allow the blood of Jesus to heal me of my hurt. I thank You Father that Jesus bore my grief's and carried my sorrows on Calvary, He was wounded for my transgressions, the chastisement of my peace was upon Him and by His stripes, I am the healed. I weep not as those who have no hope because my hope and confidence is in You, God! I trust You with my life and for the spirit of heaviness, I will exchange it for the garment of praise. I will praise You God in the midst of every situation because I know You perfect all that concerns me and Your blood purifies, pardons and protects me in Jesus name.

# Overcoming Grief and Sorrow

In this chapter, I want to share an experience that all of us have faced or will face in our lives and that is, the transition from this life of someone we love and care for.

On July 26, 1994, my mother-in-law who had lived with us since 1990 went to the hospital for her routine visit and to have her porte cath moved: a minor procedure which she had many times before. The young lady we hired to take her to and from the doctor picked her up that morning and said she would call us when everything was over.

Later that afternoon, we received a call from my sister-in-law stating that she had just left the hospital, and 'the surgery went well, and Mama was doing well'.

Approximately an hour or two later, we received an urgent phone call from the young lady who was caring for Mama for the last couple of years saying, "come to the hospital right away." Upon our arrival at the hospital, the young lady was in the hall crying stating that Mama passed away.

The lumps in my heart and stomach were then and still now, unexplainable. In all my wildest dreams, I never thought of Mama leaving us so swiftly. I also never envisioned her not coming back home and enjoying the comfort of her room that she loved so much.

The hospital allowed us to see her body before the funeral directors came. I saw a peace on her face that I had never seen before. Mama was really gone. Her going to be with God was painful enough, but immediately the thought rushed through my mind that we would have to explain to our children that Mama would not come home from the hospital, but had gone to a better place. The thought of explaining Mama's death to the older girls was not nearly as heart wrenching as having to explain to our nine year old daughter that her favorite person in the whole world, besides her dad and I, had gone to be with Jesus. Our daughter and Mama were actually the best of friends. They were like two long time friends who shared all their experiences with one another.

I, too, had a special love for Mama because as I said she lived with us for four years and she was never a burden. She was a wonderful mother-in-law who never butted into our (Ira and my) personal lives. I genuinely loved her because she was a unique part of the wonderful man I have for a husband.

I could not ever remember anyone so close to me transitioning from this life. When mama died, it was as though I not only felt the loss of mama but the pain of my baby girl losing her friend. The pain was extremely real to me as I saw my little girl cry so much that it seemed there were no more tears inside of her.

I knew I had to apply that same Word I had so boldly taught to others in our ministry, who had loved ones transition in the past. As difficult as it was, I had to go on with my life and confess and believe that God's Word must work for me in this situation. I also had to be an example and instruct my little girl to apply that same Word to her life.

Indeed we overcame that situation by confessing and believing God's Word. The entire ordeal strengthened my walk with God and proved to me that God is indeed faithful to His Word.

On January 28, 1995, I received a distressful phone call from my nephew saying that my mama (granny, DaMama) had fallen in the bathroom and papa (my dad, DaDaddy) could not get her up and he was crying. My immediate response was, "I am on my way."

Driving over to their home, which was about seven to ten minutes away, the thought never came to my mind that

DaMama was dead. As I drove up, I saw my god-sister (Berna) standing outside in tears and it still never occurred to me that DaMama had gone home to be with the Lord. As I approached my sister she said, "It doesn't look good. The paramedics are here and they have been working for a while and they have no pulse or heartbeat." I went into the house and there I saw my mama (DaMama) lying on the bedroom floor lifeless. DaMama was indeed dead. How could I deal with this? Only six months and two days ago, Mama (my mother-in-law) had transitioned and now, DaMama.

As I stood there in my parents' home, the thoughts of grief and sorrow tried to overtake my mind. I was at a crossroad of trusting God or just throwing in the towel and forgetting all the Word I had taught, been taught and had even lived through over the past six months. As difficult as it was at first, I decided not to throw in the towel. I continued to confess the Word daily. Even though the pain of the grief initially was quite intense, I put pressure on my mouth. As the tears rolled down my face, I diligently confessed and believed God's Word. After all this time, I can truthfully say, the Word has totally brought peace.

# SCRIPTURES ON OVERCOMING GRIEF AND SORROW

*"Surely he hath borne our griefs and carried our sorrows; yet we did esteem him stricken smitten of God and afflicted. But he was wounded for our transgressions; he was bruised for our iniquities; the chastisement of our peace was upon him and with his stripes we are healed." (Isaiah 53:4 KJV)*

*"Wherein ye greatly rejoice, though now for a season, if need be, ye are in heaviness, through manifold temptations: that the trial of your faith, being much more precious than gold that perisheth, though it be tried with fire, might be found unto praise and honour and glory at the appearing of Jesus Christ. Whom having not seen, ye love; in whom though now ye see [him] not, yet believing, ye rejoice with joy unspeakable and full of glory: Receiving the end of your faith [even] the salvation of [your] souls." (1 Peter 1:6-9 KJV)*

*"And Nehemiah, which [is] Tirshatha, and Ezra the priest the scribe, and the Levites that taught the people, said unto all the people, This day [is] holy unto the Lord your God; mourn not, nor weep. For all the people wept, when they heard the words of the law. Then he said unto them, Go your way, eat the fat and drink the sweet, and send portions unto them for whom nothing is prepared;*

*for [this] day [is] holy unto our Lord; neither be ye sorry; for the joy*
*of the Lord is your strength." (Nehemiah 8: 9-10 KJV)*

*"Therefore the redeemed of the Lord shall return, and come with*
*singing unto Zion; and everlasting joy [shall be] upon their head:*
*they shall obtain gladness and joy; [and] sorrow and mourning shall*
*flee away." (Isaiah 51:11 KJV)*

# CONFESSION ON OVERCOMING GRIEF AND SORROW

Father, I thank You on Calvary, Jesus already bore my grief's and carried my sorrows. He was wounded for my transgressions and the chastisement of my peace was upon Him and with His stripes I am healed. I think only those things that are true, honest and are of a good report. I weep not as those who have no hope because my hope and confidence are in the Lord. I have joy unspeakable and full of glory. The joy of the Lord is my strength. Sorrow and mourning must flee away from me according to God's Word.

I receive the everlasting joy upon my head in Jesus' name. I choose to offer unto You Father the sacrifice of praise which is the fruit of my lips giving praise and honor to You. I praise You Father because I know You are the God of all comfort and you promised to comfort me in every situation.

I receive Your comforting power in my life now. I thank You Father for Your Son Jesus, the Holy Spirit and the Word that promises You will never leave me or forsake me. I am not alone because the Holy Spirit is with me, walks along side of me and comforts me in every situation.

## OVERCOMING PARENTAL ILLNESS

DaMama (my mother) had gone through a very degrading illness (Alzheimer's) for about five years, yet, I never allowed myself to think thoughts of her not being at home when I went to visit her.

I am so committed to the confession of the Word of God, that I developed a simple confession for my mother over time she had learned to make the confession daily with the help of my sister, my children and me. We had the nurse we hired to care for her helping her with the confession. Even though DaMama was diagnosed with Alzheimer's, I believed she did not go through the horrible things most Alzheimer's patients go through because we helped her to confess the Word. The doctors, nurses and friends of our family were amazed at DaMama's memory, her loving spirit and her total disposition throughout her illness. I will share her confessions here so that you can also see God's Word work in your family members' lives.

# DAMAMA'S CONFESSION

Jesus is Lord over my spirit, soul (mind, will, emotions, imaginations, intellect) and my body. Jesus has been made unto me wisdom, righteousness, sanctification, and redemption. I can do all things through Christ who strengthens me. I do not fret, worry, or have anxiety about anything. I can cast the whole of my care on the Lord.

I have the mind of Christ and hold the thoughts, feelings, and purposes of His heart. I hear the voice of the Good Shepherd. I hear my Father's voice and the voice of the stranger I will not follow. I roll my works upon the Lord. I commit and trust them wholly to Him. He will cause my thoughts to become agreeable to His will, and so shall my plans be established and succeed.

I let the Word of God dwell in me richly. He who began a good work in me will continue that work until the day of Jesus Christ. I thank God daily that I prosper even as my soul prospers. I trust in the Lord with all my heart and I lean not to my own understanding, but in all my ways, I acknowledge Him and He will direct my paths.

Today, I fix my mind on whatever is true, whatever is worthy of reverence and is honorable and seemly, whatever is just, whatever is pure, whatever is lovely and lovable, whatever is kind and winsome and gracious. If there is any virtue and excellence, if there is anything worthy of praise, I will think on, weigh and take account of these things. I am a believer and not a doubter. I hold fast to my confession of faith. In Jesus' name

# Overcoming Generation Curses/Inherited Diseases

Of course you know, the devil has tried to torment me with the thoughts of me having Alzheimer's. I confess God's Word over my children and myself daily; I believe and act on these Scriptures and confessions daily.

*"No weapon formed against me shall prosper; and every tongue that shall rise against thee in judgment thou shalt condemn." (Isaiah 54:17 KJV)*

*"He that dwelleth in the secret place of the most High shall abide under the shadow of the Almighty. I will say of the Lord He is my refuge and my fortress; my God, in Him will I trust." (Psalms 91:1 KJV)*

*"Because thou hast made the Lord, which is my refuge, even the most High, thy habitation. There shall no evil befall thee, neither shall any plague come nigh thy dwelling. For he shall give his angels charge over thee to keep thee in all thy ways." (Psalms 91:9-11 KJV)*

*"In You, O Lord, do I put my trust and confidently take refuge; let me never be put to shame or confusion! Deliver me in Your righteousness and cause me to escape; bow down Your ear to me and save me! Be to me a rock of refuge in which to dwell, and a sheltering stronghold to which You have appointed to save me, for You are my Rock and my Fortress. Rescue me, O my God, out of the hand of the wicked, out of the grasp of the unrighteousness and ruthless man. For You are my hope; O Lord God, You are my trust from my youth and the source of my confidence. Upon You have I learned and relied from birth; You are He Who took me from my mother's womb and You have been my benefactor from that day. My praise is continually of You; I am as a wonder and surprise to many, but You are my strong refuge. My mouth shall be filled with Your praise and with Your honor all the day. Cast me not off nor send me away in the time of old age; forsake me not when my strength is spent and my powers fail. For my enemies talk against me; those who watch for my life consult together. Saying, God has forsaken him; pursue and persecute and take him, for there is none to deliver him. O God, be not far from me! O my God, make haste to help me! Let them be put to shame and consumed who are adversaries to my life; let them be covered with reproach, scorn, and dishonor who seek and require my hurt, But I will hope continually and will praise You yet more and more; My mouth shall tell of Your righteous acts and of Your deeds of salvation all the day, for their number is more than I know, I will come in the strength and with the mighty acts of the Lord God; I will mention and praise Your righteousness, even Yours alone. O God, You*

*have taught me from my youth, and hitherto have I declared Your wondrous works. Yes, even when I am old and gray-headed, O God, forsake me not, [but keep me alive] until I have declared Your mighty strength to [this] generation, and Your might and power to all that are to come." (Psalms 71:1–18 AMP)*

*"The glory of young men is their strength, and the beauty of old men is their gray head [suggesting wisdom and experience]." (Proverbs 20:29 AMP)*

*"And the Lord said My spirit shall not always strive with man for that he also is flesh yet his days shall be an hundred and twenty years." (Genesis 6:3 KJV)*

*"Christ hath redeemed us from the curse of the law, being made a curse for us." (Galatians 3:13 KJV)*

# PERSONAL CONFESSION FOR OVERCOMING GENERATION CURSES/INHERITED DISEASES

No weapon formed against me shall prosper. Because I dwell in the secret place of the most High, I abide under the shadow of the Almighty, I will say of the Lord, You are my refuge and my fortress; my God, in You will I trust. Therefore no evil shall befall me, neither shall any plague come nigh my dwelling. I am protected by the blood of Jesus; because I have allowed the blood of Jesus to cleanse my conscience, I only think on those things that are true, that are honest, and that are of a good report. My mind is alert, my body is strong, and I have a sound mind. I live a long life and a life of purpose. The number of my years shall be 120. I walk in total health and wholeness. In Jesus' name

# Building Self-Esteem

As a believer, one of the greatest challenges you have to overcome is not thinking of yourself as God sees you. For many years we ran a weekly ministry as well as resident drug treatment program. It was for addicts and their families. We saw that people would come to the weekly classes just to receive the assurance that in spite of their bad decisions God still loved them.

The truths listed on the next few pages should be confessed daily to build the believer's self-esteem. It is critical for the believer to see himself or herself as God sees him or her. John the Baptist saw himself as God saw him and spoke in agreement with the way God saw him (John 1:19-23). The discipline to speak God's Word will transform your thinking. It will change how you see yourself and your faith level will soar. As you see yourself differently, you will respond to others differently.

# CONFESSIONS FOR BUILDING SELF-ESTEEM
# 15 FREEDOM TRUTHS

1. I am a New Creature predestined for greatness. I1 Corinthians 5:17

2. I am a Child of God fully accepted by the Father. John 1:12

3. I am loved by God regardless of how I perform. Romans 5:8

4. I am forgiven and will not be tormented by my past errors. I John 1:9

5. I am an overcomer and my faith is changing my circumstances. I John 5:4

6. I am a giver and God is causing people to help me prosper. I1 Corinthians 9:8

7. I have authority over the devil and no demon power can hurt me. Luke 10:17

8. Abundance is God's will for me and I will not settle for less. John 10:10

9. I am healed and sickness will not lord over my body. 1 Peter 2:24

10. God is on my side; I will not fear. Psalm 118:6

11. The Holy Spirit is my helper; I'm never alone and I have the peace of God. Philippians 4:7

12. I am blessed and it's a matter of time before things change. What I see now is only temporary. Ephesians 1:3; I1 Corinthians 4:18

13. I have the wisdom of God; I hear the Father's voice; my steps are ordered by God and the voice of a stranger I will not follow.

14. I am set in the Body of Christ and I know that I am valuable and important to the work of God. 1 Corinthians 12:20-25; Ephesians 4:11-12

15. I choose not to be offended and I am being delivered out of all afflictions and persecutions. Matthew 5:10-12

# CONFESSIONS ON SEEING YOURSELF AS GOD SEES YOU

These confessions will help you to establish who you are. Daily you should remind yourself of who you are from God's Word.

I AM...

1. A Child of God. Romans 8:16

2. Redeemed from the Hand of the Enemy. Psalms 107:2

3. Forgiven. Colossians 1:13, 14

4. Saved by Grace through Faith. Ephesians 2:8

5. Justified. Romans 5:1

6. Sanctified. 1 Corinthians 1:2

7. A New Creature. I1 Corinthians 5:17

8. Partaker of His Divine Nature. I1 Peter 1:4

9. Redeemed from the Curse of the Law. Galatians 3:13

10. Delivered from the Powers of Darkness. Colossians 1:13

11. Led by the Spirit of God. Romans 8:14

12. A Son of God. Romans 8:14

13. Kept in Safety Wherever I Go. Psalms 91:11

14. Getting All My Needs Met by Jesus. Philippians 4:19

15. Casting All My Cares on Jesus. 1 Peter 5:7

16. Strong in the Lord and in the Power of His Might. Ephesians 6:10

17. Doing All Things through Christ Who Strengthens Me. Philippians 4:13

18. An Heir of God and a Joint-Heir with Jesus. Romans 8:17

19. Heir to the Blessings of Abraham. Galatians 3:13, 14

20. Observing and Doing the Lord's Commandments. Deuteronomy 28:12

21. Blessed Coming In and Blessed Going Out. Deuteronomy 28:6

22. An Heir to Eternal Life. I John 5:11, 12

23. Blessed with All Spiritual Blessings. Ephesians 1:3

24. Healed by His Stripes. 1 Peter 2:24

25. Exercising My Authority over the Enemy. Luke 10:19

26. Above Only and Not Beneath. Deuteronomy 28:13

27. More than a Conqueror. Romans 8:37

28. Establishing God's Word Here on Earth. Matthew 16:19

29. An Overcomer by the Blood of the Lamb and the Word of My Testimony. Revelation 12:11

30. Daily Overcoming the Devil. I John 4:4

31. Not Moved by What I See. I1 Corinthians 4:18

32. Walking by Faith and Not by Sight. I1 Corinthians 5:7

33. Casting down Vain Imaginations. I1 Corinthians 10:4-5

# MANIFESTED PROSPERITY CONFESSIONS

*"Thou has caused men to ride over our heads; we went through the fire and through the water: but thou broughtest us out into a wealthy place." (Psalm 66:12 KJV)*

*"You caused men to ride over our heads [when we were prostrate]; we went through fire and through water, but you brought us out into a broad moist place [to abundance and refreshment and the open air]"*

As you can see from the above Scriptures, it is the will of God for believers to walk in wealth and abundance. However, just because it is God's will, we will not automatically experience the power and will of God unless we do what is necessary to bring His will to pass in our lives. The following confessions were written to help you formulate a faith confession regarding wealth and prosperity.

Father, in the Name of Jesus, I thank You that promotions don't come from the east or the west, but You are the Judge who puts down one and picks up another. Therefore, Father, I believe You are ordering my steps and giving me favor so I am promoted on my job to _____(state the job title you desire). Father, I thank You the king's heart is in Your hand and You turn it whatsoever way You will. I thank You Father that those who have to make decisions concerning my promotion are sensitive to Your voice and obey Your voice. I thank You Father for my new position with better benefits, increase in income and abundant favor so I can continue to promote the Kingdom of God in the earth. I thank You Father I hear Your voice and obey Your voice as You give me wisdom to enhance my skills so I am ready for promotion. I thank You Father You are my source and You give me wisdom to tap into the right channel so I increase. I hold fast to my confession of faith as I travel to my wealthy place. In Jesus name

Father, in Jesus name, I thank You for giving me seed to sow, I thank You Father You promised to multiply my seed sown. Therefore, I believe I receive supernatural abundance in every area of my life. Father, for those persons You are speaking to concerning giving to me, I thank You they are free to obey Your voice and my increase is released to me. Father, for those persons who owe me, I thank You they are sensitive to Your voice and they have the necessary finances to pay me what is owed to me. I thank You Father that I am sensitive to hear Your voice and for those debts You want me to forgive, I obey You and release those debts. I thank You Father that I have sown my seed in faith and I am on my way to my wealthy place. In Jesus Name.

Father, In Jesus Name, I thank You for a debt free lifestyle. I have sown for the debt freedom of the ministry that teaches me the Word and I agree that our ministry is debt free. I thank You Father that whatsoever good any man doeth the same shall he receive of the Lord. I thank You Father for wisdom in purchases and the discipline to stay out of debt. I thank You for supernatural debt cancellation, supernatural increase and supernatural wisdom to handle my affairs in a manner that pleases You. I thank You Father that You are moving on the heart of my creditors and debts are being cancelled. I thank You Father, because I have sown my seed in faith with purpose of heart, You cause all grace (favor) to abound toward me and my life attracts the favor of God.

Father, I know it pleases You when I have more than enough, therefore, I believe all my debts are paid and I am ready to distribute more of my resources into the Kingdom of God in the earth. I thank You Father that I am on Your mind and You increase me more and more, me and my children. I am walking in wealth and prosperity as I enjoy life in the wealthy place. In Jesus name

Father, I thank You, You have a financial plan for the believer's prosperity called Tithes and Offerings. I set my heart to participate in Your plan to bless my life. I have given the tithes of my increase and I believe I receive the windows of Heaven blessing for my life and my family. I thank You Father for creative wisdom and insight into financial affairs. I have given for the support of the man and woman of God who teach me the Word of God, therefore, I believe I receive a first class lifestyle. I give to spread the gospel in the earth, therefore, I believe I receive the maximum return on my seed. I confess this ministry is debt free and I give for the support of the debt freedom of this ministry. Therefore, I thank You Father for supernatural wisdom, supernatural increase, and supernatural debt cancellation in my life. I have vowed and given my vow, therefore, I can decree a thing and it is established unto me and the light of God's favor shines upon my path. I thank You Father, I believe I receive your best in my transportation, in my life, and in my career for Your Word declares whatsoever good any man doeth the same shall he receive of the Lord. I thank You Father for abundance in my life and abundance for this ministry. I hold fast to my confession of faith. In Jesus name

Father, in Jesus name, I thank You that my life is committed to You and I have consistently sown my seeds, releasing my faith. I thank You Father that this is the day You have made and I rejoice in it. Thank You Father that You send prosperity now. I choose not to fear for the time to come for I have never seen the righteous forsaken nor his seed beg bread. I have confidence for the future because I will still bring forth fruit in old age. I increase and You cause me to be fat and flourishing. I thank You Father that I can rejoice in the time to come for my heart is fixed trusting in You I have sown my seed and I release my faith as I travel to my wealthy place. In Jesus name

Father, in Jesus Name, I thank You that I am on the path of perpetual increase. I have sown seed into good ground and I believe I receive a bountiful harvest. Wealth and riches are in my house and Your righteousness endures forever. My children are like olive plants; they are disciples taught of the Lord and they are delivered from every snare of the enemy. I am upright and my children are blessed with abundance. Father, I thank You that I rise early to seek Your face, therefore, You cause me to inherit real estate, jewels and other substances that will bring me enjoyment. I thank You Father that my harvest is on the way and the sinners are out there heaping up treasures for me. I thank You Father that I am a part of the generation that has been created to praise You. Therefore, I believe I receive all of my wealth as I enter my wealthy place. In Jesus name

Father, in Jesus name, I thank You that I am anointed to prosper. My eyes are open to see creative ways to increase financially. My ears are open to hear the best deals and my heart is pure so You can channel finances through me. I am on the path of perpetual increase as I enter my wealthy place. Wealth and riches are in my house. I declare that I am the righteousness of God. I have sown my seed for supernatural abundance and I live in daily expectation of increase. Money comes to me and my nature attracts money. The fear of lack has been broken and has no power over me. I hear my Father's voice and the voice of intimidation I choose not to follow. I am free from debt. I am the lender and not the borrower. The wealth of the wicked is being transferred to me and I commit to establish the Kingdom of God in the earth. I am ready to distribute and my life is a distribution channel for God's work in the earth. I thank You Father that daily You are loading me with benefits. I am anointed to prosper. I am on Your mind because You want to increase me more and more. Abundance is Your will for me because it pleases You when I prosper. I call increase, abundance and prosperity to come to me now. In Jesus name

# Blessed Pastor and Church

Bishop Hilliard and I have seen for more than 30 years, what can happen when God's people unify behind a visionary and the vision. Many Christians find it easy to point out the problems and shortcomings of their church but won't use their faith to see the church grow and become what God created it to be.

We trust you desire the church you are a part of to grow and prosper to fulfill its God-given purpose. Here is a confession that we have put together to assist you in using your faith for church growth.

## CONFESSION FOR PASTOR AND CHURCH

Father, in the Name of Jesus, I thank You that I am fully persuaded by Your Word. I know who I am and what I am capable of doing. I am a new creature, predestined for greatness. I am loved by You, God, regardless of how I perform. I take the shield of faith and quench every fiery dart of the wicked and cast down every thought of insignificance, inferiority, insensitivity, intimidation and insufficiency with the Word of God. The fear of lack is broken and has no power over me. I choose to win in every situation and I am passionate about my future and the future of my church, my children and my career. I believe You are faithful to every promise You've made. You promised no weapon formed against me will prosper. You promised You would deliver me out of all my troubles. You promised You already bore every sickness in Your own body on the tree and with Your stripes, I am healed. You promised You would increase me more and more. You promised You would daily load me with benefits. I believe what You promised and I am winning over all obstacles, defeats, disappointments and setbacks. I see my future through the eyes of faith, my future looks better than my past my best days are ahead I boldly declare I am anointed to prosper my eyes are open to see creative ways to increase financially. My ears are open to hear the best deals and my heart is pure so that You can channel finances through me. I am on the winning path of supernatural abundance and I live in daily expectation of increase. My winning attitude attracts resources to win in every area of my life. I love the church You have set me in and I decree my pastor opens his/her mouth boldly and makes known the mysteries of the gospel. I commit to support my church in every vision assignment because I am set in my church as it pleases You. I chose not to allow others to pull me out of my set place because I know You command the blessings on me at the place of unity. I have made a vow and paid my vow; therefore, I can now decree a thing and it is established unto me. I decree my church has supernatural supply in finances and in people. I believe You are drawing souls to our church from the north, east, west and south, in Jesus' name!!!

# Conclusion

It has been 30 years since I first wrote this book and I can honestly say that I am still inspired by its words and testimonies. I have seen hundreds of people experience God's best because they spoke God's Word. God's Word has benefitted me, my family and thousands of people that I will never know. I have confessed the Word of God long enough that it has become a lifestyle. The same needs to happen for you.

I trust that you will take this book and use it to overcome challenges in your life. It is a good idea to confess the Word over yourself and your family even when you don't need it so that the Word will be resident in your life and readily available should you ever encounter a challenge.

The Bible says in Matthew 12:34-35 (KJV), *"O generation of vipers, how can ye, being evil, speak good things? for out of the abundance of the heart the mouth speaketh. A good man out of the good treasure of the heart bringeth forth good things: and an evil man out of the evil treasure bringeth forth evil things."*

The Word of God is planted in our hearts (spirits) by what we hear, what we say, and what we see. As you speak the Word out of your mouth through the confessions in this book, you hear it, you say it, and as you read the Scriptures, you see the Word.

Don't be discouraged or swayed when you first start confessing the Word. The devil and others will try to torment you by saying you are lying. You are not lying; you are simply speaking in agreement with what God's Word says about you. If this book has inspired and encouraged you, write to me and let me know.

# WRITE:

Pastor Bridget Hilliard
New Light Christian Center Church
P.O. Box 670167
Houston, Texas 77267-0167
(281) 87-LIGHT • (281) 875-4448

# ABOUT THE AUTHOR

Pastor Bridget E. Hilliard is the multi-talented wife of Bishop I.V. Hilliard, they are the co-founders and pastors of New Light Christian Center Church ("One Church, Multiple Locations") located in Houston, Austin & Beaumon, TX. Committed to carry out the ministry mandate to spread the Gospel by way of television, Pastor Bridget ministers to thousands daily on local and national television stations. Her style of ministry is unique, as the compassion of Jesus flows through her preaching. She successfully ministers to men, as well as, thousands of women.

Pastor Bridget is also the founder of The Women Who Win Network, a network committed to helping today's Christian women win in life by using their faith. Her life is a continuous testimony and example of a woman living the overcoming Christian life.

Pastor Bridget attributes her success and accomplishments to almighty God and the continuous support and encouragement from her husband who she affectionately calls, Ira.

For Andy

A Girl Named Dara

## ACKNOWLEDGMENTS

I would like to thank my wonderful wife and amazing daughter for supporting me and allowing me to sneak away all the time to work on my stories.

I also want to thank my early readers—Linda Barlow, Sheri Campbell, Lisa Bolger, Cassandra Dagones, Arthur Milliken, Jonas Ball, Kris Fallon, and Riccardo Bocci. I appreciate you all taking the time to read my story and to give me your thoughtful feedback. This book is much better because of your efforts.

Thanks to my editors Elizabeth B. and Peachy Yap. I appreciate your patience wading through my endless typos and grammar mistakes.

Finally, thanks to Myriam Strasbourg for the fantastic cover art. Thank you for bringing Dara to life.

# Chapter 1

I remember the first time I laid eyes on Dara.

I was taking my first and only poetry class at UCLA, sitting in the back row and surveying the whole scene. Where some of the university's lecture halls held upward of five hundred students, this was a more intimate space, a perfect setting to explore the depths—and heights—of great poetry. I estimated there were only about thirty students in the room.

This was an advanced class, and I wasn't even an English major. To gain admittance, I'd been required to submit a sample of my poetry and a short essay on why I wanted to take the class. I suspected I'd been accepted more on the novelty of coming from outside the major and less on the quality of my submission.

I was sure I didn't fit in. The inhabitants of the room were magnificent, interesting, colorful, and deep. Every student I saw seemed to be making some artistic statement with their clothes or their accessories or the way they carried themselves. The young man seated two rows in front of me was one of the brilliant ones. With round-rim glasses and a checkered scarf wrapped high around his neck, he sat in the unimpressed way you would expect from a person being forced to watch the same movie for the third time in two days. He was talking to two cute girls, both shrouded in dark shades of brooding, yet stylish, attire.

By contrast, I was plain. I felt underdressed in a pair of blue jeans and the same green sweater I had worn three years earlier in my high school senior portrait. I believe the quote I had inset under the photo had been "Always believe in yourself." The person next to me in the class of 1992 Costa Mesa High School yearbook had taken a different approach and offered the following wisdom: "A day you're not wasted is a wasted day." Not sure how the censors let that one slip by, but the point is *I have always been boring.*

The young man with the scarf was conferring with his small congregation. I picked up on his conversation midsentence. "So how do they expect to teach us poetry? Either you already know how to write poetry, or you never will."

Damn. I didn't know how to write poetry. I mean, I tried—but it was mediocre at best. If what he was saying was true, my prospects of becoming the next John Keats were not looking very good. So much for my "Ode to a Phoenician Fern."

One of the girls waved off his comment. "That's not true."

I recognized her from my freshman dorm. I lived one floor above her and often saw her in the dining commons. Her name was Candice, but she went by Can.

"You don't think so?" he replied with a hint of mockery.

"No, I think you can teach anything to anybody."

"Yeah, well . . . ," the Scarf retorted. "Didn't you also say that New Order was better than Joy Division?"

The other girl raised her hand to her mouth to stifle a laugh as Can blushed. The Scarf eased back in his seat with a smug "I rest my case" look on his face.

The clock showed 11:03 a.m. We were a couple of minutes into our hour, and our professor was still milling about and arranging some papers on his lectern. His apparent lack of urgency had a few of us exchanging glances and smirking to one another. Just as he appeared to compose himself and command a silence across the room, the door to the classroom opened with a generous squeak.

The girl who walked in was beautiful. The entire class and even the professor looked up, then offered a collective double take.

She hugged the wall and walked toward the back of the classroom. If she was self-conscious for entering late into a completely noiseless room full of people who were blatantly staring at her, she gave no indication. Her expression was one of mild disinterest. She was dressed down in the ubiquitous uniform of effortlessly sexy girls in the early 1990s—jeans and a bodysuit. She was tall with a phenomenal figure and long straight blonde hair pulled back in a ponytail. Over her shoulder, she carried a leather bag that was large enough to transport a couple of schoolbooks, but stylish enough to not look like a schoolbag.

She turned the corner at the end of the back row and walked right to the seat next to mine. Pointing, she raised her eyebrows in a universal sign for "Is this seat taken?"

I could barely utter the words. "No, no—go ahead."

She sat and swung her bag onto the surface of her desk. Turning to me three-quarters, my new neighbor spoke quietly out of the side of her mouth. I thought I detected an accent but could not place it. "What did I miss?"

I did not know it then, but that question and the breathless moments preceding it would change the course of my life.

# Chapter 2

Our professor, Ope Opeyemi, was born in Johannesburg, South Africa, in the 1950s. He was a world-famous poet, and I had read a couple of his books even before finding out he taught a class at the university.

From reading his published works, I never could have imagined how quirky he would prove to be. On that first day of class, he dressed casually in baggy jeans and a short-sleeved shirt buttoned up to the collar. His hair was piled up and tucked into a crocheted tam. Although his face rested in a worried and weather-beaten state, he smiled easily and frequently, and the effect was comforting and infectious.

I knew from having read the biography on the inside cover of one of his books that he had witnessed terrors and atrocities that I couldn't even fathom. He had been through horrifying circumstances and lived to tell the tale—or perhaps I should say *to write the poetry*.

He didn't seem to have a formal lesson prepared. Rather, Opeyemi paced comfortably from left to right, talking about poetry in the most general sense. He smiled broadly at his students and gave off the impression that he was happy to be with us. There was a musicality in the way he spoke, and after about fifteen minutes, I started getting more comfortable with his unfamiliar accent. I enjoyed the way he pronounced the word "poetry," reducing it to two syllables: "PWAH-tree."

Among the many interesting things he said during the hour, I was most intrigued by his comments about the *act* of writing versus the *need* for expression. While living in Africa, he recounted that he often saw wild animals up close and in their natural habitat. It was dangerous, he explained, and also very humbling. By contrast, in the United States, he could see most of those same animals at various zoos and animal parks. The experience, he confessed, was neither dangerous nor humbling.

"In fact," he explained, "the very premise of a cage fills us with the false belief that we need not fear a wild beast because we *think* we can tame it and control it. Nothing . . ." He paused for effect. "Nothing could be further from the truth. A wild animal is *always* a wild animal," he cautioned. "And they are always staring back at you from their bindings and secretly waiting until they can break free and devour you."

The class collectively straightened up in their chairs at the professor's stern warning.

"Expression," he continued, "is the wild animal, and writing is the cage." Then he got very serious and posed a question to the entire class. "So why do we write?" The question was rhetorical. "Why bother?" He paused for a long moment and let an uncomfortable silence build. "Why put your real and raw emotions into a cage? Why?"

We were all silent. At this point, my beautiful neighbor reached into her bag, removed a small leather-bound notebook and a pen, and began scribbling notes on the lined pages.

"You are all English literature majors, are you not?" he asked us, never minding the fact that at least one of us was not. "So tell me . . ." He paused and let the word "me" linger in the air. "Why do you write at all?"

Silence was the only response. I was in a room full of English majors, and although they were prone to overuse their words, they said nothing.

"For this class," Opeyemi continued, "and for every day and year to follow, your assignment is to give yourself one good reason to write. You will not be graded on your ultimate answer—not by me anyway. But you may find out something important about yourself."

# Chapter 3

Class was dismissed, and I packed my notebook into my bag. The girl next to me spoke in what I believed to be a Russian accent. "I like this professor."

I was surprised that she was starting a conversation with me, but I was both pleased and relieved at the same time. In truth, I had been spending the last ten minutes of class trying to think of a good opening line.

"Me too," I blurted automatically and paused to think of a follow-up comment.

The Scarf turned to face us. He wore a pleasant expression and nodded enthusiastically in response to her comment. "He's such an inspiration, don't you think?"

My head jerked in his direction. The attractive blonde at my side ignored his comment altogether. She was occupied looking for an item in her bag. The act seemed as though it might have been a pantomime to avoid his question and any further conversation. But I didn't know—I couldn't tell if she was ignoring him on purpose or if she simply hadn't realized he was talking to her.

He looked at me for a hint and raised an eyebrow as if to ask "Is she messing with me?"

I shrugged. I had no idea of her intention or of who she even was. The Scarf stood for a moment, looking expectantly for a response, then began to make a second point. "He really . . ."

He thought better of it and turned back toward the front of the room as if something important had occurred to him. He quickly gathered his things and walked away. "Can!" he called out to the New Order fan and prior object of his light ridicule. "Hold on! I need to ask you something."

The blonde girl finished arranging the items in her bag and looked up at me. This was my first look directly at her. Any perceptions I had already formed about her beauty from watching her walk into class and sneaking sideways glances during the lecture revealed themselves as steeply underestimated. She was both cute and beautiful at the same time. Her eyes were a stunning shade of light blue. It's trite to say it, but I had never encountered a woman so lovely. And even more to the point, I had certainly never *spoken* to a woman so lovely.

"Do you always sit in the back of the class?" she asked in her Eastern bloc affectation.

I paused for a moment, somewhat mesmerized before snapping out of it. "I do, yes."

"Why?"

"I don't know."

"I do it too. I like to observe the entire class. I learn from the professor and from watching the students." She waved broadly, indicating the room in front of us.

"I like that," I said. "You're better off learning from a whole class than from one single person."

"I'm Dara."

"Jeff." I stood and extended my hand in a formal greeting. She flashed an amused look before shaking my hand.

"You have a class now?" she asked.

"No, I'm done for the day."

"Would you like to come to lunch with me?"

The offer took me by surprise. "Now?"

"Of course. Do you not eat lunch?"

That was pretty much how it began. Before I knew it, we were on our way to a small kiosk in the middle of campus that served teriyaki bowls. Dara assured me this was the best meal on campus and there was a shady bench where we could sit and watch the students walk by.

I'd never been a ladies' man. I was okay to look at and could be charming, usually by accident only. But my amorous adventures were not the stuff of legends. I was social and had a lot of acquaintances on campus, both male and female. Every couple of months, I would hear about a girl who thought I was attractive or interesting and had asked one of her friends about me.

In my freshman year, one cute young coed had come up to me at the end of a lecture and handed me a small strip of paper with her name and number on it. Her name was Stacy. We were both in our first year, and we lived in separate dorms. We had not officially met yet, but we saw each other around campus. She was petite and cute, and a few of my guy friends in the dorm were aware of her and counted her among the "hot girls" in the freshman class. For whatever *that* was worth.

On the day she handed me her number, she was wearing a stylish plaid baseball cap. She peeked up at me from below the bill and smiled shyly before walking off. Understand that we were both about eighteen years old at the time. In the early 1990s, offering me her number was not an invitation for a cheap hookup. At that time, her actions were an unspoken, but bold, request to maybe talk on the phone or go get coffee. I don't know why, but I never called her.

In the same way I was surprised that Stacy had given me her number out of the blue, I was also surprised that Dara had started up a conversation with me in class. And truth be told, I was nothing short of shocked that she had asked me to join her for lunch.

Walking through campus with Dara was a strange experience. She received many stares and double takes from men and women. I hated to admit it, but walking alongside her was an ego boost. She kept her eyes on the ground in front of her and made a point of it *not* to acknowledge any of the attention.

In time, I would learn how and why it had become so natural and maybe even necessary for her to ignore all the men that forced an orbit around her.

# Chapter 4

The teriyaki bowls were more impressive than I expected. I ordered their signature item and received a heavy Styrofoam bowl packed with rice, lettuce shreds, and a generous breast of chicken cut into vertical strips and slathered with teriyaki sauce. Dara ordered the same and paid our tab with a brand-new $20 bill she pulled from an expensive-looking wallet she had retrieved from her bag.

She led me a little farther back into campus, to a small courtyard off a pathway between two of the university's original brick buildings. "I always love to eat here when the weather is nice. This is my favorite place to be on campus."

I had walked this common thoroughfare between buildings on several occasions but had not known about this small space. We found the bench she had described unoccupied in the speckled shade of a large tree. As promised, it sat at an angle and offered a view of the walkway, where we could observe students scurrying back and forth to class or other such destinations.

"In spring," she continued, motioning to the walls of the courtyard around us, "this whole area will bloom with flowers, and it's very pretty."

We sat there, eating and talking for a while. The conversation was comfortable, and I found myself silently questioning what exactly was happening. Why had this beautiful woman randomly selected the seat next to mine and then proceeded to buy me lunch and lead me to this quaint little secret spot? We had been together for about an hour since our class had let out, and she had not offered one even remotely romantic or suggestive comment. If anything, Dara's tone was informal and even abrasive at times. I did not take offense. I assumed the sharp tone was a result of English being her second language.

Dara was from Belarus. I had heard of the country in high school geography. I knew this was a nation nestled between Russia and Eastern Europe and at one point had been a part of Russia. I also knew that the capital city was Minsk, but beyond that, I knew nothing else. She had lived in Minsk for part of her life, and although she was impressed that I knew her city, she did not seem too comfortable discussing her home country. She spoke of it only enough to declare that spring in Belarus was breathtaking and that Belarusian food was the best in all the world. She said she had been in the States for two years and those were the only things that she missed about her motherland.

I asked about her family, and Dara quickly deflected the question, preferring to discuss a point about the formation of Belarus as a nation. I got the message and did not push the subject any further. She admitted that most people in the States had not heard of Belarus and they usually assumed she was Russian when they heard her speak. She never corrected anyone and told me she believed it was better that people knew less about her anyway.

I was so curious about this last comment but felt like it was a doorway into a deeper conversation with Dara that I was not ready to have. I only smiled and said, "A little mystery is always a good thing."

She nodded, agreeing with my sentiment, but could not stop herself from calling me out on the irony. "But it seems you are not so mysterious."

"I guess I'm not."

"Maybe we can fix that." She cocked her head and raised her eyebrows slightly, giving me a conspirator's look. I had no idea what she could have possibly meant by the comment and assumed it was an attempt at humor, so I laughed a little in return.

We sat for a while longer and covered a varied and platonic list of topics. Any person watching from afar and reading our body language would have assumed we were a couple of old friends catching up over a meal and nothing more. But my heart did flutter from time to time, and I fought the constant urge to stare at her.

I was eventually able to calm down and just take the conversation for what it was. Dara was interesting and comfortably opinionated. She discussed literature and poetry, and it was obvious that she was well-read. I assumed she was an English major, but when I asked, she said, "Not exactly."

I tried to press the issue and ask her what her field of study was, but as with many other topics, she was elusive and discussed only the English classes she had taken. I admitted that I was studying political science with the goal of getting into law school, but I loved literature and poetry. Whenever my schedule could afford the time, I would enroll in these off-major classes, even though the credits wouldn't contribute to my graduation.

"If you love English, why not change your major?"

"This is just something I love. I will always love to read and study great writers, but I'm not interested in pursuing this as a career."

"You wish to be a lawyer?"

"A judge," I corrected, "at some point down the line."

"You dream to become a judge that reads great books in his free time?"

"Something like that."

"These are good answers." Dara showed genuine appreciation. "Good to have such strong goals."

"What about you?" I asked. "What are your goals?"

"My goals are not interesting," she replied, evading my question. "Why do you take this poetry class? This is a class for writing, is it not? Are you writing poetry?"

Whenever she tried to change the subject, her accent seemed to be a little thicker, and her phrasing seemed to become more awkward. I wondered if it was a device to disarm me and steer the conversation. I didn't care. If she had topics she was avoiding, I was happy to give her space.

"I am definitely not a poet, but I couldn't pass up a chance to take this class and learn how to write from such a great poet. I've read many of Opeyemi's books."

"You wish to write more poetry if you can learn?"

"Sure. If I could learn how," I answered honestly, "I would love to."

"You heard his question today: 'Why do you write?'"

"I heard him, yeah."

"So . . . why do you want to write?" she asked matter-of-factly. "Why is this important for you?"

"I don't know. He asked us that question a couple of times today, and I couldn't think of a good answer."

"Can you give *any* answer?" she pressed.

22

"The only answer I can think of is all of these great writers from the past, they had a voice, and they stood for something—and they wrote important things."

"You wish to write something important?"

"Maybe. I really don't know." I met her eyes. "What about you, Dara? Why do you want to write? I assume you took that class because you like to write."

She leaned in a little closer, lowering her voice. "I don't write anything. I love poetry, of course—very much. I didn't even know this professor was a poet and an author, but I will read his poems."

Dara and I continued like this a little while longer until early afternoon. The shadows were starting to lengthen, and the warm air gave way to a hint of an autumn chill. I didn't want to, but I had to excuse myself.

"Well, I'm sorry to do this, but I have to get going pretty soon."

"You have plans? Am I keeping you?" Dara asked flatly.

"My roommates and I are in a band," I said, stacking our used bowls and looking for a garbage can where I could throw them away. "We have a show coming up, and we need to practice."

We had been booked to play a gig at the Beta Beta Chi fraternity, otherwise known as BBX. We had plenty of time until the show, but we had not played since before summer break and were running the risk of embarrassing ourselves if we didn't practice. We'd agreed we would get together at our apartment later that day and work on some songs.

"That sounds like fun."

"It is." I wanted to add something more but couldn't quite think of what.

"Thank you for having lunch with me."

"No problem!" I said, probably with too much enthusiasm. "We should do it again."

"Maybe after class next week?" she suggested.

"Sounds good."

Dara remained in the courtyard. She told me she was going to hang out for a little while longer and then head back to her apartment. We said our final goodbyes, and I began the walk back to my place.

I wasn't sure what had just happened. *Was that a date?* Was our lunch, loosely set for next week, a date? Why, out of everyone in that class, had she chosen to walk right up to me and invite me to join her for an intimate conversation in her secret spot on campus?

Dara was blindingly attractive, and any reasonable person would quickly agree she was way out of my league. Maybe the John Hughes movies were right. Maybe the goofy, boring guy did have a chance with the femme fatale. Maybe she'd singled me out because of some inexplicable animalistic attraction. I was average-looking by LA standards, but maybe I was the model of manly beauty in Belarus.

Whatever the reasons were, I didn't care. I just felt great. The conversation had flowed naturally, and we had a lot of interests in common. Dara could be a little matter-of-fact in her demeanor, but she was sincere, and she asked me interesting questions. More than anything, I was happy to have gotten through the entire afternoon without saying anything too embarrassing or stupid. For a young man of twenty years, surviving an encounter with an attractive woman without sticking my foot in my mouth was quite an accomplishment.

I was a little disappointed that I would have to wait a week to see her again and felt remiss that I had not asked for her number. But I knew where she would be next Wednesday at 11:00 a.m. I was already counting down the days.

# Chapter 5

My roommate Francis had already set up his drum kit in our living room.

I noticed the new addition right away. "Hey, Francey, you got a second snare."

He spoke without taking his eyes off the issue of *Sports Illustrated* he had stolen from our neighbor's welcome mat. "I did. That's the good news."

"Uh-oh. What's the bad news?"

"Kerry didn't come back to school. He's still in Minneapolis. We have no bass."

My other roommate, Dylan, called from his bedroom, "Stop worrying about it!"

Clearly, this discussion had been going on for a while prior to my arrival. Kerry was a good friend who had played with us at a couple of shows. He was famous around campus for being the guy who walked around from class to class in a dress. He added a lot to the band and made us way more punk rock, but apparently, he would not be joining us for any gigs anytime soon.

Dylan exited his room and walked into the living room. His guitar was slung around his shoulder, and he was carrying a glass jar full of colorful guitar picks in one hand and several pages of printed paper in the other. I noticed he had already set up all our amps near the drum kit.

"I think we should prepare to go on with just two guitars," Dylan said, making his case. "I'm not sure we can find a bassist that will be comfortable with our style, but we'll try."

"You mean because we suck?" I added for effect.

"Actually, because *you* suck," Dylan corrected me. The words were harsh to the untrained ear, but he knew I was unfazed by the banter— and anyway, he wasn't wrong.

Dylan was a great guitar player. He had been practicing and playing in small coffee shops for the last seven years. He had never been in a band before, and despite our many musical flaws, he liked that we were getting a few gigs here and there. Francis was new to drumming, but it came naturally. He could keep the tempo of any song with machinelike precision. Of the three of us, he was the best singer, but he was too shy to sing and would only occasionally join in on harmonies.

I was the liability in the band. I couldn't sing or play guitar. But the whole thing was my brainchild, and Dylan and Francis and I were all best friends, so they stuck with me.

I loved music and had always wanted to be in a band. So last fall, in a moment of inspired lunacy while searching for a Halloween costume in a secondhand store, I saw a guitar/amp combo for $150 and a two-piece drum kit for $100. I spent *all* my money on the equipment and begged a stranger with a pickup truck to drive me back to my apartment.

When my roommates saw the instruments, they were game to set everything up and give it a go. Francis had never actually played the drums until I insisted that he try it, and he was a natural. We borrowed a hi-hat cymbal from a friend (who had yet to ask for it back), and voilà! Dutch Candy was born.

Friends often asked where we came up with the name, and we always gave some silly answer. But the truth was it all originated with Douglas Handy, an elementary school friend of mine. During the summer between third and fourth grade, we went to a basketball camp led by a strange older man who apparently had been really good at basketball in the 1950s. Every day, he wore extremely tight polyester shorts that were uncomfortable to even look at, and he tried constantly to get the campers to shoot free throws underhand.

During chalk talk sessions, he would often pull campers from the bleachers to join him on the court and demonstrate a play or a formation. On one occasion, he picked my friend out of the crowd and asked him for his name, to which my friend quietly replied, "Doug Handy."

The camp leader's hearing was already failing, so he thought the young boy said his name was Dutch Candy, and he almost lost his mind. "Dutch Candy? What kind of name is that?"

The camp erupted in laughter; and the entire population of campers, coaches, counselors, and even the ladies who served us lunch went out of their way for the entire day to greet Doug and add their own stupid submission to a growing list of horrible puns. "Hey, Dutch Candy, looking sweet!" or "Hey, Dutch, way to clog up the passing lane!" and "Come on, Dutch, let's see a windmill dunk!" Or my personal favorite: "Let's go, Dutch! Split the defense like you're splitting a bill!"

My friend showed a brave face until we were dismissed for the day, but the episode was more traumatic than he let on. He refused to return to the camp the next day, and after a couple of angry phone calls, his mom got an apology from the crazy old coach in the polyester Daisy Dukes and a full refund of the tuition. I made out quite profitably from the whole affair as well. I knew as soon as I'd heard the phrase "Dutch Candy" spoken aloud that I would turn it into the name of a kick-ass rock band.

Fortunately, Dylan and Francis loved the name as much as I did. For Halloween, we dressed up as the members of KISS and performed a small set at our friend's Rocktober party. We practiced three songs for the entire week leading up to the event and miraculously played our best set ever in front of about fifty mildly interested partygoers. After we played, we joined the crowd to mix and mingle and have a few drinks. To our surprise and delight, we had women walking up to us and shamelessly fawning over us. It lasted only one night, but the attention was a fast-acting and highly addictive drug.

Dutch Candy was out of the wrapper.

We became mini celebrities, mostly in our own minds. In our attempt to keep the dream going, we booked another half-dozen shows throughout the remainder of the school year. For the most part, we were always met with praise or appreciation.

Dylan even met his girlfriend, Naomi, at a friend's St. Patrick's Day party last March, where we played a couple of punk rock covers of U2 songs and drank pints of green beer. It wasn't accurate to say that Dylan *met* Naomi at that party. Rather, that was the day when Naomi admitted that she finally saw Dylan in "that way"—meaning he hadn't ever been attractive to her until she saw him onstage speeding through a knockdown rendition of U2's "With or Without You."

So if anyone ever tells you that rock 'n' roll can't help you score chicks, they are lying. It should also be noted that Naomi was attractive and very stylish, but she was also high-maintenance. One time, she got in a fight with Dylan because she thought he should keep her favorite diet soda in the refrigerator for whenever she came over. She lectured him that a relationship was about the little things and that he needed to do those little things for her or he wasn't really trying. I guess that made sense, but when I heard her berating him about it, it sounded more like the ramblings of a crazy person. He bought a couple of six-packs and always kept a few cans on the door of the refrigerator for when she came by. Every single time (and I mean *every single time*) she came over, he offered her one, and she always refused. They never discussed the topic beyond that.

To me, Naomi was amusing to observe and maddening to engage. I kept my distance from her but didn't mind having her over so often. She was not boring, and I admired her confidence and sense of self-worth.

Also, she was extremely social and very active in the Greek system at the school. She belonged to a sorority called Delta Delta Gamma, and she always bragged that ΔΔΓ (or DDG) really stood for "drop-dead gorgeous." She wasn't exactly wrong. She had a lot of attractive and outgoing friends. From time to time, she would pop in to say hi with one or a few of her sorority sisters in tow, and I had no problem with that.

Aside from capitulating on the diet sodas and a few other silly things, Dylan gave his girlfriend a run for her money. He typically let her have her way to a point, and then he would dig in and call her on her selfishness. In my ten-cent psychological assessment, I think she liked the idea of dating someone that called her on her bullshit. She was a strong personality and appeared to appreciate other strong personalities.

Despite her silly quirks, Naomi was a big supporter of our band and encouraged us to try to play more shows. The BBX show was our first of the new school year, and it was set to be our biggest ever. They wanted us to play for thirty minutes, and we reasoned that would require about eight songs. We had made that plan about two months ago during summer break, but we had yet to rehearse. Today was the day we were going to bring it all back to form. Probably not, but that was the plan anyway.

Dylan was all business. "I noodled around, and I have a little surprise for you both. I put together a *set list*, for lack of a better phrase." He handed a stapled bundle of pages to Francis and me. "I played through everything, and we can easily fill sixty minutes if we had to. Everything is a basic four-chord progression."

"Thank you," I said in acknowledgment of the comment, which was no doubt intended for me since I was incapable of playing anything other than a basic four-chord progression. I looked through the list of songs, and I was impressed. "Dylo"—I called him by his nickname—"this looks awesome!"

Francis also flipped through the song list. "Why are we preparing sixty minutes if we need only thirty for the show?"

Dylan and I shared a quick look. This was all part of the process. Francis always had to question the plan first before he could commit to it.

"Don't you want to play other shows after the BBX show? It's better to have more material."

"You sure we don't need a bass?"

"Yes, we need one, okay?" Dylan released an exasperated sigh. "Let's just learn these songs, and we'll look for a bass to fill in later."

I ran to my room and grabbed my thrift store guitar, which was now covered in stickers of every style and size. As I joined my roommates in our living room, we plugged in and set up facing the large picture window, which looked out onto Kulby Avenue. Dylan had printed out the tabs and chords for me and set them up on a music stand. I felt like a toddler who needed help getting dressed for school, but I appreciated that he was making it easier for me.

We practiced for the better part of three hours, interrupted a couple of times by neighbors and a few friends who happened to be passing by. Anyone who wanted to stick around and listen was invited in. Nobody stayed for long.

We agreed we would play through the whole list to warm up. Most of the songs were rough the first time through, but we eventually fell into a groove. We still sounded horrible, but I could see a light at the end of the tunnel. I reasoned that if we practiced like this four or five more times, we could probably pull off a decent show. My playing was just a shade below mediocre, which was good for me; and Dylan even commented that I must have been practicing, which I had not. He didn't realize I was still floating from the afternoon I had spent getting to know Dara. If there was a little extra electricity in my playing, it was because of her.

We were all tired, and our fingers hurt. It was time for a break, but we agreed to leave the instruments in place and planned on rehearsing every Wednesday and Sunday going forward. Francis suggested we all walk down into Westwood and get pizza. We pulled on jackets and set off into the chilly evening air. It was a Wednesday night in Westwood, and we had music in our souls and pizza on our minds.

# Chapter 6

We met up with some friends at dinner and decided to stop by Harrington's Pub before coming home. I had a few drinks, but nothing too heavy. I spent most of the night hoping against hope that Dara would magically walk in through the front door and find another seat next to me.

My roommates noticed I was a little disengaged and called me out on it. I assured them that everything was okay and that I was only suffering a small headache from playing too loud during rehearsal.

"And you want to be a rock star?" Francis remarked, shaking his head in mock disgust.

Dylan had a few too many drinks, and we ended up getting kicked out because he reached across the bar and used the phone without permission. He was trying to call Naomi at midnight to get her to bring a couple of her friends to join us at the bar. I admired his pluck. I think her roommate answered the phone from a dead sleep, and Dylan ended up in a mild shouting match with her. He tried to keep his voice down, but the noise drew the attention and ire of a bartender, who up until that point had been distracted by a conversation with some patrons on the other side of the bar. It was time to wrap things up anyway.

Walking out and saying goodbye, I heard a vaguely familiar song on the jukebox that opened with a basic nursery rhyme piano melody before layering in Lou Reed's vocals. I was at a loss and couldn't place the tune. Lingering by the door, I listened a little more closely and eventually recognized the voice of Michael Hutchence. I determined this was more than likely INXS and not the Velvet Underground. I had never realized the similarities between the two bands before that. The chorus kept repeating the words "Beautiful girl, stay with me. Beautiful girl, stay with me." As if I wasn't already preoccupied with Dara enough . . .

I got home at about one in the morning. When I finally got back to my room, I pulled open the bottom drawer of my dresser, where I kept my CD collection. I fished around and pulled out *Listen Like Thieves*, *Kick*, and *Welcome to Wherever You Are*. There it was, the eighth track on *Welcome to Wherever You Are*.

I fit my headphones over my ears, slid the disc into the top tray of my CD player, advanced to the eighth song, and pressed play.

"Beautiful girl, stay with me. Beautiful girl, stay with me." The line was taunting me.

I listened to the song a second time all the way through and decided it was time to sleep.

# Chapter 7

I woke up on Wednesday morning before my alarm sounded and jumped right out of bed. I had never been so eager to attend an 8:00 a.m. class. I had already showered the night before. So all I had to do was wet my hair, push it into shape, and pull on my jeans and T-shirt. I tucked a well-thumbed volume of *I Cry Bomjt* by Ope Opeyemi into my book bag and was on my way.

My first class of the day was a direct requirement for my major. I was taking a class on the Supreme Court. Two days prior, during our last lesson, Professor Kinkade had told the entire class that we could take a midterm and a final exam or that we could elect, instead, to write a twenty-five-page paper on any past or present justice from the Supreme Court.

There was no point in going to the class if self-study would comprise the full weight of my grade, but I was a good soldier, and there I was at eight in the morning with a cup of Kerckhoff coffee steaming beside me. Apparently, I wasn't the only student who suspected attendance was unnecessary. Over half the attendees from Monday's class were nowhere to be found.

Walking from my political science class to poetry class required only a short stroll across Dickson Court. I had an hour to kill, so I took the walk slowly and stopped briefly to catch up with an old friend I recognized from freshman year, Dan D'Angelo. He was smoking a cigarette under a shady tree outside of Schoenberg Hall.

"Hey, Dan Dan!" I caught him by surprise with his old nickname.

He and I had both lived in the dorms and worked several shifts together in the dining commons kitchen. He was a music major, and I recalled fondly how he used to drum these crazy beats on the plates and cups as they came around a slow corner on the widely turning conveyor belt that delivered the dirty meal trays from the dining room into the back kitchen. The job we'd endured was both disgusting and humiliating. Anyone walking past the pass-through could see directly into the receiving station, where I was often standing in my magenta UCLA dining commons staff shirt, a moldy black apron, and a hairnet. I never understood why plate scrapers were required to wear hairnets, but those were the rules.

"Jeff, what's going on?"

"Just had a little time to kill between classes. I thought you moved to Europe."

"I wish," Dan Dan chuckled and dropped his spent cigarette to the ground, where he promptly smashed it with his foot. "I was in Paris last year, interning at the Philharmonie de Paris." He overstressed the accent when stating the proper name.

"And now you're back for good?"

"I hope not." He pulled out another cigarette. "I'm trying to save money to move back. I loved it."

"The internship or the city or both?" I asked, waving off the pack of cigarettes he was now tilting in my direction.

"The city. I loved Paris. I'd go back there just to live." He lit his cigarette and took a drag. "I promised my parents I would come back to school, but I already regret it."

"Sorry to hear that."

"It's okay. I'm taking a French class and am getting a ton of hours."

"Where are you working?"

He thumbed toward the building behind him. "Schoenberg. I'm getting like sixty hours a week to basically babysit this place."

"How did you arrange that?"

"We have a lot of expensive equipment, so I'm like the music department mall cop."

"Doesn't sound so bad. Are you working right now?"

He offered a satisfied smile and took another drag. "As a matter of fact, I am."

Only Dan Dan could pull off a deal like that. I was impressed and certain he would make his way back to Paris. We exchanged numbers and parted ways, agreeing to get together again soon.

I felt a rush of adrenaline just entering from the outside into the hallway of the English department building. I did not see Dara anywhere in the mass of zigzagging students all frantically finding their classrooms. I turned the handle and pushed in the door leading to my class. I hoped I would find her sitting alone in the back row, waiting for me to join her. She wasn't there. Only a handful of the students had arrived and were noisily taking their seats. I took my place in the exact same position as last time.

There were still seven minutes until class began, and I busied myself by pretending to go through my notes from the last lecture, if you could call it that. I kept one eye on my notebook and one eye on the door. No sign of Dara, but I did notice when the boy in the high-reaching scarf entered the classroom, followed closely by Can. They assumed the same seats two rows in front of me. The Scarf noticed I was sitting in the last row. "You're all the way back there."

I didn't know how to respond. I settled for a simple "Yeah."

Can looked back and gave me an emotionless smile. She offered a curt wave at the end of a half-extended arm. This was, I thought to myself, the bare minimum greeting that could still be considered polite. I returned her gesture with a warmish "Hi, Can."

"You guys know each other?" the Scarf asked, turning to Can.

"We were in the dorms together."

"Yeah, I never did the dorm thing." I could tell it was a source of pride for him. "I'm Anson, by the way."

"Jeff," I replied.

"Nice to meet you, Jeff." He waited a beat. "Where's your friend today?"

I saw Can smirk to herself ever so slightly.

"Not sure."

We were now one minute before the top of the hour. Opeyemi was standing center stage, smiling and rubbing his hands together. "Good morning!"

His words relayed genuine excitement. He was a man who enjoyed his job.

Class began, and Dara was nowhere to be seen. I couldn't stop myself from glancing up at the door every thirty seconds or so until it finally sank in that she wasn't coming. I was glad Anson had asked about her, or I might have doubted if she really existed.

With my mind now free to focus on the lesson, I turned my attention to Professor Opeyemi. He pulled a book out of a leather satchel and turned to a page marked with a yellow Post-it note. He continued making a point that I had been daydreaming through. "This is a piece I wrote when my second son was born. He is my audience, and I want to tell him that life is not what you think. These words were my attempt to prepare him for this world."

He held the book up at an arm's distance and began to read the pages aloud.

*Do not believe the rules they force upon you*
*You may choose to follow*
*You may be forced to follow*
*But do not believe*
*Do not believe*
*Do not believe*

*I tell you these things, my son*
*Not with sadness nor fear in my heart*
*I tell you these things as a hopeful optimist*
*The world is glorious*
*The world is glory*
*But we people are fools*
*There is no shame in knowing who you are*
*No shame in being who you are*
*They will force you to scrub off your spots*
*With a wire brush*
*The very act will make you bleed and believe your spots are not*
*beautiful, perfect*
*But they are beautiful, perfect*
*And so are you*

*As you are*
*And always*

*Do not blame them for this*
*They simply don't know*
*These are the same men fixated on control*
*Men who breed wolves into pets*
*And pets into demons who taste blood*
*And blood into litigation*
*And litigation into shame*
*And shame into currency*
*And shame becomes currency*

*You may be forced*
*You will be forced to follow these rules*
*But never*
*Never believe them*
*These are the same men fixated on control*
*That told the earth she was the center of the universe*
*And that the sun and stars revolved around her*
*And VY Canis Majoris becomes a fact we momentarily memorize*
*For a test*
*When we should choose to kneel and humble ourselves*
*At the majesty of random chaos*
*And the majesty of greater powers*
*And the reality of our futility*

*Futility is more valuable than you may know*
*Always own your futility*
*They will ask you to loathe your futility, poverty*
*They will call it shame*
*These men fixated on control*
*Will hide the grand majesty of just being here*
*And sell you a superhero superhuman*

*Just so that they can control who gets knocked down*
*And why and when*

*You may be forced*
*You will be forced to follow these rules*
*But never*
*Never believe them*
*These are the same men who will point a gun at you*
*And force you to hate your black face*
*A gun*
*Gun, hammer, knife, chain, whip, gavel, money, blood, shame*
*Do not believe the rules they force upon you*
*You may choose to follow*
*You may be forced to follow*
*But do not believe*
*Do not believe*
*Do not believe*

The class had gone silent. Opeyemi closed the book and picked up his lecture in midstride. "Do you remember the question I asked the last time we were together?"

A moment passed, and a smattering of voices offered different versions of his question from the last class. "Why do you write?"

"Yes, yes . . . I asked you why you write." He walked to the window and looked up at the sky beyond the building, posing a question to nobody or everybody. "So why did I write this poem?"

He kept his gaze out the window. Some part of him seemed to slip away. Several ambitious hands raised and remained in the air for a full five seconds until Opeyemi turned to again face his congregation. "No, no, put your hands down. I asked you *why* I write. This is not a question to answer. This is a question to think about. Maybe you think you know why I write these words, but I believe you do not know. Just *think* about why I write these words and then think about why you wish to write your own words."

We still had about ten minutes left until the end of class. Opeyemi decided to quit while he was ahead. "Go," he encouraged us. "Go and live your wonderful lives!"

He grabbed a few papers off his lectern and stuffed them, along with his book, back into his bag. He broke directly for the door and stopped abruptly as a thought occurred to him. He addressed the class to share his revelation. "Next week, I will read more poetry to you." Then he was gone.

Any disappointment I was feeling from having been stood up by Dara was partially abated by the almost-spiritual experience I had just had in class. I was walking with my arm extended, about to push open the door, which would lead me into a gorgeous Southern California day. I readied my eyes for a flood of much-brighter light.

"Jeff!" It was Dara's unmistakable voice. I spun around to see her walking toward me. "Hey, I was looking for you."

"I was in class."

"I thought you would be, so I waited here."

"You waited for me?"

"Can you still go to lunch?"

We tried to pick a place to eat, but after both admitting that neither of us was very hungry, we decided to cancel our lunch and take a walk instead. We wandered aimlessly into North Campus. I told her a little bit about the class she had missed and tried to explain the poem that Professor Opeyemi had read aloud.

She interrupted me. *"Never Believe."*

"Pardon?"

"What he read to you today—this was part of a much-longer poem called *Never Believe*," Dara continued. "It was a hundred-page poem that he wrote for his two sons. His first son died while Opeyemi was being held in prison for a made-up crime because he opposed a local warlord. His second son was born a year later, and he wrote the poem to celebrate life and grieve death. He wrote it over thirty years ago."

I stopped in my tracks. Last week, Dara had confessed that she was not familiar with our professor's writings. I had misunderstood something because she now seemed to be an expert on the subject. She caught the confusion on my face.

"You wonder how I learned this?" she asked, her accent slightly more pronounced. "I took your advice and read a few of his books. I said I would."

I pulled *I Cry Bomjt* out of my bag. "I brought this one for you to read."

"This, I have not read," she admitted. "It is the last book he has written. I know this much."

"You can take it for a while if you want to read it."

She took the book and turned it over in her hand. "You think it is as good as his early writing?"

"I don't know, but from some of the criticism I've read, it is supposed to be more optimistic than his earlier writing. His outlook of the world seems to have improved over time."

She put the book into the same fashionable bag she had toted to class the previous week. "Thank you. I will read this."

We continued meandering until our aimless feet brought us past the large research library and to the southwest corner of the fabled UCLA sculpture garden. Without communicating the plan, we walked onto the well-paved pathway leading into the garden.

We took turns commenting on the sculptures, and I learned that Dara was very cultured and fairly opinionated. The conversation was interesting, but she could be a bit rude and dismissive. She didn't say anything overtly mean, but she didn't place a lot of value on any of the opinions that weren't hers.

I was becoming infatuated, so I made up excuses for her in my mind. *That must be the way people in Belarus talk to each other.*

She veered us down the first left turn. "This is my favorite."

"It looks like an abstract heart."

"A bird goddess," she said, correcting me.

I was getting perturbed by her constant corrections, and I defended myself, saying, "Well, it's all a matter of interpretation."

"You are wrong." Dara turned to me. Her voice was sharp, but her blue eyes were calm. "This piece is called *The Bird Goddess* and was made in the late '70s by Vladas Vildžiunas, a Lithuanian sculptor. He lived only thirty kilometers from Belarus."

"Here," she instructed me. "Stand where I am standing."

I would have preferred she'd gone about her tutorial a little more delicately, but I realized that she knew what she was talking about, and the mention of this sculptor being from her part of the world made me wonder if this was personal for her. I afforded her some leeway and complied with her request.

"Here," she said as I closed the five feet between us. "Look from right here."

She put her hands on my shoulders and turned me to face the work of art from her preferred perspective. The mere placement of her hands on my shoulders sent vibrations through my body. As much as my mind was recoiling at the harshness of our conversation, my body was enraptured by her touch.

"You see?" she asked, extending her arm past my ear and pointing to a sharp jetty-like shape protruding from the top center portion of the sculpture. "The sun is perfect right now. You see the shadows? You see her looking down?"

Dara spoke those last words almost in a whisper. I did see it. The piece was a depiction of a winged and feminine figure. I got momentarily lost trying to interpret the other shapes in the composition. I could see the downcast and delicate face, but below that, I wondered if her arms were folded across her body or if she was holding a child. I could not tell.

"You're right," she said, catching me off guard. She stepped even with me and looked intently at Vildžiunas's work as if seeing it for the first time. "I see the heart. I should not have said you were wrong before. I see it now."

As if she had read my mind, Dara's tone changed from that point. I couldn't say she was sweet, but she smoothed some of the rougher edges. We continued our walk around the great works of art until finally coming to rest on a small flight of shallow steps near a rectangular pool at the northeastern end of the garden. In all, we had wandered and discussed art for a couple of hours at that point.

At the center of the rectangular pool was a bronze fountain composed of a stack of rounded box-shaped figures gradually increasing in size as they went up. I thought the uppermost shape looked like a vacuum tube television from the 1950s. Water was rushing in a flat stream out of wide-open cutouts on three sides.

I playfully suggested to Dara, "This piece is called *The Leaky TV*. I believe this installation was commissioned by the Howard Radio Company in 1957 to get people to stop watching television and to go back to radio. The artist is suggesting that too much TV will cause your brain to spill out of your head."

Dara looked at me, dumbfounded. She did not know I was joking. I could tell she was weighing what she should say next. Eventually, her need to set the record straight won. "This is *Obos 69*, made in 1969 by a Japanese artist. I forget his name."

I smiled. "Dara, I'm kidding!"

"Oh . . . I see." She smiled back at me. "You made that up."

"I thought it looked like a TV with water flooding out of the screen, so I made up a silly story."

"You were making a joke."

"Exactly."

Dara was quiet for a minute, then perked up. "Did you really think that *The Bird Goddess* looked like a heart?"

"That was true," I assured her. "I thought it looked like a heart at first, and then I saw the figure and the wings."

We were both quiet for a moment. She tilted her head and looked at me sideways. "I believe I am a curious person. When I am interested in something, I tend to throw myself into it."

"Like with Opeyemi's poetry? Last week, you didn't even know who he was."

"Yes, just like that."

"You're passionate about learning."

"And escaping," she added.

The comment seemed odd and a little heavy. She peeked over at me and smiled to lighten the moment.

"I like to research things too," I offered.

Dara brushed some unseen dust off her knee. "Someone once told me the world is an open book. You understand this?"

I nodded. "An open book. Like an open-book exam? Yeah."

"So many great people have been through the world before us and left so many valuable ideas and works of art. We can find all the answers. We just need to look."

"Was that a friend?"

She cocked her head. "A friend?"

"You said 'someone once told' you . . ."

"No, not a friend." She looked down and paused. "I don't have so many friends." Her tone was flat and untroubled. She was stating a fact.

"Your friends are all back in Belarus?"

"I do not have many friends in Belarus or here." If this was a point of unhappiness for her, she didn't show it. "But anyway, I am content."

While we were on the steps talking, no less than three male students made comments in our direction. Nothing was ever very direct or discernible, but it was always apparent. Dara never gave it any notice. Even when I rolled my eyes at the most obvious offender, who offered a low "woot woo" whistle, Dara took pains to ignore both the whistle and my reaction and remained focused on whatever we had been discussing.

46

Catcalls notwithstanding, the afternoon was pleasant. Just being with her was exciting for me. On a few occasions during our conversation, our knees touched momentarily. Although I did not dare reveal my excitement outwardly, an electric shock surged through my body. At one point, I felt a strong urge to reach over and put my hand on the warm, smooth skin of her leg. But I could not touch her. I wanted very much to touch her, but I could not.

Dara caught me eyeing her watch, and she positioned the face so we could both more easily see. It was already 2:45 p.m. "I was supposed to tell you when it was two thirty," she noted. "I'm sorry."

"It's okay, but I need to go. Can I walk you back if you're going that way?" I pointed in the general direction of Westwood Village.

"I'll stay here for a little while."

"Hey, do you think . . . ," I began.

"What?"

"Do you want to get together this weekend or something?"

She was frank in her reply. "This weekend is not good, but I will see you next Wednesday. Maybe we will have dinner then?"

"Okay." I was surprised she had just kind of asked me out to dinner. "Next Wednesday works." I built up a little more nerve. "Do you think we could exchange numbers?"

"Yes." Dara reached into her bag and pulled out her notebook. "I will write it for you." She spoke while lightly stabbing and swiping the paper with the tip of her pen. "You are lucky—I never give my number to anyone."

She tore off the corner of the page where she had written her name and phone number.

"Thanks." Her characters were all recognizable to me, but they were different. Her *1* looked more like an *A* without the crossbar, and her *9* more closely resembled a lowercase *G*.

Her pen was poised above the page and ready to write. "Now you give me your number."

I walked back to my apartment replaying the wonderful afternoon I had spent with Dara. As pleasant as our time together had been, something was whispering to me in the back of my mind. Something didn't quite fit. Dara was not like the other girls I knew in college. As much as we chatted and shared ideas, there was still a disconnect between her and me. Even though she had been next to me in the sculpture garden, she was also out of reach.

# Chapter 8

I wandered into the kitchen for the third time in an hour and stared again into the limited and rotting selection of food on my assigned shelf in the refrigerator. I wasn't sure if I was hungry or bored or a little bit of both. I closed the fridge and walked back out of the kitchen.

"I have bagels and cream cheese if you're hungry!" Dylan called from his room, startling me.

"You're home?" I called through his door. "I thought you had to get the exhibit ready for tomorrow." A number of fine arts students were showing their summer projects for an exhibit on campus. Dylan was supposed to be helping set up the exhibit space.

"You can come in!" he called. I found him lying in his bed, stretching and yawning himself awake. "We pulled an all-nighter last night. I went straight to my 8:00 a.m. class from the studio."

"You made it to your 8:00 a.m. Friday class. I'm impressed."

"Dude, I always make that class."

"We're two weeks in," I reminded him.

"Have a little faith."

"So are you all done setting up?"

"Everything's ready, and my installation's in place. The other artists will finish setting up their stuff tonight, but I don't care about that."

"That's the spirit," I teased. "So what's the plan tonight? Or are you going to catch up on sleep?"

"No, I'm good. I got back here around noon and took a nap. What time is it now?"

The square red letters on the digital alarm clock read 6:43. Twilight was peeking through the window, casting a blue hue on the room.

"Shit, it's later than I thought." Dylan sat up onto the edge of his bed. "I saw Francey on campus, and he said there's a little party at Y&T's tonight. They asked us to head over. It's supposed to be starting up around 9:00 p.m."

"A party? Or is it just the same stoners sitting around getting high and complaining about corrupt governments and evil corporations?"

"What's the difference?" Dylan quipped.

"Good point. I'm in. You want to eat first?"

"Yeah, I'm supposed to call Naomi. Let me do that and get dressed. I'll be ready in fifteen minutes."

Y&T was an affectionate nickname we had given to our friends Yuri and Todd. The two of them were a quasi-famous pair of partiers on campus. They were almost always together, and they eventually accepted the joint nickname.

They were several years older but still lived in Westwood Village and partied with the undergrads. It was weird, but also not weird, if you know what I mean. Where most undergrads were in the "eighteen to twenty-two years old" range, Yuri and Todd were both probably twentyeightish. I often warned them to be careful because they always had people over to their place, and many of them were underage. They were both nice people and never forced anyone to do anything, but I figured they could get in big trouble if someone found out that they had supplied booze or weed or worse to a nineteen-year-old. They agreed but ultimately never changed.

The rumor was that Yuri was pursuing his doctorate in philosophy and had a 4.0 GPA. Similarly, Todd was a law student, also with a 4.0 GPA. Todd was one of the most effortlessly intelligent people I had ever met. Not only was he book smart, but he was also very wise and doled out great advice when the occasion would arise.

Yuri was a left-leaning radical who believed, with every fiber of his being, that the path forward for America was to adopt a Socialist doctrine. He looked and dressed like the quintessential '90s neo-hippie. He had shoulder-length hair, round-rim glasses, beaded necklaces, and long droopy pants that dragged on the ground behind his shoes until they wore out flush against the floor. He smoked comical amounts of pot. There was never a single time when I saw him at his place or on campus when he was not high.

In most ways, Todd was Yuri's opposite. He kept a gun safe in the apartment, but nobody ever saw any guns. He had a poster of Ronald Reagan in his room, and I was told that he was a founding member of the Real Republicans club on campus. Somehow, despite their conflicting points of views, the two of them were best friends. Todd did not smoke near the amount of pot as Yuri, but he did drink significantly more—and he also dabbled in the use of harder drugs.

Todd's look was buttoned up. He was all about polo shirts, deck shoes, and well-groomed hair. It just so happened that his parents were rich. His dad was a lawyer and an architect (don't ask me how or why), and his mom came from serious money. Todd was always flush with cash; and he always had weed, drugs, and food at his place. He was more than willing to share on all accounts. He had two different cars—a Chevrolet Corvette and a Ford Explorer—tucked into the parking garage of the apartment complex. He was also very popular with the women, but there were a few rumors about some of his strange perversions floating around. I never paid much attention, though, because he always seemed so normal to me.

Of the two of them, I got along a little better with Todd. We had more in common, and we hung out more frequently. He could shed the party persona whenever I needed a decent wingman, and he knew how to conduct himself when parents or other adults were visiting from out of town. He was also more athletic, and I could count on him to join me on a trip to the gym or for a pickup game of basketball.

"All right, you ready?" Dylan called from his room.

"I am." I shut off the TV and jumped up off the couch. "Where do you want to eat?"

"How about Buck Fifty Sub?" Dylan suggested.

Buck Fifty Sub was a low-cost sub shop occupying a small shack in close proximity to the border between Westwood commercial and Westwood residential. Any owner daring to take up residency in that little food shack would be facing stiff competition from the adjacent food shack, Tommy Burger, which had, at that time, become a legendary UCLA landmark. Buck Fifty Sub was holding its own, and I preferred it to its greasy neighbor because they used actual vegetables in the sandwiches. I had gotten sick from my last attempt to eat Tommy Burger about one year ago and was still trying to avoid that from happening again. Although Dylan had not gotten sick, he was with me on the prior occasion, and the experience was even more memorable for him.

I believe it was about two in the morning, and Dylan and I were wrapping up an overindulgent night of barhopping. He had recently broken up with his ex-girlfriend, Gwen, and we were using the night to

52

help get his mind off her. It was a horrible idea because as we were bouncing around from location to location, we kept seeing all the places and people that reminded him of her.

I wanted to go home, but he insisted we stop at Tommy Burger and get some chili cheese fries. We each got an order and stumbled across the street, shuffling sloppily and munching on goopy cheesy chili fries. Sucking our fingers clean and talking to each other through mouthfuls of food, we looked like disgusting Neanderthals. We were on the sidewalk and had just passed the gas station to begin our gradual ascent up Levering Avenue when, of course, fate somehow put Dylan's ex-girlfriend and three of her best friends in an open-air jeep driving down the road toward us. I saw them first and thought, *Oh shit.*

They were playing, at an aggressive volume, Smart E's "Sesame's Treet," a remix of the *Sesame Street* theme song. I don't mean to judge them for their musical taste, but there is not a scenario where either Dylan or I would ever be caught dead listening to such a moronic song. No offense to morons.

Dylan heard them before he saw them. "What kind of shit music is that?"

I tried to divert his attention so he wouldn't see them and pointed to an imaginary item in the other direction. "Whoa, dude, look at that!"

It would have worked. But one of the passengers in the jeep—in a voice that was meant just for her friends, but loud enough for us to hear— asked, "Is that Dylan? And Jeff?"

That immediately got Dylan's attention, and he twisted his neck over in their direction. There was a slow-motion moment when they rolled right past us, and all our eyes met. They all looked so damn good, and we looked like sloppy monkeys on our way back to a cage. Obviously, they had done a great job of cheering up their friend, but all of that was about to get obliterated . . . for everyone.

We then heard another softer, but still audible, voice, which I recognized as Gwen's. "Just go . . . please."

The car picked up a little more velocity and motored away. Dylan realized what had happened and took offense. Without thinking, he wheeled around on his left foot. Then with the momentum of a full-body spin, he windmilled his right arm and heaved his remaining paper basket of chili cheese fries in the direction of the jeep.

I was not a math major, but I'd aced high school geometry. In my expert opinion, the trajectory of the fries was directly on target. The messy and high-calorie warhead lifted off at the perfect angle, where it would squarely meet the open interior of the vehicle at about forty feet down the road. By an act of God, or pure luck, the projectile clipped a No Parking sign about halfway between us and the intended target—sending the chili, cheese, chopped onions, and fries into a whirlybird pattern of disgusting buckshot. Even at that distance, I felt a slight splatter coming back to reach us. I think that was when I started to feel sick to my stomach.

I stared at Dylan, who remained hunched over from his follow-through. The moment sobered me up a bit and revealed how stumbling drunk my friend was. He shifted his weight from side to side and labored his head up to look at me and slur, "Did I get 'em?"

"I . . . don't think so, but we should probably go."

At maybe noon the next day, Dylan popped into my room. He was bright and had regained his life force. I was still a bit queasy. "Hey, dude, I just had a crazy phone call with Gwen. She said that we saw them on the road last night and we threw our food at them."

"*We*?" I asked.

"What do you mean?" he asked, playing coy.

"You don't remember this?"

"No . . . I mean, I kind of remember seeing them, but that's it."

I brought him up to speed on the story as best I could remember it, and he stood in the doorway, looking serious. I knew he remembered most of it, but I played along. "Does any of that sound familiar?"

"Okay . . . I have to confess something."

"This should be good." I braced myself. "What?"

"Gwen was so pissed. I guess they got sprayed by chili and cheese. Jenny had to go get her whole car cleaned inside and out, and they all got it in their hair and on their clothes. It was just a mess." Dylan went quiet after that.

"So let me guess . . . ," I started. "You couldn't bear to admit doing that to her, or she would have never spoken to you again?"

"Something like that."

"So you told her I did it?" I already knew his answer. He stood in the doorway for a moment, saying nothing.

I don't know which one of us cracked first, but we both just started laughing like crazy. It was a full-on hysterical fit. We laughed to a point where we couldn't speak. Eventually, Francis walked in to find out what the hell was so funny. We couldn't tell him anything because we couldn't talk, and eventually, he asked, "Oh, is this about the chili cheese fries that Jeff threw at Jenny's jeep?"

The fact that he somehow already knew the story made it even more hysterical to us. We continued like that for maybe ten minutes and then spent the rest of the day musing over what it must have been like to get rained down upon by so much disgusting food.

Fortunately, there would be no similar fireworks or falling-outs while walking back from the food shack on this night. We ordered two subs each and two more for Francis, in case he came back before we left for Y&T's. We walked back to our apartment following our typical route, and when we got to the same general area as the scene of the crime, Dylan asked, "You remember the time you threw the chili cheese fries at Jenny's jeep?"

I snorted in mild derision. "Do you?"

Francis, as we suspected, was waiting at the apartment and watching TV when we pushed open the front door. He was appreciative of the sandwiches. We spread out on our couches, eating and half watching the movie *Airplane!* "I am serious, and don't call me Shirley."

"Hey, so what did Naomi say about joining us at Y&T's?"

"She didn't commit one way or the other." Dylan frowned. "I don't think she likes going there. She's not into the incense and lava lamp thing."

I was fine with that. The only reason I liked having her around was because of her friends, but on this night, I couldn't have even looked at another girl.

I had Dara on my mind and almost nothing else.

# Chapter 9

Naomi did end up coming over to our place, and she brought a couple of her friends from her sorority, Carey and Maya. I had heard about Maya from Francis. He was not the type to overstate things and wouldn't gush over his crushes, but it was clear from his comments that he was interested in her. They were both economics majors, and Maya had a reputation as a great student. Francis had a couple of classes with her the previous year. He'd angled to get into her study group but never had the nerve to ask her out.

They apparently had some chemistry because Maya walked right over to Francis on the couch and said, "Hey, Francis, I haven't seen you since school started."

They spent the next several minutes ignoring the TV and catching up about their econ classes and how they'd spent their summers. I overheard her telling him that she'd taken a yoga class over the summer and was trying to get space in the John Wooden Center, where she could invite students and teach a class.

I admired her gumption. Her discipline for practicing yoga was enough by itself, but the desire to teach a class and share what she knew with others was even more impressive. Francis was a workout buff, and I was sure Maya's passion for fitness appealed to him. The fact that she was lean and toned was probably also appealing. I had known Francis for two years, and he always fell for girls who were athletic and had dark hair and a dark complexion. She seemed like his ideal match. I hoped she felt the same.

I had met Carey on several occasions, but we'd never spoken much to each other. She was always pleasant and had a reputation as a caring girl. She was known for being heavily involved in philanthropy, and I had heard that she had an interesting background, but I didn't know much more than that.

It was shallow to say, but Carey wasn't what I considered to be conventionally pretty, and she didn't put any extra emphasis on her looks. She preferred a more natural approach to beauty, and I rarely ever saw her in makeup. She wore her hair straight and flat, and when I saw her out with her friends, she was almost always dressed down in a T-shirt or a sweatshirt and baggy jeans. This austere approach to fashion was not entirely uncommon for young women in the mid-1990s.

She did, however, have very unique eyes that rested at half-mast. The basest among us would have called them "bedroom eyes," whereas the classy and cultured preferred the term "Bette Davis eyes." This feature gained her one of the world's best nicknames, *the Look*. I recalled on several occasions Carey arriving at a party and being greeted by a procession of friendly voices shouting various iterations of "It's the Look!"

Naomi had come to our place with an agenda. She wanted to spend time with Dylan, but she did not want to go and hang out with a bunch of stoners. So she stopped by to inform us that the three of them were going to get pizza at DJ's and then see the 9:30 p.m. showing of *Pulp Fiction*. She said they would love us to join them but that we needed to decide quickly because they had to run down to the theater and get tickets since the shows were still selling out.

Neither Dylan, Francis, nor I had seen the movie—yet. We had been hearing great things about it, and we all wanted to see it. If Naomi had selected that specific film to apply the maximum incentive for the three of us to ditch Y&T's and join them on the outing, it was working.

Dylan put up a pretty good defense. "We just ate."

"So?" Naomi countered. "DJ's is a bar. Just come and have a couple of beers while we eat."

Francis was the first to fold. "Yeah, sure, I'll go."

He was like that. He always just did what he wanted and never bothered asking what everyone else thought. I'd always admired his independent mind.

Dylan followed his lead. "Okay, I'll go with you guys. If we get back early, maybe we can check out Y&T's later."

A proud smile appeared on Naomi's face.

"Come on, Jeff," Carey addressed me directly, surprising me a little. "It'll be fun, and this is supposed to be a great movie."

"I'm gonna have to pass." I had already made up my mind. "I'm going to head over Y&T's. Sorry, guys." Any other time, I think I would have been more interested, but I didn't want to spend the night on a forced triple date. I wasn't that interested in Carey, and besides, I thought I could ask Dara to see *Pulp Fiction* the next time we were together.

I thought I saw a flash of disappointment cross Carey's face, but she laughed it off. "It's fine. I'm sure I can find another guy on the way to the theater."

"Well, Jeff's not going to find another girl like Carey," Naomi chided. "That's for damn sure."

Dylan grabbed a jacket, and Francis changed his shirt and applied a light sprinkling of cologne, and the fivesome headed on their way.

# Chapter 10

Y&T's was a two-minute walk from the back of our apartment complex, straight up Veteran Avenue. I could see up to the top-floor apartment from the street and recognized the unmistakable silhouette of Yuri and a few of his friends out on the balcony of his room. The lights were dimly lit, and "Love Her Madly" by the Doors wafted down to greet me fifty feet below.

Yuri and Todd lived in a magnificent building that had a well-maintained gym and pool and was surrounded almost completely by palm trees. Compared to the typical run-down buildings through the whole of Westwood Village, theirs was a standout with respect to design, spaciousness, and upkeep. They lived in one of only three extralarge apartments on the top floor. By comparison, all the other floors, which shared the same general footprint, had six apartments each.

I'd tried to explain to them that they lived in a penthouse, but Yuri's Socialist leanings would not allow him to live in a penthouse, so he'd explained to me that he lived in a large apartment where all were welcome. Since I was one of the welcome parties, I let it go at that and agreed with his logic.

They had a formal entryway leading to a set of double doors with potted mini palm trees on either side. I always felt like I was entering a tiki bar when I visited. Tonight, the right door was wide open, and I let myself in.

Their place was large and expansive. They had a completely modern kitchen (which they put to good use), a massive living room with a thirty-six-inch television, three bathrooms, and four bedrooms. Yes, both Yuri and Todd had two rooms each. They each had their own bedroom with an en suite bathroom, as well as a second room to use for their own purposes. Yuri had converted his second room into a pillow-lined Chill Room, where he would smoke pot, read books, debate politics, and meditate. Todd had converted his into a professional office that housed all his legal volumes and law school materials. This was the site of both his gun safe and the Ronald Reagan poster.

As I had anticipated, the front room was dimly lit, with the incense burning and no less than two lava lamps visible. Naomi would have walked right out. The room was fullish, and Todd greeted me immediately.

"Jeff! Glad you could make it, buddy! It's great to see you! Are Dylan and Francis with you?" he asked, looking over my shoulder at the front door. Todd had a square jaw and a radiant personality. He made everyone feel like they were best friends with the high school quarterback.

I had to break the news. "No, they are on a double date. But they may show up later."

"That's great! Did Naomi finally set Francey up with one of her friends?"

I was impressed at his powers of intuition. "Yeah, that's exactly what happened."

"Not Carey, was it?"

"No," I chuckled a little, given my last exchange with her at my apartment. "It definitely was *not* Carey."

"Well, part of me would love to see them tonight, and part of me hopes they can both find something better to do—if you know what I mean." His meaning was clear.

Todd ushered me around and got me acquainted with several of his friends and colleagues. I realized that some part of his exuberance that evening was likely chemically induced, and I was getting a lot of the same vibrations from his buddies. After getting to know a few folks and ping-ponging my way into and out of various frenetic conversations, someone asked me if I'd like some blow. I politely declined, and he went on his way.

Todd cornered me a moment later and presented a brand-new golf club—a state-of-the-art driver with a graphite shaft and a clubhead the size of a cantaloupe. We spoke for ten minutes or so about how excited he was to have the new set of clubs. If memory served, he had gotten his previous set less than a year prior, and we'd played a week after he'd gifted me his old set. We loosely agreed to schedule a golf date within the next couple of weeks when something else abruptly stole his attention away, and he buzzed over to chat with another guest. Todd and I were usually good about keeping our golf dates, so I made a mental note to follow up with him in the next few days.

I hadn't yet seen Yuri, so I made my way to the Chill Room, sliding into position on some unoccupied pillows. He was seated in the middle of the room, chatting with about six other people I didn't recognize. The room smelled intensely of marijuana, and I gathered that juxtaposed with Todd's more energetic party in the living room, Yuri had been shepherding an entirely different flock of friends into and through a more mellow plant-based high. I wasn't much of an indulger myself, but I had a wide-open mind on the subject and was never uncomfortable around people who were under the influence.

Yuri saw me, then leaned over from his position to squeeze my hand tightly and smiled. "Jeff, it's good to see you! I'm so glad you could join us. Do you need anything?"

"No, I'm good for right now."

"Great! My friends just got back from the Zen temple on Mount Baldy." He motioned to others in the room, but to no one in particular. "We're just about to play some of their recordings of the monks' chanting."

A cross-legged figure behind Yuri nodded kindly and said in my direction, "Please, stay for this. Feel free to join in if you feel moved to."

"Thank you," I returned.

"Yuri," the figure continued, "will you pour our guest some tea?"

Yuri shot a finger into the air and nodded slightly. He turned to his side and presided over a rustic wooden slab that held a simple earthenware teapot and a stack of earthenware cups at the side. At this moment, I noticed that all the other inhabitants in the room either clutched identical cups in their hands or had them set off to the side of their seated position. Yuri held the teapot by the swinging handle and poured me a portion of tea with a flourish. He held the cup momentarily to his forehead, bowing to it, and then extended it to me.

I grabbed the tea and looked at it cautiously. I had no idea what was in this cup, and there was no way I would drink it without a little more investigation. Yuri had replaced the teapot and turned his expectant gaze back upon me. I assumed he was waiting for me to take my first sip. I wanted to be bold and play along, but I had to ask. So I whispered to my friend, "What is this?"

Yuri laughed slightly. "Tea. Only tea, harvested from the small tea farm at the monastery on Mount Baldy."

The figure behind him spoke up again. "For their evening reflection, the monks at the monastery will drink this tea and give dharma talks long into the night. They allowed us to pack some with us before we traveled back down the mountain. We are sharing it with our friends here today."

It seemed like a believable story, but I assumed there was only a 10 percent chance that the "tea" *wasn't* spiked with something mildly hallucinogenic. I nodded appreciatively and took a small sip. I was willing to see what one small sip would do. The contents of the cup tasted as though someone had strained lukewarm tap water through a coffee filter full of topsoil.

All other occupants in the room were seated cross-legged on pillows and propped up against a wall with their eyes closed and a look of bliss across their faces. I followed suit and crossed my legs. I made myself very comfortable, reclining on a large pillow I had placed against the wall. Leaning back slightly, I closed my eyes. I heard the unmistakable sounds of a cassette tape being slipped into the slot of a tape player and closed tightly. I listened for the distinct sound of the play button's depression. The grind of spinning reels was eventually overtaken by the sound of a single guttural foreign voice releasing a melodic flow of sounds that were filled with meaning, but indecipherable to my ignorant Anglophone ear. In a word, the earnest sounds bouncing off the walls in that small room were *stirring*. Eventually, other similarly toned voices joined in near-perfect synchronicity, adding a wildly satisfying harmonic quality to the chanting.

I remained in place, peacefully content to smell the incense and enjoy the unusual sounds. I felt myself relaxing deeply and sinking farther into the pillows. For good measure, I took just one more sip of my tea. The second sip was considerably more appetizing. Delicious, in fact.

# Chapter 11

I sat in place for a comfortable and extended period; and due to the rhythmic nature of the recording, I might have drifted slightly into a light sleep, where I was both relaxed and vaguely mindful of the happenings around me. I was aware of the moment when the recording ended and the room turned to a crypt-like silence. Enjoying the quietude and comfort of my surroundings, I slid back even farther into the pillows and allowed the pleasant vibrations to flow freely through the many levels of my conscious and subconscious mind.

I kept my eyes closed and my focus steady. I tuned in to another horizon, which would become observable only to my lidded eyes. This field of perception was not like the typical visible light spectrum. In fact, this new spectrum was delicate and would flee from view when disturbed by even the faintest hint of the visually observable world. With that world tuned out, I was now able to sense an undefined object in the distance. This was not a tangible object, but rather an emotional object—something akin to hopeful sadness.

"Jeff!" A woman's voice startled me, and my eyes immediately shot open. I was still in Yuri's Chill Room in the exact same position. All the other occupants were either passed out or asleep, and everyone clutched their cups tightly in their hands.

"Jeff!" I recognized the voice as belonging to Dara.

I rose quickly and walked into the living room, where, to my surprise, every other attendee of the party had fallen asleep or passed out. I was mildly horrified at the scene and couldn't help but conjure an image of Jonestown in my mind. Had the Zen Buddhists poisoned everybody with their crazy earthenware tea? Was I the only one who hadn't drunk their entire serving?

"Jeff, come here please! I need to see you."

I rushed onto the balcony. I saw Dara standing on the street. I called down to her, "Dara? What are you doing here? How did you find me?"

"I am the moon," she said. "I see everything in the dead of night."

I didn't understand. "Why are you here?"

"I need *you*. I need you to come down here."

"Okay, I'll come right down." I turned to walk back through the apartment.

"Jeff, no!" The urgency in her voice spun me back around. "No, we don't have time . . . You have to jump."

"Jump? I'm four floors up."

"Trust me . . . You can fly if you trust me."

"What are you talking about, Dara?"

With that, she pressed her hands down slowly to her sides and began to float off the ground. I couldn't believe my eyes. I couldn't believe what I was witnessing. "What the hell, Dara? You're floating off the ground!"

"What did you think was going to happen, Jeff?" She levitated higher, her hair beginning to float around her. "When I found you in class that day, didn't you know it then? Couldn't you sense something was about to change? Didn't you wonder why the secret courtyard opened in front of you? Weren't you curious as to why the great statues knelt before you?" She began to glow. "Just jump down to me, and I'll explain everything."

I placed one foot on the railing and hoisted my other knee up to steady myself. When my balance felt sure, I pushed up into a standing position. "You want me to jump from here?"

"Yes. Put one foot forward, and we'll be together."

I stepped off the ledge and momentarily felt as though I could hover. The illusion wore off almost immediately, and I began to plummet. Panic coursed through my entire body. The fall lasted much longer than I had expected. I used the extra time to look all around me and could find no sign of Dara anywhere. At the moment of impact, my eyes shot open, and I was back in the Chill Room. There were fewer people in the space than before. Instrumental music played in the background.

Yuri spoke. "Welcome back. How was the ride?"

"I don't know," I answered honestly. "How long was I out?"

"Not sure. Three or four hours maybe."

"What was in that tea?"

"Your hopes, your dreams, your secrets, and your fears," he answered cryptically.

This was not the time for fortune cookie Yuri. I couldn't handle any more. The walls felt as though they might have been closing in, and I had to get out of there. "I have to go."

"You okay? You need water?"

There wasn't a chance in hell I was about to drink anything else in that apartment. I stood up and walked straight for the door. I was relieved to find that everyone remaining in the living room was still very much alive. I might have heard a couple of calls in my direction, but I left without acknowledging anyone or anything.

The fresh air of the street did wonders for me. I lingered outside of my apartment for a moment to clear my head and collect my thoughts. From the street, I saw the soft glow of the television lighting up the living room ceiling through the front window. I assumed Dylan or Francis had passed out watching *Point Break* again.

I walked in and saw Dylan and Naomi curled up on the couch, watching *Like Water for Chocolate*.

They both turned to me when I walked in. "Hey, guys," I said. "How was *Pulp Fiction*?"

Naomi paused the movie and turned on a lamp near the couch. "It was good." She smirked at me, and I thought that was odd. "So . . . who's Dara?"

I looked to Dylan for an explanation.

"There's a message for you on the machine."

I looked down at the answering machine, and sure enough, the digital message display was showing a bright red *1*. That it was glowing steadily and not blinking was a clear indication that someone had already listened to the message.

If you didn't live through 1994 and never shared an answering machine, then you probably don't realize the extent to which you could get into your roommate's personal business. I placed the tip of my finger down on the playback button.

"Jeff, it's Dara. I really want to leave work early tonight. What are you doing right now?"

Dylan seized on the urgency in Dara's message. "Damn, I like the way she said 'right now.' Who is that?"

"Is that a Russian accent?" Naomi asked nosily.

"Shhh." I wanted to hear the time stamp.

The digital voice announced it as "11:13 p.m."

Naomi continued, "Who leaves work *early* at 11:13 p.m.?"

I realized she had probably dissected this recording thoroughly at this point. "What time is it now?" I asked.

Naomi looked at her watch. "A little after two. You can't call her now."

"Why do you say that?"

"You'll look desperate," she explained. "She called you, and she was too late, and you were already out having fun. Too bad, she'll have to plan better next time."

I realized that Naomi was thinking about this like a woman. A guy's brain was wired a little differently. Two in the morning seemed like a perfectly reasonable time to call her back.

I headed to the hallway leading to my room. "Night, guys."

"That's it?" Dylan asked.

"What?" I shrugged.

"That's all we get? You aren't going to tell us who that was?"

"Just a girl I met in class."

"And she's calling you in the middle of the night?"

"I guess so."

I did end up calling Dara that night but got an answering machine. Despite having rehearsed my opening line if she answered *and* a nonchalant message if I got the machine, I stumbled a bit. I managed to tell her I was sorry I'd missed her and that I was attending an art exhibit on campus the next night if she wanted to join me.

# Chapter 12

Saturday was kind of an in-between day. I spent most of the morning in a fog owing to, in part, having stayed up so late and, in part, having consumed whatever mild hallucinogen had been slipped into my beverage the night before. I made a note to reach out to Yuri at some point and ask him to come clean with me.

I lay in bed all morning and some of the afternoon, hoping that the phone would ring and Dara would return my call from the wee hours. I reasoned that I couldn't call her again until she called me. I smirked a little at the realization that Naomi had been right about not calling her right away. She always seemed to be right, and it was getting annoying.

I faintly recalled hearing the front door being pulled open and thumped closed a couple of times while I drifted in and out of sleep, and I wondered if anyone else was in the apartment with me. At some point, I needed to get up and go get something to eat. I tried not to obsess over the thought that Dara had an invitation on her answering machine and there might be even the slightest chance she would attend Dylan's show that night.

Pulling on a pair of jeans and a ratty T-shirt, I shuffled out into the living room and got a little blood flowing. The place was empty, and I already knew there was nothing for me to eat in the fridge. I opted for instant coffee in a "#1 Grandma" mug and drank it out on the front stoop, allowing the sun to warm me up.

Within about ten minutes, Francis came rolling down the hill on his bike. He skidded gratuitously up to the curb, leaving an impressive skid mark on the asphalt behind him. "You're alive."

"I am indeed," I assured him. "Where are you getting back from?"

"I went to Wooden to work out, and then I went on campus to get lecture notes."

"Have you eaten?" I asked.

"No, I was going to make myself something now."

Francis always had food on his shelf in the refrigerator, and I was always jealous. I was good about never eating it, but some days I was tempted. Today, I had another idea. "How about I grab my bike, and we ride over to Mexico Fresh instead?"

He liked the idea, and soon, we were pedaling back up the same hill he had just coasted down from. We chatted on the way, and I learned that he had also heard the mysterious accent on our answering machine from the night before. He explained that he had arrived home about an hour after Dylan and Naomi because he had walked Maya and Carey back to their sorority house. That was just like Francis—he always did stuff like that. Where you might think that level of thoughtfulness would have helped him in his romantic pursuits, he was more likely viewed as a supernice guy; and too often, his overchivalrous behavior ended up getting him "friend-zoned" with the fairer sex. I was hoping that wouldn't be the case with Maya.

"So . . . ?" I asked.

He knew I was asking him about Maya, but he played dumb. "What?"

"Is there some potential with Maya? How did that go when you walked her home?"

"I was just walking her home. Besides, Carey was with us."

"You think anything would have been different without Carey there?"

"Maya's nice. She's a really cool girl." Francis never shared much information, and today would be no exception. He quickly changed the subject. "You should have come with us last night. Carey was asking about you."

"I hope she wasn't offended," I said sincerely.

"She was joking about it. I think it bothered her a little," Francis recounted. "Dylan and I wondered why you turned her down until we heard the message. Do I know this mystery girl, by the way?"

"I doubt it," I answered. "She's just someone I met in class."

"The message was pretty direct . . ." He hesitated. "Is there something going on with you guys?"

I tried to sound disinterested. "No, we're just friends."

I could tell he wanted to ask me more about it, but he let the topic drop. We ate lunch and stopped at Spotlight Records on the way home. Francis wanted to pick up a copy of the *Pulp Fiction* soundtrack. He told me the movie was amazing and unlike any other he had ever seen, and he insisted he couldn't think of another film to compare it to.

We rolled back up to our place, and Dylan was on the phone, surrounded by a couple of overstuffed plastic bags from a party store. I saw a wrapped stack of clear plastic champagne cups peeking out over the crest of the bag.

Dylan blurted, "Jeff, are you coming tonight?"

"Of course I'm coming. Why?"

He shook his head and rolled his eyes. Covering the mouthpiece of the phone, he whispered to me, "Girl stuff."

I went back to Francis's room, where we were going to dive into the newly purchased CD. This was the kind of compilation that featured excerpts from the movie. I'd always hated those novelty tracks. What was the point? While 2 percent of people listened to them, 98 percent instinctively pressed the advance track feature on their CD players. We did the exact same thing and started on the third track, "Jungle Boogie," which began with a crashing gong and brass section before settling into a smooth and funky groove. Best I could tell, there were only a few lyrics repeating over and over, but the product was effective. This was only the first song, and I could already see why Francis had gone out of his way to buy the album only a day after seeing the movie.

Dylan poked his head into the room. "Hey, you guys think you can help me tonight?"

"Sure, what do you need?" I asked as Francis lowered the volume.

"I have to set up some refreshments at the show. I forgot about it until my professor called this morning. It won't take long if we all do it."

"What time do we need to head over?" I asked.

"Starts at seven," he said, thinking out loud. "I guess we should get there at five forty-five, so we should leave here at five fifteen?"

"Are we walking?" Francis asked.

I'd been thinking the exact same thing and hoping that somebody had access to a car. The exhibit was being held on North Campus, near the sculpture garden, and would require a solid thirty minutes of walking. Something told me we would be carrying bags of goodies and supplies, so I thought that might add a little extra effort as well.

"Yeah . . . I don't have Naomi's car, if that's what you're asking."

"That's what I was asking," Francis admitted.

"Hey, speaking of silly questions," I transitioned, "why did you ask me if I was going to this thing tonight?"

"Oh," Dylan said dismissively, "Carey wanted to know. She might come with Naomi tonight, but I think she was embarrassed by yesterday."

"Why? Because I didn't go to the movie?"

"I guess she was more into it than you think. She feels like she asked you out, and you turned her down in front of her friends."

"I had plans," I protested. "She asked me at the last minute."

"Dude, I can't explain how girls think! Anyway, I think Naomi told her you had a mysterious Russian girlfriend. So she'll get over it."

I didn't believe that Carey was asking me on a serious date. I figured she'd just gotten her ego slightly bruised because she had been with her friends when I'd said no to her invitation. I should have been more thoughtful about that. It wasn't that she cared so much about going out with *me*, I reasoned. It was probably more that she'd had to be a fifth wheel, and that had made her uncomfortable.

The walk to North Campus posed a bit of a challenge. We carried a veggie tray, a case of twelve bottles of wine, and all the party supplies— plastic cups, plates, napkins, and such. We kept exchanging our burdens because whoever got stuck with the case of wine could make it only about a hundred yards before they needed to switch. About five minutes into our journey, we thought of many ways by which we could have made the process considerably easier. Specifically, we regretted not bringing a skateboard to set the wine on and push along easily beside us. By the time we figured that out, we were just far enough away from our apartment that we didn't want to turn around.

Janss Steps presented the most difficult and uncomfortable obstacle. As soon as we crested the top step, we cut a hard left over to Royce Hall and found a rolling chair left unattended against the building. The wheels of the chair were not perfectly suited for gliding along brick walkways, but anything was better than lugging those bottles even one step farther.

We were the first to arrive at the exhibit hall, and I was impressed with how the hall had been completely converted into an art gallery. The large room was clearly a teaching facility and had several counters and sinks lining the walls. But aside from those unmovable mounted elements and a severely paint-splattered floor, every other notion of a classroom had been removed and replaced by various works of art and temporary walls.

We went right to work setting up the hospitality tables and cleaning up stray items here and there. Prior to our arrival, someone else had dropped off soda, cookies, sparkling cider, and a few bottles of champagne. All in all, the event would be well stocked, and I could see a relief spreading across Dylan's face as we put the last pieces into place with more than thirty minutes to go before the official start time.

Leading up to that night, I had heard little about my roommate's submission for the exhibit. All I knew was that he had created a series of sculptures he wished to keep secret until the unveiling. In my opinion, it had been worth the wait. His installation was occupying a relatively large footprint near the front of the exhibit. It consisted of three clay sculptures of human heads, arranged in a row and individually perched on five-foot high white pedestals. Each head, which was about one and a half the size of a normal head, depicted the same male model—an older schlub of a man closely resembling the ancient Roman philosopher Seneca. I had seen a book with his likeness on the cover in Dylan's room last year and wondered why a Bacchanalian art major would have ever taken an interest in the Stoics. Now I knew.

The likeness on the one to the far left was breathtaking. I had no idea Dylan was capable of such realism. I almost expected the mouth to open and the man to start speaking to me. The creases in the forehead, the strands of hair, the sagging jowls, even the impression of the large man's labored breaths—it was all so perfect.

The middle sculpture was not so precise, but still compelling in its imperfection, and it still bore a strong resemblance to the first figure. Looking more closely, I saw what I believed to be the indentation of knuckles from a balled-up fist on the left cheek and the faint impression of the top of an aluminum can against the upper forehead.

The final work in the collection was a rough impressionistic rendering of the first sculpture. On one hand, it was an incomplete work and unpleasant to look at. On the other hand, it completed the regression of realism from the first and second sculptures. Viewing the third piece in this context made it even more impressive. I noticed unusual marks and scars on the third sculpture through the outer glaze. I thought I could make out a faint mesh divot from having been struck by the head of a microphone and a nasty brown smudge where the artist, my roommate, might have stubbed out a cigarette.

"Do you like it?" Dylan asked, snapping me out of my observations.

"It's amazing!" I confessed, my eyes still searching the third sculpture for little hidden items. "This is one of the best works of art I've ever seen. Not just from you . . . ," I gushed. "From anyone."

"Thanks," Dylan said, accepting the compliment graciously. "Any thoughts or first impressions that you want to share?"

I'd meant what I said. I thought the entire composition was terrific, and I was impressed my friend could create such a mind-blowing work of art. As much as I loved art and as much as Dylan and I could talk for hours about our opinions on art, books, movies, and music, I was not sure I wanted to discuss this specific piece with him. In all our other discussions, there were never any right answers. We were just two anonymous dudes arguing over the meaning of song lyrics, with no referee to interject and award points for the winning opinion.

In this case, there *was* a right answer. I had immediately jumped to a conclusion about the meaning of his work, and for about one full minute, I was diving deeper and deeper into my interpretation. I realized that with a single word, the artist, who was standing three feet away, could shatter my perception—and I was not sure if that was a good or bad thing.

I offered him only a little, just to test the waters. "I'd prefer to think a little more about it. But so far, I see this as your statement about the regression of society over the last two thousand years."

"Not bad . . . You're pretty close." Dylan sounded neutral. "You can think more about it. We can discuss it later if you like."

"Okay," I replied, accepting his offered draw. "What's it called?"

Dylan smiled. "You're gonna laugh."

"Uh-oh."

He beamed. "It's called *Mick Jagger*."

Gradually, other artists started showing up and wandering about the room. Dylan was in his element, speaking with fellow artists and talking about new ideas for upcoming pieces and shows. I was proud of him and admired that he had found a noble place where he so deservedly belonged. He had a gift and was using it. I suppose everyone has a gift tucked away in them somewhere. Sometimes it bubbles right to the surface, and the world both recognizes it and appreciates it immediately, without reservation. Life for these people can be very fulfilling, so long as they recognize their good fortune and never take it for granted.

For others, their gift may be hidden or locked away under layers of doubt, confusion, difficulty, laziness, or other circumstances. These folks are no less worthy than the others, but their journey is significantly different. Neither better nor worse, but markedly different. Sadly, for this group, their lives may resemble tragedy if they choose to secretly dislike themselves for *not* being one of the beautiful or fortunate ones.

Francis and I shambled around, looking at the many other displays. Predictably, some were superb and powerful, while others fell flat and failed to inspire. We were closing in on 8:00 p.m. at that point and nearing the end of our second circuit through the gallery. Francis was ready to be done with the event and started offering crude and cutting remarks about the works he found to be less than worthy. I found his antics amusing but begged him to keep it to himself as the crowd was littered with artists, their friends, and their families. Francis suffered from "inside versus outside voice" issues, and I was sure his comments were perceptible to everyone.

"All right, Francey, I get it. You're done with this place," I capitulated. "Let's head back to the front and see what Dylan's up to."

"You think he's ready to go?"

"I doubt it, but we should go check in with him before we take off."

We turned the corner of a temporary wall and nearly walked straight into Naomi, Carey, and another girl I didn't recognize. Naomi received us warmly. "Hey, boys!"

We all greeted one another politely. I was cautious about anything I said to Carey because I still felt bad about the previous night. The other young woman joining them was named Keisha. She was also a Delta Delta Gamma and an art major as well.

"Are you showing anything tonight?" I asked my new acquaintance.

She smiled broadly, glowing with genuine enjoyment. "No, I didn't know about this show. This is so cool!"

Naomi interjected, "Keisha has a few of her own pieces up in Fowler Hall."

"Fowler Museum, on campus?" I asked, raising an eyebrow.

Keisha nodded. "I created an updated collection of African masks to fit modern-day Los Angeles."

"She was in an article in the *LA Times* over the summer," Naomi reported. "And she's supposed to be featured in a CNN piece about up-and-coming artists next month."

"That's really impressive!" I said. "That collection sounds interesting. I have a class in Fowler this quarter. Where can I find it? I'll look for it."

"I'm surprised," Naomi quipped. "I thought you would be more interested in Russian art."

Francis understood she was teasing me, but based on the blank looks on both Keisha's and Carey's faces, I assumed they had no idea what Naomi was talking about.

After a moment passed, Keisha picked up on my previous comments regarding her work and explained the location of the masks in Fowler Museum. I made a note to look for them the next time I went to my anthropology class.

"So . . ." Naomi gave a mischievous grin. "What do you guys think of Dylan's family portrait?"

I had no idea what she was talking about. "What family portrait?"

"His sculptures!" she laughed. "I assumed it was the three of you."

Her comment kind of blew my mind. I had not considered that as an option at all. Was she serious? Were those three sculptures really supposed to be the three of us? We had known one another for a little over two years. I highly doubted Dylan was about to cast our heads in lead just yet.

"If that's supposed to be the three of us," Francis replied, "then I'm the first one. Not either of the messed-up ones. Okay?"

It was unclear if Francis was serious or playing along with Naomi at that point.

Naomi continued, "I think he wants to use it as the cover art for the Dutch Candy album."

"I don't think that's supposed to be the three of us," I said, laughing a little. "But now that you mention it, I kind of *love* the idea of using that as an album cover."

Keisha smiled. "She's kidding . . . I spoke to him for fifteen minutes, and he said the piece was a statement about how mankind's philosophies have changed over time."

"I liked it," Carey, who had been conspicuously quiet, chimed in. "It's nice. Dylan said that so far, everyone assumes it is supposed to be interpreted from left to right, but it can be read from either direction. I thought that was interesting because we can interpret how we are changing and if it's for the better or for the worse."

"That's nice." Keisha smiled at her friend. "I always find that art is most impactful when it encourages the observer to draw their own conclusions and interpret the meaning for themselves."

We continued our conversation in that vein for a little while longer. Naomi, Carey, and Keisha were all very smart and very deep thinkers. I found myself listening a little more than talking at this point, but Francis wasn't having any of it. After about five minutes, he finally interrupted the flow of their discussion, wondering aloud what was going on that night and where everyone would be headed after the show. He added, perhaps a little too obviously, that Maya had mentioned that they were all going to a big fraternity party. He left the comment hanging in the air, hoping that someone would fill in the blanks and offer an invitation to join them.

"I'm heading back to the house after this," Carey confessed.

"You are?" Naomi pouted. "You're not going out?"

"I don't think so," Carey replied sheepishly. "I'm busy tomorrow."

Naomi turned to Keisha. "How about you?"

"I'm up for anything."

Francis realized that there would be no invitation to join them, and we eventually parted company with the girls as they continued their way through the remainder of the exhibit. Dylan was standing near the front door, settled into a lively discussion with a happy mass of artists and admirers. Neither Francis nor I felt like interrupting him. He caught sight of us and toasted in our direction with one of the plastic champagne cups from the party store bag. I gave him a small salute and motioned that Francis and I were leaving.

# Chapter 13

Dara arrived at class before me. My eyes met hers immediately after passing through the propped-open door. She pressed her lips into a tight smile. She was sitting in the back row, in the same seat as when I had met her on the first day of class.

I noticed Anson, Can, and a few of their friends huddled and chatting in the rows ahead of her. Students were creatures of habit and found comfort in occupying the same general seating chart from class to class.

I'd rehearsed a Belarusian greeting. "Dobry dzień."

"Dobry dzień. You learned Belarusian," she beamed.

"Not exactly. Did I say it right?"

"Perfect."

"That's all I know."

"Well, it's a start."

We chatted idly, waiting for class to begin. I didn't have the nerve to mention her late-night voice mail, and we managed to navigate our prelecture banter without making any mention of either of our phone calls.

I felt mildly self-conscious speaking in such proximity to Anson and Can. I felt like they were each individually taking momentary breaks from their own conversation to eavesdrop on Dara and me. I didn't have what everyone called "game," and I felt like everything I was saying was both awkward and uninteresting. I noticed Can sneaking a glance back at me at one point. I almost stopped in midsentence but managed to catch myself and finish making my point.

Professor Opeyemi was brilliant as usual, but then again, I wasn't the best judge of his lectures. To me, everything he ever said in his class was profound. I was sure I placed more emphasis on his lessons than they demanded. But I was only visiting from the political science department, and every word he uttered was a pleasant deviation from the banalities of a never-ending debate about the efficacy of a two-party system of government.

As promised, Opeyemi spent the class reading samples of poetry. More specifically, he spent the full hour gushing over the works of a few poets whose poems he counted among the most beautiful ever written in the English language. His first sample of a great poem was "The Tyger" by William Blake.

The professor recited the verses from memory, and the class sat motionless. After completing the poem, he spent a quiet moment staring ahead and contemplating the words and their meaning. Yes, it was odd and awkward, but it was so very Opeyemi that you couldn't help but love it.

Predictably, he began his analysis of the poem in a familiar fashion. "Why," he wondered aloud, "does Blake take the time to write these words?"

Unlike the previous two classes, an earnest discussion broke out, and the class began to share insights and opinions. Can was among the first to speak, and she attributed the central theme to Blake's belief in a higher power. She mused that each stanza contemplated a direct question about who could have created something so inspiring and divine.

Other students emphasized Blake's reliance on inquiry and pointed out that every line in the poem was phrased as a question. To this point, Anson made a comment about Socratic poetry. Most of the class snickered at this, but I didn't understand what he meant.

Opeyemi allowed the conversation to continue for a while before breaking in and revisiting his central theme. "Why would a man ask us to contemplate these things? Why would he ask us how the tiger became so fierce? Why does he ask these questions?"

A dark-haired boy with thick glasses and a collared shirt buttoned all the way up to his neck finally asked, "What's your interpretation?"

His question was postured just on the cusp between annoyance (from having been asked the same rhetorical question over and over) and genuine interest.

The professor was deep in thought, crossing his arms in front of him and looking toward the floor. "There is one woman in this class who believes that in this poem, Blake is pointing to the tiger as proof of God's brilliance and majesty. This is a good reason to write."

He let silence fill the air. "But I do not believe in this kind of thing, I am sorry to say. I wish I did."

In front of me, Anson's head snapped over to Can's direction. She showed no reaction to our professor referencing her comments or beliefs.

Opeyemi released a sigh and continued his commentary. "What I believe, what I feel in my heart, is that this man is asking us—he's *pleading* with us to answer the questions in his poem. He wants to ask us all, where does the fire come from?"

He stood, facing the class. "He wants us all to find the source of that fire for ourselves."

He spread his arms to the class like a preacher adding emphasis to the final point of a sermon. "This is what I believe."

Dara and I walked out in relative silence at the end of class. We walked down the hallway and out into the bustling university campus. Then she turned to me and asked as casually as if she were asking the time, "Do you still want to have dinner?"

"Yes, but it's a little early."

"I can meet with you later. You have band rehearsal on Wednesdays, do you not?"

I was impressed that she'd remembered. "Yeah, until maybe five or six."

"Okay, we'll meet in Westwood at six thirty. I live close to the village. Can you meet me on the street at Gayley and Weyburn?"

I knew both of those streets but didn't have a clear visual in my mind of exactly where that was. But I knew I could figure it out. "I can find it."

# Chapter 14

Francis was seated on the front stoop of the apartment, reclining on the steps and speaking on the wireless phone as I approached. He nodded his head in greeting and continued his conversation as I squeezed past him and into the apartment. I gathered from his goofy smile and tentative speech that he was talking to a girl, probably his movie date from the previous weekend.

Dylan was hovering around our amps and tinkering with the cables. He noticed the additional light filling the room as I opened the front door but remained focused on his task.

"Dylo, are you performing surgery on the amps?"

"Something like that. I keep getting static, and I think it has to do with this connection." He demonstrated removing and then reinserting the quarter-inch TS connector. An audible buzz cut out and then resumed in time with his actions.

"Hope you bought her dinner," I offered, thinking I was funny.

I could tell he was losing his patience. "It's driving me crazy!"

"Try my guitar cable and see if it's the amp or the wire—"

"I already did that. Both cables buzzed, so I'm pretty sure it's the amp."

"Plug it into a different outlet on the other side of the apartment," I suggested.

"What's that gonna do?" He sounded annoyed, but I heard a hint of hope in his voice.

"I don't know. We got the neighbors on the other side of that wall. Maybe they have something over there that's interfering."

"You think they just brought in a new deep freezer on their side?" His voice dripped with sarcasm. "And it's pulling from our power supply?"

I laughed even though he was mocking my idea. "I don't know. Just try it."

He retrieved an extension cord from our hall closet and disappeared into my room, presumably to plug it in, and then walked the female end back out to the amp. "This is a dumb idea."

"Dumb enough to work . . . ," I encouraged.

He plugged it in, and the red light went on. The amp was completely silent. He had probably just spent ten minutes frustrating the bejesus out of himself to get rid of that irritating buzz. I was sure he was beyond annoyed that I'd walked in and, within ten seconds, provided an implausible, but effective, solution. He looked at me, searching for the perfect thing to say. He finally settled on "Go fuck yourself."

"You're welcome," I offered cordially.

"All right, let's get going," he grunted.

I went back to my room to drop off my backpack. I reentered the living room to find Dylan sitting in a chair and tuning his guitar. I grabbed my own guitar and plugged it in.

"Hey!" I called. Gaining his attention, I then lowered my voice a bit. "Who's Francey talking to?"

"I think it's Maya," he replied, matching my low volume.

"That's good, right?" I asked, giving a thumbs-up.

Dylan shrugged. "We'll see . . ."

The comment caught me off guard. "Why do you say it like that?"

"I don't think the movie date was a huge success."

"Did Naomi tell you something?"

He nodded. "Maya doesn't like him *that* way. And besides, she started dating one of the baseball players."

"That's too bad. Does Francey know?"

Dylan shook his head. "I don't think so."

"So this phone call"—I pointed to the front door—"probably isn't helping him?"

"Probably not."

"Well, let's get started then. I'll go tell him to wrap it up."

I walked over and poked my head back out the door to give Francis a two-minute warning. It seemed like every one of us one had somewhere to be after rehearsal, so we got warmed up and sped through a few of our songs. We sounded great, and the improvement since the first rehearsal was obvious.

Francis seemed to be the X factor. He'd always been stiff in the past but was starting to branch out and began adding a little more attitude. A new swagger was coming through in the way he hit the drums. Without a doubt, the new sound was elevating everything Dylan did. I felt like the two of them were hitting another level. By contrast, I was still doing my best to just play the right chords in the right order and on time.

We decided that we had enough time to take a quick break and then go to work on the eight-song set list for our upcoming show. Dylan went into his room and produced three sheets of paper with a new shorter subset of his rehearsal songs listed on the pages in bold letters.

"You already picked out a set list for the show?" Francis asked. It was unclear if he was protesting or simply curious.

"I did," Dylan replied, taping the sheets of paper to the ground in a perfect spot so we could see them when we resumed our positions. "Jeff, can you do these songs from memory, or do you still need the chords?"

"I'm good. I got it all memorized." I actually didn't have it *all* memorized, but I kept that to myself. I figured it would be a good test to see if I could make it through the eight songs.

"Right. Well, I have the chords in red next to the songs just in case."

"That's probably a good call." Francis just entered the living room from the kitchen. He made the comment with just enough ridicule to make it clear he was teasing me. I took no offense. He sat down heavily on the couch. He was drinking a bottle of fruit juice that he had retrieved from his shelf in the refrigerator. Beads of perspiration had covered most of his forehead, a result of having exerted himself on his small drum kit.

"Jeff," he began after a big gulp of the cool red liquid, "whatever happened with that Russian girl from the answering machine?"

Francis was not usually one to pry about such matters. His comment caused Dylan to jerk his head sharply and turn his interest away from taping down the set lists. I suspected Dylan was as curious about Francis asking an uncharacteristic question as he was about my reply.

I decided I would share a little. "Actually, I'm having dinner with her tonight."

They both visibly leaned forward from their respective positions. Francis asked the first follow-up question. "Is she really from Russia?"

I thought the question was a little strange, but I had to admit I was excited to talk about her. "Not exactly. She's from Belarus."

"Belarus?"

I interpreted from his tone that he was asking me to tell him more. I didn't have too much to add. "It's close to Russia," I explained. "I don't know much about it. They declared their independence from Russia a few years ago. She explained it to me, but I didn't get it all."

"Her name is Dara, right?" Dylan asked.

"Yeah, Dara," I replied.

"So what's the deal? Are you dating her? The message sounded urgent. Kinda seemed like . . ." Dylan left the point unfinished.

"There's nothing going on. We just met in my poetry class. We've hung out on campus a few times. That's all."

"Whoa!" Francis had picked up on something. "So tonight's the first off-campus date?"

"I guess, but I'm not sure if it's a date," I admitted.

Dylan fired off the next question. "Did you ask her, or did she ask you?"

"She asked me." I knew they would read more into that, but it was true.

Dylan cut me off, asking, "So *she* asked *you* to go to dinner?" He shared a look with Francis. "What does she look like?"

"Yeah, is she hot?" Francis blurted, putting a finer, if not cruder, point on the question.

"You guys wouldn't even believe me if I told you."

"Wait." Dylan exchanged another look with Francis. "What does that mean? Is she, like, beautiful?"

I was at a loss for words, and I was grinning like an idiot. "I can't even describe it, you guys. I really can't."

"So she's beautiful?" Dylan pressed the topic. "Can you tell us anyone she looks like?"

I hadn't thought of a comparison to that point, and nothing came to mind. "I can't think of anyone. She looks like . . ." I was stumped. "A tall blonde Russian model."

Dylan's response was unfiltered. "Fuck . . ."

"Where are you guys going to dinner?" Francis asked.

"Well, I'm not going to tell you. The way you guys are acting . . . I don't want you to show up and spy on us."

"Yeah, I don't blame you." Dylan laughed at himself. "Does she have any supermodel friends you can introduce us to?"

"What about Naomi?"

"I'm not saying I need to date them. I just want to hang out with some supermodels."

"She's not a supermodel," I protested. "See? This is why I wanted to keep this to myself."

The conversation continued. I confessed to them that we were only friends and the relationship wasn't romantic at all, but I was sure they didn't believe me. They kept referencing the answering machine message and insisting that "friends" didn't leave those kinds of messages in the middle of the night. I tried to change their minds, but the more I attempted to set the record straight, the more they believed that I was hiding something. On one hand, I didn't want them jumping to conclusions. On the other, I was encouraged by their insistence that something was going on.

To be honest, I was excited to think that Dara and I could have possibly been a couple—even if only in the imagination of my idiotic roommates.

# Chapter 15

When Dara told me that she lived close to Westwood, she wasn't exaggerating. Her apartment complex, Gayley Gardens, was roughly across the street from Buck Fifty Sub and Tommy Burger.

She asked if we could eat at Montecito Pizza Kitchen. The restaurant was a new addition to our small college town, and Dara told me she found herself eating there several times a week. "They have a couple of salads that I like," she explained. I was happy with her selection.

She insisted that we take our food to go and said we could eat on the balcony of her apartment. Of course I agreed. The thought of a dinner date at her place was spectacular. Gauging from her demeanor, she was not inviting me back for anything more than a friendly dinner and our typical conversation about books and movies. Regardless, I couldn't help myself from becoming extremely excited about being alone with her in her apartment. Despite my elevated heart rate and racing mind, I played it cool and tried not to talk too much or say anything too embarrassing. I was fairly successful.

We walked about five minutes from the restaurant to a weathered staircase that clung to the side of her building. She motioned for me to follow her up the stairs. "I'm just up here."

I estimated that her building was less than a ten-minute walk from my own apartment. She turned left at the top of the stairs, and I followed her down a short external hallway that looked back over at a partial view of Westwood. "Nice view."

She dug her keys out of her bag, signaling to me that her door was probably right ahead of us. "Thank you. It's even better inside."

I waited in her alcove as she unlocked her door and pushed it open. I was struck immediately by the colors. The door was bright purple and flanked by a couple of comfy-looking patio chairs on each side.

The apartment was small, but colorfully decorated in a remarkable and eclectic manner. Dara meshed many motifs and styles. Where I would have made a mess of trying to pair moroccan tile patterns with paisley, she had created something incredible and was now living in her own work of art. All the walls were painted a different color, and the floor-to-ceiling curtains were printed in an oversized floral design in a bold primary color that looked like something from the Andy Warhol window covering collection.

Dara immediately pulled the curtains apart, and sunlight flooded the apartment. A slice of Westwood was visible beyond the small sitting area, which was big enough only for a bistro set.

"We can eat out here," she said, opening the door. "What would you like to drink?"

"Just water."

It occurred to me that everything in her apartment was high quality and quite expensive. She had a huge L-shaped pillow-top sofa, which took up most of the living room. In keeping with the overall theme of "mismatched, but matching," she had adorned it with an armada of pillows in varying shapes, sizes, colors, and patterns. Opposite the sofa stood a wall-mounted entertainment center stocked with a multiple-CD changer, VHS player, state-of-the-art TV, and large speakers. Two entire shelves housed a well-organized library of CDs and VHS tapes. Many of the selections were still wrapped in the original boxes. I made a note to look through her collection after dinner and see what treasures might be hiding within.

In a quick glance, I saw a CD cover that I recognized—Mary J. Blige's *What's the 411?* (which was a good sign)—and another one that I did not recognize. The cover depicted a rectangular photograph running horizontally across the bottom and a coffee stain ring positioned above it. The artist's name was Jeff Buckley.

I saw several books scattered about on the shelves, on the colorfully tiled coffee table, and even on the small dining table beyond the sofa closer to the kitchen. The kitchen itself was an open space tucked around the corner from the living room, and it was well appointed with chic stainless appliances. It all seemed a bit high-end for a college student living on their own. I was starting to get the impression that Dara was well-off and had a taste for finer things.

"Can you put that out there?" She was referring to the food I carried and pointed behind her to the balcony as she crossed to the kitchen. "I'll get our drinks and some regular forks."

I ventured farther into the apartment. "This is nice," I complimented her. "Did you paint it yourself?"

"No, it was the painters. Why?"

"I mean, did your landlord do it? Did you rent it this way? Or did—"

My question sparked a memory. "At first, they were so upset. His wife said she was going to kick me out, but they let me stay if I promised to paint it all beige before I leave."

I was impressed. "You did this without asking?"

"Well, it looks so much better than beige. Who wants to live in a house with white walls? Isn't that where they put crazy people?"

A center hallway led farther back into the apartment, ending in a stunning poster of Toulouse-Lautrec's *Reine de Joie*. Red and yellow doors, which lifted their exact Pantone colors from the four-color lithograph, faced each other at the end of the hall. Dara had mentioned on a couple of occasions that she lived alone, and my assumption was that the red door opened to her room and the yellow door to her bathroom.

Well-stocked bookshelves covered the wall of the hallway almost completely. The sheer number of books in her space seemed almost out of place. They were neatly organized for the most part, with a few disheveled sections. She had large hardback classroom editions, small pulpy paperbacks, and everything in between.

"Dara, you have so many books!" I exclaimed.

She glanced over from the kitchen and admitted sheepishly, "I know. I love books."

"Where did you get all these?"

"Around. I go to bookstores and thrift stores. They always have cheap books. Each store gets new books on one certain day of the week or month. I show up first thing in the morning and spend hours picking whatever I like."

"Have you read them all?"

"No," she said with a sigh. "I've read some of them, but not all of them. I think even if you cannot read all the greatest stories, you should put them on a shelf in your home, and at least you can be near them."

Just then, she remembered something. "I almost forgot—I wanted to give you *Never Believe*. It is brilliant to read."

We ate out in the open air overlooking Westwood. Dinner was comfortable. Dara seemed more relaxed in a familiar environment. Her style of speaking was less abrasive, and she seemed to be nicer.

We sat quietly, watching the sky turn from blue to purple. The air became cooler. For days, I had already been forming an opinion about Dara and how she was potentially "out of my league." I know it's horrible to say, but most people can understand the sentiment. She just had this *thing* about her, a certain je ne sais quoi that I couldn't put into words. It was evident in the way she carried herself, in the way she dressed, in the way looked—and, most apparently, in the way that people looked at her.

Sitting with her on the balcony of her luxurious apartment only further confirmed my feelings about her elevated status in my mind. This wasn't a bad thing. I believed, in time, I could get there too. But if I was being honest, I wasn't there yet. I wondered all the time why she was taking an interest in me.

"This is a nice apartment."

"Thank you."

"Do you mind me asking you a personal question?"

"You can ask." Implication being she wouldn't necessarily answer.

"Are you . . . Is your family well-off?"

"Well-off?" She either didn't understand the phrase or was pretending not to understand to avoid the discussion.

"Wealthy?"

She released a humorless laugh. "No, not wealthy."

I got the distinct sense that the conversation was over.

Dara stood up. "I'm going to have a glass of wine. Do you want one?"

I wasn't much of a wine drinker, but how could I say no? "Sure."

"Great." She got up and cleared some of the mess from the bistro table. "I'm cold. Let's drink it in the living room."

"Okay," I agreed, getting up and clearing the remaining items from the surface of the table.

"You can leave it. Just pick out some music to listen to."

"Sounds good." I passed through the apartment to the entertainment center. "Hey, I noticed this disc when I walked in. Who's Jeff Buckley? Is this any good?"

"This is one of my favorites right now. You know Tim Buckley?"

"The folk singer? From the '70s?" I asked, unsure if I had it right.

"Yes, him!" she called from the kitchen. "This is his son! He's very good!"

"All right, let's listen to this." I read the cover of the album aloud, "*Live at Sin-é.*"

Dara appeared from out of the kitchen with two glasses of red wine. She handed me one. "Sin-é is a club in New York City. The disc is already in. Just push play."

I scanned the CD changer, successfully found the album, and then pressed the play button. Dara sat on the couch behind me. "What kind of music is it?"

"You'll see. Have a seat." Her words were matter-of-fact and *not* come-hither. I did not get a sense that she was seducing me with a bottle of red wine. Rather, she was only inviting me to join her for an after-dinner discussion.

I sank into the comfortable sofa and took my first sip of the wine. I'd had red wine on a few prior occasions, but it hadn't really been my *thing*. This, however, was delicious. "Wow, this is really good."

"I know," she agreed. "I like this one."

"Are you a wine expert?" I knew there was a better word to use, but I couldn't think of it.

"No, no," she said quickly and sharply. "I know nothing about it. I just like what I like."

We sat without speaking. Ethereal moaning interspersed with the high-pitched plucking of electric guitar strings lilted in the background as the first song on the CD slowly came to life.

Dara rested peacefully with her foot tucked under her other leg. She was staring vacantly toward a spot on the floor and periodically sipping on her wine. She was content in that moment. I got the sense that she was comfortable and seeping serenely into some recess of her mind that only she could enter. I feared I might have been in the room with her, but not really *with* her. I searched for something to say.

"This is nice. Do you do this every night?"

She smiled ever so slightly, but more than trying to relay pleasant agreement, her expression seemed to imply a note of amused annoyance and maybe even embarrassment for me. I immediately read that this moment, for her, was for quiet contemplation. My anxious desire to talk must have seemed, on some level, a little desperate.

It was unfair for her to make these rules on the fly and shut off communication, but I was so enamored by both her *and* the moment that I had no choice but to accommodate her every unexplained whim. I took her cue and backed off. I let the moment and the music take over. I turned inward and just listened, resigned to reemerge only when she decided to reengage the discussion.

In the background, an earnest and beautiful voice took flight. The vocals were towering and sincere. The lyrics were poetic in the highest order and spoke of love and pain.

"Do you like it?" she asked.

"Very much."

"It's poetry to me."

"What's the meaning? It's a love song?"

She still had not looked at me since we had begun speaking again. "For me? It's a love song, but it reminds me of my mother and father. Is that strange?"

"It's not strange. You can't control that, right? If it reminds you, then it reminds you."

"I think you're right." Dara looked at me. "What does the song make you think of?"

*You!* I wanted to scream. *The song and the wine and the dinner on the balcony and the sky turning purple and the crazy way you decorated this place without permission . . . All of it, now and forever, will make me think of you, you beautiful, mysterious, and fascinating girl! You! It all reminds me of you.*

But I didn't say any of that. "Um . . . not sure. I need to hear it again, but I like it."

"I'll let you borrow it."

"You don't have to do that. I can always get one at Spotlight."

"It's very rare. I doubt they have it. At least I can make you a copy."

"Okay, fine. You can make me a copy."

We settled back into silence and listened to the rest of the song. Dara offered to no one in particular, "Wine always makes me sleepy." Her glass was empty. Eventually, she stood up. "I'm going to have one more. Do you want another glass?"

I was just starting to feel the slightest percolation of a buzz. It was soft and warm and pleasant. "Sure."

She had already walked around the arm of her sofa and disappeared into the kitchen. I heard the satisfying scrape of a half-full wine bottle being lifted from a counter. She began speaking to me from the kitchen. "Why is it you love poetry so much?"

I watched her walk back toward me. Damn, she was gorgeous. She held the bottle in front of her. "Hold out your glass."

I complied. She filled my glass and then her own. She set the bottle on the coffee table and sat back down on the sofa. "So . . . why do you love poetry?"

I was thinking of how to respond to the question since she had called to me from the kitchen, but I still didn't have an answer. "I don't know . . . It makes me feel good. It makes me . . ."

"What?" She encouraged me to finish the point. "What were you going to say? I want to know."

"It inspires me. It makes me want to find . . . something."

"I like that." She took a sip of wine. "Makes you want to find something. What?"

"It's silly. But I think that poets—great poets—they reveal something truthful, and they uncomplicate it so that we all can see it."

"You think they reveal something true?" she asked.

"They take complex issues and simplify them. Remember the William Blake poem?"

"'The Tyger.' Yes, I remember. From class."

"That's what I love," I confessed.

"And do you want to write like that?"

"I don't know. You asked me this before," I said, referring to our first lunch together. "I don't know why I want to write. I don't even really know *if* I want to write."

Dara fell silent. She tilted her head and regarded me. I took the break in the conversation as an opportunity to take a long drink from my wineglass and recollect my thoughts. She eased back a bit into her seat and retrained her gaze on the anonymous spot on the floor. I sensed she was traveling somewhere in her mind again. I wanted to keep her there with me and asked the first question to pop into my head. "What about you? Why do you love it?"

"Poetry?"

"Poetry or any of this." I waved my hands in the direction of the books on her coffee table and the bookshelves peeking around the corner of her hallway.

She didn't meet my eyes, but she was thinking. Finally, after a moment of silence, she let the answer slip. "My father."

There was a hint of longing in her voice. She did not elaborate beyond that. On our previous outings together, she had conspicuously avoided the topic of her family—her father in particular. Tonight, however, she had now made mention of him twice in less than thirty minutes. I was curious and wanted to understand a little more about the impact this man had on her life. "What about your father? Did he love literature and poetry as well?"

Dara nodded. "He did. I know this much. He was a brilliant man and a professor."

Something about the way she said "I know this much" gave me pause. "Did he—"

"Can we not talk about this tonight?"

"Of course," I replied a little too eagerly. I was programmed to say yes to her and give her what she wanted. Of course I would agree to her request, but I was curious why she had said "tonight." Did she assume that we *would* talk about this at some point?

"Do you want to watch a movie? I have a new movie that I want to watch. I think you'll like it."

"Sure. What movie is it?"

"*Out of Africa*. Have you seen it?" she asked. "I just got it, and I've never seen it, but I've wanted to."

I had heard of this movie. It'd been a major blockbuster from about ten years earlier. I didn't know much about the film, but I did have a vague notion that it had won several awards. Until that moment, I had not had any desire to see it. However, the thought of sitting alone in a dark room with my beautiful Belarusian friend and watching an epic love story was too much to turn down.

Dara had already retrieved the unopened VHS tape and begun removing the cellophane wrapper from the box. "I wanted to see this for a while, but I didn't have anybody to watch it with."

"Can I see the box?" I asked, arm extended. She handed it back to me. I recognized Robert Redford and Meryl Streep sitting together in tall grass on the cover. The back cover revealed a short synopsis and a running time of two hours and forty-one minutes.

Dara held the wine bottle perched at an angle above my glass. "More?"

"Please."

She walked to the front door, flipped off the light, and pulled two blankets from an old chest at the side of her entertainment center. She tossed one in my direction and threw the other on the space where she had been sitting on the couch. The blanket was plush and gave off a faint, but pleasant, flowery scent. I reasoned from her simple action that she would remain on her section of the L-shaped sofa.

"I'll be right back. Do you need anything?" She turned and tucked around the corner.

Everything was happening so quickly. I tried to make sense of the dynamic. We were about to sit together for the next three hours on near-opposite sides of the sofa watching *Out of Africa*. I was consumed with the hope that she would scoot herself around the coffee table and join me on my section of the sofa facing the TV. At a minimum, I wanted to sit close to her and not six feet apart. I would let her watch the movie and spare her the pathetic attempts at a high school make-out session. I just wanted to sit next to her and maybe share a single blanket. I was happy to be with her and to have this wonderful night together. But the idea that she wasn't willing to cozy up to me and watch a movie was almost too much for my fragile male ego to bear.

Dara reentered the room. She had changed into sweats and a sweatshirt. I could tell instantly by the sway of her breasts that she had removed her bra. I was twenty and conditioned to notice such things. The hint of her nipples cast small shadows off the sideways glow of the TV. Dara settled into her side of the sofa and pulled the blanket up to her neck.

I tried for five minutes to accept my fate sitting so far away from her, but the longing eventually got the better of me, and I decided to float up one single balloon to get her to join me. "Are you sure you don't want to sit on this side so you can see the screen head-on?"

"This is fine," she said without looking at me.

# Chapter 16

I wasn't sure what time it was when Dara woke me up. The glow of the blue television screen filled the room like the light of the moon.

She shook me gently. "Jeff, we fell asleep."

It took me a moment to get my bearings, but I eventually came to my senses. She slipped my shoes off and scooted my feet from the surface of the coffee table to the sofa. "I'm going to sleep. You can stay if you like."

"Okay."

Dara shook me again, and I opened my eyes once more. The room had brightened considerably, and I searched for the source of the bright white light before realizing that morning had arrived. She was sitting on the coffee table, leaning toward me and dressed for her day. She laughed a little. "Did you like the movie?"

I noticed that I had a slight headache. "It was amazing."

"You were really sleeping."

"Was I snoring or doing anything gross?" I worried aloud. My voice was a little hoarse.

"Breathing a little heavy, but it was cute." It was the first time she had ever said anything endearing about me. "Hey, I have to go, but you can stay as long as you want. I made you coffee."

I noticed a steaming cup resting on the table next to her. "Thank you."

"Help yourself to anything in the kitchen. The bathroom is the yellow door at the end of the hall. When you go, just lock the door behind you, okay?"

"Okay." I was still a little startled. My mouth tasted bitter, and my headache was growing more intense. I guess this was the fabled wine hangover I had heard so much about but had never experienced. I rubbed my eyelids to wake myself up. Dara picked up her bag and headed for the door.

"Hey . . . !" I called to her, and she turned back to me.

I wanted to thank her for having me over and ask her if she wanted to go out this weekend. I also wanted to ask her if she'd been dreaming about me last night like I had dreamed about her. But none of it would come out. She stood waiting for me to say something.

"Yes?" she asked.

"Um . . ."

Dara laughed. "I'll see you later, okay?"

"Okay," I agreed. Then she opened her front door, walked out of the apartment, and pulled the door closed behind her.

I sat up and took a sip of coffee. As exciting as it was to be in Dara's apartment, it was also weird. I decided I shouldn't linger too long. I did have to use the bathroom and was relieved to see in the mirror that my bed head had not flown to embarrassingly unruly heights through the night. I did, however, notice my teeth were purple and there was a pronounced wine stain on my white shirt just below my neck. A rookie move, to be sure.

Exiting the bathroom, I faced head-on the red door leading to her bedroom and *all* my fantasies. I was curious if she had locked it or if she trusted me to not go into her room. I fought the urge to turn the handle—just to check. Instead, I returned to the living room, where I noticed for the first time that she had rubber-banded two Ope Opeyemi books, a recordable cassette tape with the words "Jeff Buckley" scrawled on the spine, and a paper note on top that read "Jeff." I folded both of our blankets and returned them to the chest where I had seen her retrieve them the night before.

I finished my coffee on her balcony, taking one last look at the view of Westwood before grabbing my books and music and quietly departing from her place.

# Chapter 17

"Jeff?" Dylan called out to me as soon as I walked through the front door.

"Yep." I'd known my early-morning return would not escape his scrutiny, and I expected a small barrage of questions to follow. What I hadn't expected, though, was that Naomi would be the first to spring from his doorway and lead the inquest.

"So . . . ?" She was grinning from ear to ear. "Where were you last night?"

She was already dressed for classes and holding a travel mug. She took a sip. I smelled coffee.

I decided to be honest. "I fell asleep watching a movie at Dara's place."

"That's a good one!" Dylan called from his room. His voice was still scratchy, and I assumed he was still lying in bed.

"Just watching a movie?" Naomi asked suggestively.

"That's it."

She noticed the stain. "Did you spill red wine on your shirt watching a movie?"

"Actually," I said, pulling on my shirt to get a peek at the ruddy blemish, "that's exactly what happened."

Her tone changed to pouty. "You're not going to tell me what happened, are you?"

"Naomi." I had her full attention now. She was listening intently. "Nothing happened. I wish it did, but it didn't. We watched a movie, and I fell asleep. That's it."

"And you spilled red wine?"

"Yes, and I spilled red wine on my shirt."

"You're lucky. I have to go to class." She pointed at me playfully. "I know there's more of a story here, but I don't have time." She called to Dylan, "Sweetie, I'm going to go! Call me later?"

"Okay, have a good day!" Dylan called back.

"Can you find out what happened with Jeff last night and tell me later when you call?" she asked, smirking at me like a spoiled brat.

"I'm on it!" Dylan called back to her.

Naomi smiled a satisfied smile. She picked up her bag and left the apartment.

"Well . . . How was it?" Dylan spoke the words without raising his voice. I could see his shitty grin in my mind as he spoke. I walked back to my room. I needed a nap.

# Chapter 18

Dara was waiting in the back row of poetry class for me on Wednesday. She was smiling broadly and watching me as I walked over to take the seat next to her.

"You look like you're in a good mood."

She beamed. "I am!"

I had never seen her this happy. Her smile was infectious, and I felt the corners of my own lips tilting upward. "So what's up? Anything you can share?"

"There's a string quartet from Belarus playing in Southern California!"

My smile dipped slightly. I hadn't expected that answer. I hadn't assumed a string quartet could make anyone so outwardly happy, but I played along. "That's great! Where are they playing?"

"I don't know." Her brow furrowed momentarily. "It's unclear, but I hear they may be on the UCLA campus. I have to find out."

"When?"

"I don't know that either," she admitted. "They're supposed to be touring the area for a couple of weeks."

"How'd you hear about it?"

"I work with a girl from Russia, and she told me." Dara was still smiling from ear to ear. "They are playing many songs from *Faust*. You know this?"

"It's the story by Goethe, right? I didn't think it was a musical."

She laughed. "No, not a musical. It is a composition by an important Belarusian composer, Antoni Radziwiłł." She held her hands up in front of her in mock prayer. "I *have* to see this!"

"You know, I have a friend that works at Schoenberg." She straightened up in her seat at my mention of this. "We could check after class to see if he's there and if he knows about the show."

"You think he will know?"

"Yeah. If anyone does, he will."

At the front of the room, Opeyemi had a slight twinkle in his eye and began his lecture with a question. Not his typical question, but rather a new question, which was no less impossible to answer. "Who knows what makes a great poem?"

The class fell silent.

"Anyone?" He smiled and challenged us with the trademark lightness in his voice. "Does anyone know what goes into a great poem?"

On the right side of the room, a hand belonging to a girl with jet-black hair and pronounced cat-eye eyeliner rose halfway before returning to a resting position on her desk.

"Okay, let's try something different . . . Who can tell me the name of a great poem?"

The class was still reticent to speak up.

"Hey, this is easier than you think," Opeyemi encouraged. "I read a great poem for you last week."

"'The Tyger'!" an unidentified student called out.

The professor pointed in the direction of the voice and smiled broadly. "Yes."

"Is this all a matter of opinion?" Anson blurted from a couple of rows ahead of me.

"Yes," Opeyemi agreed. "So give me your opinion."

"*The Cat in the Hat,*" Anson quipped. The class laughed, and a fair amount of tension fled from the room.

Opeyemi looked out the window for a moment and let some silence build, restoring the tension. He commented dryly, "Dr. Seuss . . . You know he was not actually a doctor?" A few laughs followed, and the professor continued, "But I wonder, is that a serious answer or a joke? Are you unwilling to have your real opinions heard? How can you—any of you—expect to write if you are afraid of sharing your opinions?"

The question was posed to the class but might have been partially intended for Anson.

"'Still Here' by Langston Hughes." Anson spoke the words clearly and deliberately.

Opeyemi responded immediately, orating the poem from memory.

*I been scared and battered.*
*My hopes the wind done scattered.*
*Snow has friz me,*
*Sun has baked me,*
*Looks like between 'em they done*

*Tried to make me*
*Stop laughin', stop lovin', stop livin'—*
*But I don't care!*
*I'm still here!*

The class clapped at this. The professor smirked. "Please tell me you're applauding the poem and not an old man's memory." The class broke into laughter, and then Opeyemi turned his gaze to Anson. "Well done! That is an excellent poem. 'I'm still here!' This is a poem that will apply to all of us at some point in our lives." He was pensive for a moment and then snapped out of it. "Anyone else? Would anyone else like to offer what they believe to be an excellent poem?"

A girl, the same girl who had gotten shy about raising her hand before, called out, "'I Heard a Fly Buzz—When I Died' by Emily Dickinson!"

Can reached up with both hands and began snapping her fingers in approval. I recognized the gesture as something I had seen Naomi and her sorority sisters do when they approved of something. I took it to be a subtler, less distracting form of applause.

The lecturer stared blankly at the girl. "I know of that poem, but I don't *know* it. Can you recite it for us?"

The Dickinson fan exchanged a glance with the girl next to her. I recognized her expression as one of trepidation.

Opeyemi continued, "Please, I want to hear this poem that you find to be wonderful. Do you know it? Can you recite it?"

She nodded, then straightened herself up. "I heard a fly buzz when I died . . ."

As best I could tell from the quick recital, the poem was told from the point of view of the author on her deathbed. Her world is ending. She is surrounded by grieving loved ones. She is awaiting the presence of her

115

king. She's giving away all her possessions. And in the midst of all those very human contemplations, she hears a fly buzzing. She describes the buzzing as "blue," "uncertain," and "stumbling."

The class applauded. A few others had joined in Can's practice of snapping instead of clapping. Opeyemi stood with his hands clasped behind his back, staring at the floor for a prolonged moment. The class settled their collective gaze onto him.

"So," he finally began, "she came back from the dead to tell us there was no king—there was only darkness and the sound of a fly."

He wiped his hand over the front of his face as if removing a layer of filth and confusion. "That is heavy. I think I will read that again tonight and think about that some more. I thank you for sharing this poem. I think we can agree with you that that is a great poem. Very powerful!" He pressed both of his palms together and bowed in the young woman's direction as a demonstration of thanks.

The class covered five more poems, including selections by Maya Angelou, Sandra Cisneros, Robert Frost, Allen Ginsberg, and, finally, W. B. Yeats. Opeyemi admitted he didn't like the latter poet very much but conceded that his poem "Politics" was quite poignant.

*And maybe what they say is true*
*Of war and war's alarms*
*But O that I were young again*
*And held her in my arms.*

"So this is what I wish to pose to you," the professor announced to the class. "I would like to invite any one of you to write one great poem. Write one great poem and read it in my class, and you are guaranteed to earn an A in this class or in any other class you may take with me between now and whenever you graduate."

He spoke as an aside to a couple of students sitting in the front row.

"Does that seem like a good deal?"

That was a good deal, and the challenge was intriguing, but mostly symbolic. Opeyemi had a reputation as a teacher who gave out A's like Halloween candy at the end of October.

A boy toward the front of the class—the one who had suggested Robert Frost's "Stopping by Woods on a Snowy Evening"—asked the question everyone was thinking: "How will we know if it's a great poem?"

"Simple," Opeyemi explained. "The class will determine that."

He smiled. "I just asked for a sampling of great poems, and you were all right on the mark. I think we covered seven poems, and there was little disagreement on the greatness of the selections. I trust that we, as a group, can apply the same standards of quality and come to a consensus when evaluating the work of our peers. After all, are we not all just people—the same as these poets you admire?"

# Chapter 19

Dara and I were lucky to bump into Dan Dan right away. He was smoking a cigarette outside the front entrance of Schoenberg and standing in a loose circle of classmates. They were breaking up their conversation and disbanding in different directions. Dan Dan noticed Dara and kept his eyes glued on her as we walked toward him. He noticed me only at the last second.

"Hey, Jeff. What's up?"

"Dan, this is my friend Dara. We were actually coming to see you."

They greeted each other. Dan Dan took a long drag from his cigarette and turned his head to exhale a blue plume of smoke away from our direction.

"I didn't think you'd be so easy to find," I admitted.

"I told you last time, I practically live here now."

He dropped his cigarette and crushed it with his foot while pulling a pack from the front breast pocket of his oversized flannel shirt. He turned his eyes toward me. "Smoke?"

His cigarette of choice was Marlboro Reds—nasty little things. "No thanks."

He looked at Dara and held the pack up in her direction.

"Thanks." She accepted a cigarette and the temporary use of his lighter.

"No problem."

Dan Dan had heard about the quartet from Belarus and understood that they were fantastic. He reported they would be playing at Schoenberg tomorrow night and Sunday afternoon. Plus he'd be working tomorrow night and could get us great seats if we wanted to come by and ask for him around seven thirty.

Dara was beaming. I could tell she was excited, and we should accept the invitation without hesitation. "Do we need to pay you or make a donation to your favorite charity or anything like that?"

"You insult me." Dan Dan smiled. "I'd love to have you both as guests."

I walked with Dara through campus and onto Strathmore, where we followed the lightly winding and hilly street as far as Weyburn Place. Along the way, she was chatty. I could tell she was excited about the following night's show, and I felt great that I was the one (with Dan Dan's help) to give her such a highly coveted gift. We discussed Opeyemi's lecture and the nature of great poetry.

"I think a great poem," Dara stated, "or any great work of art should inspire action or change."

I thought for a moment about what those words meant. I had always heard that art could and should be inspiring, but the phrase had become a platitude in many ways.

"I don't know." I paused, searching for a way to articulate my thought. "I think there's a lot of great art that don't inspire. It's enjoyable and entertaining, but you can't really say it inspires people to change their life or take action."

"That's just it!" She was excited about making her point and waved her hands as she spoke. "Great art *will* inspire. It will whisper something into your ear and change your view of the world. That's the difference."

"You heard the poems in class today. Did you think those were great works of art? Could they inspire you to take action?" I asked.

She cocked her head and went silent for a moment. "I need more time to think about it. But yes, many of those poems were great if you slow down and think about the words and their meaning."

We were both quiet for a moment. Then I asked, "Are there any poems or other works of art that you consider to be great?"

We had reached the point where we were about to head in separate directions. Dara turned to face me. "Of course! The next time we are together in my apartment, I will show you."

Before we parted ways, I told her I would come by her place the following evening and we could walk to the concert together. She set off down the long alley. I watched her for a moment and then continued the rest of the way to my apartment.

# Chapter 20

Dan Dan came through in a big way. He set us up with tickets in the middle of the third row, which, he insisted, provided the best possible acoustics for live music in the auditorium. There was a nearly audible gasp in the hall when Dara entered through a door with both Dan Dan and me in tow.

In a word, she looked amazing. She had her hair up in a messy bun, with small locks framing either side of her face. She wore an elegant fur-collar coat over a pencil skirt and a simple bodysuit. Upon arriving at our seats, she whispered to me, "Can you help me with this?" Turning her back to me slightly, she slipped her coat off her shoulders; and I assisted her in removing it the rest of the way, revealing her breathtaking silhouette. Every eye in the room was upon her—and rightfully so.

I had worn khakis and a sports jacket I'd borrowed from Todd. The jacket was made from a rich material and emblazoned with some meaningless crest on the breast pocket. I was glad I had put in the extra effort. I was sure more than a few people snuck brief glances at me to understand how and why I could have been here, escorting such a tremendously beautiful woman to this event.

Despite her strong resemblance to royalty and the elegant air about the way she sat upright in her auditorium seat, Dara was as giddy and playful as I had ever seen her. Upon taking our seats, she reached over to squeeze my arm with both hands and said something in Belarusian. I had no idea what she was saying, but I felt a sense of carefree joy emanating from her.

She sat transfixed throughout the entire show. At various moments in the program, she reached over and whispered comments to me in either English or Belarusian. I had never been a huge fan of classical music to that point, but the stars aligned in that moment, and I learned to appreciate the art form in one single sitting. I wished the moment would never end. But after nearly two hours, the houselights eventually came back on, and we were expected to leave our seats.

Dan Dan was able to get us a quick meet and greet with the musicians after the show, and Dara jumped at the opportunity to chat with her fellow countrymen. They spoke enough English to accept my hearty praise of their superb artistry, but eventually, the conversation shifted to their native tongue. Of course, I didn't understand a word of the exchange; and after a moment, I excused myself and drifted over to Dan Dan to chat with him for a moment. Dara subtly reached over and squeezed my hand before I completely broke free of the conversation. At the time, my heart skipped a beat, and I wondered feverishly what message she might have been sending me. In reality, the gesture was probably more about keeping the four musicians from offering any unwanted attention and less about sending me a message.

I barely made it to Dan Dan before he blurted, "Dude, don't take this the wrong way, but your girlfriend is gorgeous!"

"Actually, she's not my girlfriend."

"Whatever." He was not worried about splitting hairs. "Then your *date* is gorgeous!"

"Uh . . . thanks."

"She's not . . . ," my friend began but paused, searching for the right words. "She's not actually a student here, is she?"

I knew what he meant. She didn't look like a typical coed, and I could understand why he was asking. I assured him, "Yeah, we have a class together."

Dan Dan pulled his pack of cigarettes from his pocket and rolled his eyes. "I have to change majors."

# Chapter 21

On our walk home, Dara recounted the rest of her conversation with the members of the string quartet. They'd discussed the current state of politics in her home country as well as some of the latest trends and popular TV shows, movies, and songs. She was excited to have had a chance to commune with other Belarusians. She seemed so content, and I was happy for her.

I wanted to keep chasing the good feelings. "Do you want to stop in Westwood for a drink?"

In my peripheral vision, I caught a glimpse of her face scrunching up. I reacted, perhaps too abruptly, to her expression. "What? Not interested?"

"I don't like to go into Westwood."

I was quite fond of various haunts and hot spots just south of campus and suggested that I could show her a few places she might like. Secretly, I hoped that I could take her to a few of the most popular Thursday-night locations and potentially show her off. I hated to admit it, but I reasoned that being seen out on a date with such a striking woman would do wonders for my status among my peer group.

Dara seemed on the verge of accepting my offer but ultimately demurred and instead promised me, "Some other time, just not tonight."

"Not up to your high standards, huh?" I was joking, but also a little serious.

"It's not that. I just feel out of place."

"In Westwood?"

"It's not my scene. The people in those bars are not my crowd."

My voice shrunk. "Gotcha."

With that simple comment, she had inadvertently confirmed what I had been feeling and fearing for a couple of weeks. Technically speaking, *I* was part of the Westwood bar scene—the very same scene Dara claimed she didn't belong. I knew she wasn't saying that scene was too good for her. She was saying—without saying it—that she was well above anything that small college town could offer her.

I guess I already knew all of this. It was obvious in the way the men on campus couldn't control their comments when they walked by her, and it was obvious even in the way Dan Dan doubted that she could be a student at the university. Everything about this woman—from her looks to the way she carried herself to her expensive tastes—suggested that she was playing a more advanced game. My biggest fear was that I was merely on the sidelines and not actually playing alongside her.

The quick dismissal of the Westwood bar scene had slightly diminished our overall mood. I sensed that something else was on Dara's mind. She had been so happy during the show, and the afterglow was still with her now, but I could tell something more serious was on her mind not far beneath the surface. We walked in silence. Eventually, our footsteps brought us back to her apartment.

She smiled. "If I promise not to make you watch another three-hour movie, do you want to come up for a while?"

She already knew my answer.

Dara's apartment was exactly as I remembered it, but a tad messier. Several of her books were now scattered over her kitchen table.

"Can I trust you with another glass of wine?" she teased.

"I promise to go a little slower this time," I reassured her—and myself. I took the same position on the sofa as on our last encounter.

Dara bumped around in her kitchen for a moment until finally producing the unmistakable pop of a cork being extracted from a wine bottle. She called from the other room, "I picked another red!"

"Sounds good!"

She brought out two glasses in one hand and a bottle of red wine in the other. She set the glasses side by side on the coffee table and splashed each one up to the same level. I was impressed with her haphazard precision. The unnamed preoccupation that I'd sensed on my friend during our walk back from campus had only intensified since entering her apartment.

"You put a few candles out," I observed.

"I was reading last night. I like to read by candlelight. I used to read by candlelight when I was young." She leaned over the table and picked up a book of matches. "I'll light them."

"Okay," I said automatically.

Dara lit a cluster of three colorful candles and set the book of matches down beside them. "Do you mind listening to some classical music?" she asked, turning to her entertainment center. "Tonight's show has given me a taste for it."

"I don't mind."

She pressed a few buttons on the CD changer, and a rich piano arrangement played low in the background. It was melancholic from the first note, but I just rolled with it. "This is Beethoven. His fourteenth piano sonata."

If I hadn't known any better, I would have said Dara was trying to seduce me. She'd invited me up to her apartment, lit candles, put on soft music, and poured me a glass of red wine. This appeared to be the final page from a playbook on beguiling men. But I *did* know better, and my skepticism of her amorous intentions was confirmed when she resumed her space far away from me on the sofa. She sat fidgeting for a moment.

"I have something I want to show you," she said, then walked over to her kitchen table to retrieve a stack of books and loose-leaf papers. She wedged her way around the low table and swept past me to take a position on the sofa close by my side. Her bare leg brushed against my knee as she passed.

"What's all this?" I asked, trying to act natural, but my heart was racing.

"I told you I would show you a great poem." Dara began arranging the books and notes on the table in front of me. "Have you ever read any Belarusian poetry?"

"I don't think so."

"I wanted to show you this." She touched my knee to make the point. "This is my favorite."

I felt like we were the only two people in the world. "Okay."

She held up the booklet. "Read this." Her tone was serious.

There were several scraps of paper sandwiched between the pages, presumably marking her favorite and most memorable entries in the small tome. Dara opened to a marker in the middle of the booklet and handed it over to me.

"Here," she instructed, pointing to a series of narrow stanzas beginning halfway down the right-side page. "The poet is Yakub Kolas. He is an important writer from this century, considered to be a great Belarusian poet. Tell me what you think."

I looked to the page. Dara's eyes dropped with mine, and she read silently alongside me.

*O spring, O long-*
*Awaited one!*
*You will return,*
*Come back again . . .*

Reading through the entire poem required the turn of a page. Upon completion, I turned back to the original page and began reading for a second time. My impression of the work was not as favorable as Dara might have hoped for. The verses, to me, were elegant and uplifting. But I could not say I felt particularly moved by the imagery or the writing. The poem felt more like a simple ode to springtime and nothing more. Perhaps there was a deeper message about rebirth that I was missing.

In two full readings, I was unable to find anything to grab on to. I could not tell Dara any of this, so I lingered a bit in the second reading and scrambled to think of something complimentary and insightful to say.

She sensed my hesitation. "Maybe this doesn't inspire you?"

"No . . . I like it," I assured her. "I am just thinking about it."

"This poem is not for everybody." She leaned toward me. "You think it is nice, but you do not believe it is inspiring."

"I like it," I said, trying to sound convincing.

"I would be more surprised if you loved it." She looked at me tenderly. "I told you this is my favorite poem, not yours. Can I tell you about it?"

I understood that she was really asking if she could tell me a little more about herself and not necessarily the poem. Dara was taking her defenses down, and I was being introduced to a more vulnerable side of her that I had never seen before. "Of course . . . tell me."

"Jeff, I would be more surprised if you loved this poem because, for you, you are still living in the spring of your life." Her tone was serious. "You are still there. You cannot miss what hasn't been taken from you. Belarus is very different from America, and I am very different from you."

Dara fell silent. I took a moment to process what she was saying. The subtext of her comments was that I was a naïve. I found this to be a little off-putting, but I wanted to give her a chance to make her point. "I understand."

"In Belarus, for many of us, we are not living in the spring. You understand?" She looked at me, waiting for an answer.

"I do."

She investigated the candle's flame intently. "I grew up, and I was never happy."

"Dara," I responded automatically, with a protector instinct coming quickly to the surface, "look at you. You *are* in the springtime of your life."

"No, I understand what you see when you look at me, Jeff." She paused. "Life is good for pretty girls only when they live in pretty places. Life can be bad for pretty girls who grow up in ugly places."

"But look at all of this!" I asserted, motioning to her apartment. I didn't know why I was trying so hard to tell her how great her life was. I should have just listened.

Dara put her hand up. "Please. I will share something with you." She looked into the candle again. "I never knew my father."

I was not expecting that. "I'm so sorry . . ."

"It's okay. I know he was a good man, and I suspect he was a brilliant man. My mother told me very little about him. She was a silly young woman and didn't know what she was doing. Her beauty was legendary, and she didn't understand its power. She confessed to me that she tricked him, but she tricked herself too. She told me he was a good man." She looked at her hands coyly. "Maybe he still is."

Dara's last comment struck me as odd. "Is he still alive?"

"I don't know. These books"—she motioned to the few books and papers on the table in front of her, including the one I was still holding— "this is all I have of him. These were his things."

I looked back down at the first stanza of the poem.

*O spring, O long-*
*Awaited one!*
*You will return,*
*Come back again!*

I suddenly felt strange holding such a personal possession of hers. I worried that I might damage it somehow. I placed the book on the table and awkwardly returned my hands to my knees, unsure of what to do next. "Dara, I'm so sorry."

"I've never told this to anybody."

"You can tell me," I whispered.

"I haven't lived the best life."

"But all that can change, right?"

I heard her voice cracking a little. "I'm not . . . a good person."

"I think you are."

"You 'think' . . ." She was quiet for a moment. "You don't know everything."

"Then tell me."

Dara placed her hand on top of mine and squeezed it before bringing it to her mouth and kissing it firmly. She let our intertwined hands come to rest back on my thigh while sighing audibly and settling back into the soft cushions of her sofa.

We sat in silence. I remained upright for a moment and then eased back into the cushions as well. Immediately, she leaned against me and put her head on my shoulder.

We sat together like that for several minutes, and I thought I heard her crying. She had opened up to me. In her way, she was asking me to help her carry a heavy burden. I suspected that there wasn't anybody else in her life playing a supportive role of any kind, and that made me feel sad for her.

I should have understood what she needed in that moment, but as I've already mentioned, I was a raging ball of twenty-year-old hormones. I wanted to kiss her. I wanted to reach over and put my hands on her. The urge was basic and uncomplicated. My temperature rose, and my heart began beating out of my chest. I was a male of the species in close proximity to a perfectly formed female of the same species, and my million years of genetic programming drew me to her. In those moments when she sat close to me, I was hypnotized by her sensuous and feminine features—the pout of her lips, the curve of her hips, and the flowery scent of her hair.

"I can hear your heart beating," Dara said in a voice just loud enough for me to hear.

"Dara," I said almost in a whisper.

"Hmm?"

"Dara," I repeated, hoping to get her to look up at me.

She did exactly that. She turned her blue eyes toward me, and I reached over to prop up her chin gently in my fingertips. I leaned in to kiss her. Before our lips could meet, she spoke the single word quietly, but firmly: "No."

Dara turned her head away from me and lay back to rest on my shoulder. My heart rate increased noticeably, but she said nothing. A cold, prickly chill spread across my body; and I sat there in silence, wondering what the hell I was supposed to do next.

It was her right to not kiss me. I understood that, but I was confused. I'd read into the many different times she had grabbed my arm this evening. I'd read into the fact that she had invited me back up to her apartment to read poetry and share a glass of wine. Even now, she was resting her head on my shoulder, and I felt so close to her. But at the same time, I felt so far away. There it was again—that distance.

We just sat there. My sympathetic nervous system eventually relaxed, and my pulse returned to normal. We remained like that for another half an hour at least. By the sounds of her deepening breaths, I could tell that Dara had fallen asleep. I followed her into my own troubled slumber not many moments later.

We both bolted awake at the sound of her ringing phone. I took a moment to process where I was. She sat upright beside me, and I caught her peeking at the watch on her left wrist.

"What time is it?"

"Almost one," she answered.

"Who would be calling now?" I asked the question as innocently as possible, but in truth, I was very curious.

Her words carried a hint of trouble. "I don't know."

The phone rang itself out, and silence returned. Dara eased back into her place on the sofa but was no longer leaning against me. A moment passed, and a flashing light appeared on the answering machine at the far end of the kitchen counter. She stood. "Let me see who that was."

Dara crossed the room to the answering machine, lifted the handset, and depressed a couple of buttons before pressing the phone to her ear. She peeked over at me and caught me spying. I looked away immediately, and she took two steps around the corner, out of my sight.

A moment passed in silence. "Bliadz!" I heard her exclaim softly to herself. Another moment passed, and she repeated the sound twice more. "Bliadz! Bliadz!"

She poked her head around a corner and addressed me, "Excuse me just for a moment? I need to make a call."

I heard her walk through the kitchen and followed the path of her footfalls down the hallway. I then heard the yawning of an opening door, which I assumed was her room. The sound of a door closing followed. I reached forward for my glass of wine and took a sip.

Dara's voice was faint, but I could make out at least two different phone calls. Her voice became louder and a little more agitated with the second call. The conversations were in English. I could discern only a few fleeting words, but not enough to understand what was going on. Eventually, she fell silent.

I couldn't help but wonder who it was on the other end of those phone calls. Clearly, the conversations had elicited some intense feelings in Dara. From my limited life experience, I reasoned that those types of feelings were typically reserved for the crazy emotional swings experienced in romantic relationships.

I was only speculating, of course, but my mind began to wander. Maybe Dara already had someone in her life. Would that be so hard to believe? She was worldly, interesting, and so much more. Maybe that was why I had been relegated to arm squeezes and rebuffed advances. Or maybe she was completely single and saw me only as a friend. I didn't know.

Twenty minutes and one glass of wine had expired since the moment

Dara had retreated to her bedroom. I felt uncomfortable sitting there alone and thought I should leave, but I couldn't do that without first checking on her and saying goodbye.

I felt light-headed walking the short distance of her hallway. I had to place my hand against the wall to steady myself. I noticed a faint dancing light escaping out from under her door. When I was sure I had regained my balance, I stepped forward and knocked lightly. "Dara?"

There was no reply. I placed my ear against the red-painted surface of her door to listen more intently and heard indistinct sobbing coming from inside her room. Hesitantly, I turned the knob and pushed slowly. Dara was lying curled up on her side with her back to me. She was silhouetted by a candle burning on the opposite side of her bed. I opened the door just wide enough to enter and stepped inside. She offered no reaction. I approached her and sat on the edge of her bed, propping my leg up on the mattress so I could face her partially.

"Dara, are you okay?"

She stirred ever so slightly. Without looking, she uncoiled her arm from its resting position at her chest and reached behind her back to grab my jutted knee. She squeezed and let her hand linger until finally returning it to its position in a ball under her chin. I was immediately excited and read unmistakable affection in her actions. I swung myself around to lie behind her, pressed tightly against her body, and wrapped my arms around her. My heart rate began to race, and from the simple and subtle way she pushed back against me with her hips, I knew she both sensed and welcomed my excitement. She worked her hips subtly in rhythm until finally reaching back and taking me in her hand.

Dara turned to face me. "This is it then? This is all you wanted?"

I hated the way she said it! She was minimizing me, my emotions, and my feelings for her. Of course I wanted to sleep with her, but that was *not* why I'd walked into her room. I was concerned for her. I had approached her only to give her comfort and nothing more. In one cutting remark, she had turned me into a self-serving womanizer who was interested only in getting her into bed. That was not true.

I wanted to push myself away from her and set the record straight, but before I could respond, Dara pressed her lips against mine. I could taste the wine still on her lips and the salty residue of the tears that had run down her cheek.

# Chapter 22

Friday morning at Dara's apartment was an uncomfortable blur. She woke me up at about six in the morning. I had lain awake staring at the ceiling for most of the night in a postcoital stupor, so I had probably been asleep for only an hour at that point. Dara was already dressed and visibly eager to leave the apartment. She was distant and told me I didn't need to stick around if I was uncomfortable in her bed without her. She left the room and returned a moment later. When she realized I hadn't moved, she repeated her sentiments and then left the apartment in a rush.

The message was clear: she did not want me lingering in her intimate space.

I had no choice but to get up, pull on my clothes, and leave. There was no steaming cup of coffee or any bundle of books or music for me to take home. There was nothing but a distinct and sticky feeling that I was an unwanted guest and the sooner I left, the better.

The Westwood streets were empty in the morning's dawning light. Despite my lack of sleep, I had been jarred awake, and my mind was spinning. I headed into the Westwood downtown and decided to get a cup of coffee and something to eat at a diner about two blocks away. I spent most of my time staring into the slowly receding cup of coffee and processing everything that had happened in the last twelve hours since picking up Dara from her front door and escorting her on our date to Schoenberg Hall.

My emotions were teetering on the boundary between elation and terror. In one moment, I would receive waves of excitement, like none I'd felt before, relating to having spent the night with this beautiful, interesting, and mysterious woman. In the next, I was crushed under the weight of a heavy fear that last night was a mistake and Dara's distant and dismissive attitude that morning was a sign of things to come.

Deep down, I knew Dara was out of my league and truthfully had never expected last night to happen. I'd wanted it, and I'd imagined it, but I'd never expected it. Judging by her own words, she never expected it either. She asked me, "This is it then? This is all you wanted?" That was resignation, not romance, on her part. That was the last thing I wanted to hear before our ceremony began. Those words were still clawing at me as I sat there in the empty diner, but that wasn't even the worst thing she said to me.

As much as I had completely surrendered to the moment, I could tell Dara was not with me, not even a little bit. Sure, her body was there. But her mind was far away, and she was only going through the motions. I tried to find her in that moment and talk to her so I could tell her how I was feeling, but she could barely say anything back to me. When she finally spoke, I heard her whisper maybe to herself or maybe to me, "Is this all I'm worth?" I heard it, but I had no idea how she could say it or even think it.

Was she implying that I was only interested in sex? I couldn't imagine that after all the time we had spent together, she could feel that way. I had a vague notion that the comment was not just about me. I assumed that someone else had made her feel that way at some point. I didn't know that for sure, but that was how I felt.

There were no answers waiting for me in that cup of coffee. I paid my bill and shuffled off to my apartment. I still had plenty of time to shower, change, and make it on time to my morning classes.

Of course, I was met by Naomi's voice when I pushed our front door open. I had barely even stepped into our apartment before she called out, "Did you fall asleep on her couch again?"

"Something like that!" I called back and stalked through the hall to my room at the back of our apartment.

A few more comments bubbled up from the direction of Dylan's room. But I ignored them, undressed, and turned up my shower as hot as the water could go before stepping into the steamy stall and attempting to wash off all the confusion and doubt.

# Chapter 23

Several days went by, and I thought way too much about Dara. I spent my Friday classes scribbling stanzas in the margin of my notebook. I was sure that the previous evening's encounter had provided the perfect muse for me to meet and exceed Opeyemi's challenge. After a few attempts and much editing, I was certain I had crafted a deep and meaningful poem that would both astonish and inspire the masses. I was excited to share it with Dara, my class, and the rest of the world.

I found myself vacillating wildly about my prospects with my Belarusian love interest. At times, I was confident and sure we'd had a profound connection that would only grow stronger as a result of our night together. At other times, the colors would all flip, and I could see only the futility of my infatuation and the meaninglessness of our tryst.

By Monday evening, I was a mess. As much as I'd tried not to, I had left a message for Dara every day since Friday. I'd tried to sound normal and offer plausible reasons why I was calling. I'd employed standard tactics, such as this one on Sunday afternoon: "Hey, Dara. I wouldn't bother you again, but I just got free tickets to see *Pulp Fiction* tonight and wanted to see if you wanted to go." Of course, there were no tickets. I was just trying anything.

My roommates weren't making the situation any better. From their perspective, I was going out with mysterious international beauty *and* spending the occasional night at her place. To them, I was living a charmed and fortunate life. They made mention of her almost every time I passed them in the apartment. Their comments were always silly: "So . . . when are we going to meet this KGB agent you've been dating?" And "Is she a Bond girl?"

Fortunately, on this evening, I was alone at last—and safe from their ridiculous and prying commentary. I decided to walk into town and grab a bite. I caught myself ambling down Dara's back alley and realized that I had chosen that specific and unfamiliar route because it would place me right under her balcony. From my vantage point descending the gradual slope of her alleyway, I could plainly see that the door leading to her balcony was propped open. She was letting the evening breeze flit into her apartment and likely winding down after a day of classes.

Against my better judgment, I looped around to the front of her building and took the stairs, two at a time. Even as I knocked, I knew that I would regret it, but I couldn't help myself—I had to see her.

The music inside the apartment stopped, and I heard light footsteps approaching the door. "Who is it?"

"It's me."

The sound of a chain lock sliding was followed by a click, and then her door opened, revealing Dara in a pair of jeans and a stylish cropped T-shirt. She looked so good. I saw an open bottle of wine and a half-full glass on the coffee table behind her. Next to them was a book resting with its spine facing up like a tent. I assumed I had interrupted her in the middle of reading. I hoped she would invite me in and pour a second glass.

Her voice was not angry, but it wasn't particularly pleasant either. "Jeff, what are you doing here?"

By just her tone, I sensed that she was not happy to see me, so I kept it simple. "I was walking to Westwood to get dinner. I wanted to see if you were hungry."

She released a puff of air. It was too subtle to convey exasperation, but that was certainly the direction she was going. "I already ate."

"Okay . . . I just thought I would stop by."

"Okay. Well, it was good to see you."

The scent of her apartment hit me—and it hit me hard. I was immediately flooded with the memory of my last visit. I felt a strong pang of desire for her and thought quickly of anything I could say or ask to prolong the conversation. "Hey, did you get those messages I left you?"

"I did. I've just been busy." Dara smiled an emotionless smile. "Was the movie good?"

"Oh . . . *Pulp Fiction*? The tickets, right. I ended up not going."

"Oh, I still need to see it too," she offered absently.

"Maybe we can see it this week?"

"Maybe."

I pushed the conversation a little further. "Will you be in class on Wednesday?"

"I don't think so."

"Too bad. I think I may have written a great poem. I was going to read it in class." I smiled my most charming smile. "I had a little inspiration from last Thursday night."

Dara didn't seem to get my meaning at first. She looked blankly at me, but then her expression changed to one of annoyance. "No . . . You didn't write it about me, did you? Tell me you didn't write about me."

I instantly felt sick to my stomach. She had just rebuked me in a pure, immediate, and visceral way. My pride kept me upright just long enough to laugh off her comments. "I'm only kidding," I lied. "Of course I didn't write . . . about . . . anything."

We stood awkwardly for a moment, and then it finally dawned on me that I had to be the one to say goodbye. I did exactly that and left without any further discussion.

I couldn't understand what had just happened. I understood that she had not invited me over, and perhaps it was a little inappropriate for me to show up at her door without notice, but she'd acted like I was the last person in the world she wanted to see. Why? She'd acted angry and maybe even a little repulsed. Why? I hadn't done anything bad to her. I had been a good friend to that point. I knew our last night together had been intense, but it wasn't like I'd crossed a line I shouldn't have.

# Chapter 24

I wasn't proud of it, but after the episode at Dara's door, I was feeling lovesick. I played the conversation over in my mind repeatedly. I punished myself for saying all those stupid things to her. *Why did I ask if she got my messages?* Of course she did. I knew her answering machine displayed a bright flashing light whenever anyone called. *Why did I tell her I wrote her a poem?* That was so childish, so stupid. *Why did I say I had some inspiration from last Thursday night?* I couldn't think of a grosser, creepier thing to say to a woman than "I wrote a poem about sleeping with you."

I couldn't sleep at all on Monday night. Not a wink. I slept only an hour at most on Tuesday night. Dylan saw me before I left for my political science class on Wednesday morning and told me I looked like shit. He also said I needed to cut out all the late nights sneaking over the Berlin Wall and back. That didn't even make any sense.

Only forty of the original three hundred students even bothered to attend the early-morning lecture. Professor Kinkade's offer for his pupils to write a paper in lieu of taking a test appeared to allow more than a few students to catch up on their Wednesday-morning beauty sleep. I had already resigned to write a term paper on Chief Justice John Marshall, but I just couldn't get myself to skip class.

Kinkade finally set us free, and I had an hour to kill. I timed a route to walk around campus and ended up at the door to poetry class with only a few minutes to spare. I took my seat in the back row, as usual. Anson entered the room, took his typical position in the seating chart, and glanced back in my direction. He did a double take. His eyes widened, and he asked, "Are you okay?"

Apparently, I did look beat-up. But I wasn't thinking about that at that moment. I was just excited to see Dara, and I could barely contain my emotions.

Class had been underway for about ten minutes, and she still had not shown up. I couldn't concentrate on a single thing that Opeyemi was saying. Eventually, I realized that Dara was not coming. I hated to accept it, but I came to grips with the fact that she was purposefully shutting me out. For the previous week, I had been holding on to hope that she was just busy and would eventually work her way back around to calling me. Something about the empty seat next to me finally made it clear: I had been excommunicated.

I "zombied" through the next couple of days and spent most of the time in class or in my room. Band rehearsal was the only bright spot during that time. I was moody and quieter than usual, but the emotions helped me in a strange way. I was playing pretty well.

Dara never called. I kept hoping that she would relent and realize that she missed me. In a pathetic display of fixation, I searched for books by the author Yakub Kolas in the large research library on campus. I did manage to find a book of his poetry titled *Songs of Grief*, and I could only laugh at the irony.

By the time the weekend rolled around, the banter in my apartment had ground down to an obvious halt. I suppose that the gang had caught on to my moping and were giving me some space. On Friday evening, Dylan asked if I wanted to go out with him and meet up with Naomi and

Carey at a house party. I couldn't tell if he was just inviting me out or if he was attempting to play connect the dots with Carey and me . . . again. I declined, and he asked if something was bothering me and if I wanted to talk. I declined that offer as well, and he got a little more explicit, stating that I hadn't been myself for the last week and he wondered if I was having problems with Dara.

I assured him everything was fine. My desire to keep it all to myself was probably just my pride. I was always so upbeat and confident, especially around "my boys." I didn't want to admit to them that I had just had my heart ripped out by a girl.

Dylan left, and I decided to head over to Y&T's. I wasn't surprised to hear music at their front door and find a few happy people sitting in their living room when Yuri let me in. His eyes were only half-open.

"Jeff! So glad you stopped by. What's up?"

"Nothing. I was just looking for something to do. So I just . . ."

"Well, say no more! You're hanging out with us tonight."

I was relieved to earn the invite. "Cool. Thank you."

"Is there anything I can get you?" Yuri was always the gracious host.

"Actually . . ."

"Ah yes! I know that look." He rubbed his hands together in front of him. "You came to see the apothecary."

I felt silly being so obvious. "I'm sorry, I don't mean to be a mooch."

Yuri motioned me to join him on his way to his room. "No need to be sorry. Besides, I think I owe you."

"What do you owe me for?"

"Last time you were here . . . I *may* have given you some bad information about the tea we were drinking."

"Oh, because it was laced with a hallucinogen?" I spoke the words dryly, but he knew I was teasing him and forgiving him. I was happy he acknowledged the faux pas.

He giggled, his eyes still only half-open. "Yeah, I was fucked-up, and I should have given you a heads-up."

"Are you fucked-up right now?" I asked.

Yuri laughed, "Maybe a little buzzed."

He supplied me with a low-potency intoxicant of the herbal variety. We hung out in the Chill Room with a couple of other people I had never met and spent some time catching up and talking about life. Yuri was thinking about taking the next quarter off from medical school and planned on traveling through Southeast Asia. He said he wanted to try his hand at travel journalism.

I shared a little bit about Dara, and he seemed to catch on right away. "Yeah, I see it now. Your aura is sad. You're a little bit broken up."

I probably shared more with Yuri than with anyone else at that point, but he was a good listener.

About that same time, Todd shuffled in to join us. "Jeff! What's going on? We still have to set our golf game."

"Hey, Todd," Yuri said, interrupting. "Jeff's having relationship troubles."

"You want to go to the strip club? Check out some naked ladies and get your mind off things?" Todd had a very 1988 approach to mending a broken heart. I could almost hear Mötley Crüe playing in the background of Yuri's sitar music when he spoke.

"I don't think that's gonna help," Yuri interjected.

I had been to a strip club only one time, and I'd been so nervous I could barely even enjoy myself. The whole thing had seemed weird to me. I'd gone during freshman year of college, and to that point, I had only ever seen two topless women in my life. The idea that you could pay a $20 cover and walk through an unlimited sea of naked breasts felt like I had stolen some cheat codes to the game of life. It had quickly become apparent that the $20 was just a down payment, and to remain in that room, you were either required to spend quite a bit more or suffer blatant ridicule and disdain at the hands of these beautiful women. I'd left in only five minutes without telling my friends. The woman at the front door laughed in my face when I'd asked if I could have my money back.

"Maybe another time?" I said to Todd.

"Okay, a rain check then."

I opened up a little more with both Todd and Yuri about the Dara situation, and they were both sympathetic. They didn't offer any advice but took turns sharing a couple of stories about when they had their own hearts broken. I wasn't sure what I'd expected would happen at their apartment, but I left feeling better than when I'd arrived. I guess that was worth something.

# Chapter 25

I slept until about noon on Saturday and woke up with an appetite. Feeling both rested and hungry was a welcome sensation that I had been deprived of for a little too long. I wasn't over Dara by any stretch of the imagination, but at least I was feeling a little more like myself. I lumbered out into the living room to find Francis and Naomi watching TV.

Francis spoke first. "Morning, princess. You have a nice sleep?"

My voice was groggy. "I did, yes."

"Where were you last night?" Naomi asked suspiciously. "You got in after us."

I yawned, "I was just out."

"Just out," she repeated. "You're so mysterious."

"Where's Dylan? Sleeping?"

"No, he took my car to get us lunch at Burger Burger. He should be back in a second."

"No . . . ," I lamented. "I missed it?"

"He's getting you something too," Naomi relayed. "He said he knows what you like."

That was exactly what I needed. I felt a surge of energy. Bolstered by the promise of food, I found the strength to be a little more social. "What did you guys do last night?"

"You know." Naomi was back to pouting. "You were supposed to be there. Dylan said he told you."

"The house party?" I turned to Francis, asking, "Did you go too?"

He seemed unimpressed. "Yeah, I went."

"Whose place was it?"

Naomi smirked, "You don't know them."

"Some baseball players on Gayley," Francis offered, looking at the TV. "It was a pretty big party."

He sounded dejected. I knew Maya was now seriously dating one of the baseball players and wondered if the party had been at his apartment.

"Carey knows them," Naomi revealed. "She dated one of them for a while. They were together for most of last night."

I wondered why she was bringing Carey into this. Before I could comment, a loud knocking came from the front door. I assumed it was Dylan and that his hands were full and that, based on the abruptness of the knocking, he must have kicked the bottom of the door to get our attention. I was closest, so I let him in.

My mood gradually improved over the next few days, but I still felt sad. I experienced a wave of anxiety on Tuesday night, realizing that I might be sitting next to Dara in class the following day. It had been well over a week since I had seen or heard from her.

I dressed way too nicely for classes on Wednesday and received a couple of quick glances and questions as a result. It always surprised me how people noticed when you put the slightest effort into your outfit. I wondered how bad I must have looked on every other day if a simple collared shirt caused my peers to assume I was going to a wedding. For the few people that asked, I made up a story about interviewing for a new promotion at the pool. That was enough to satisfy everyone's curiosity.

My anxiety was on full tilt by the time I stepped into the hallway leading to poetry class. Part of me wanted to pass right through the building and exit through the opposite doorway, avoiding the upcoming encounter altogether. Turns out, I had nothing to be nervous about. Dara, for the second straight week, did not show up for class. As much as I felt bad that she was probably avoiding me, I was also a little relieved. The anticipation of seeing her had built itself up so much in my mind that I was shaking nervously, certain that I would end up saying something stupid or embarrassing. At least I could relax a little bit now.

Class was unremarkable, and even Opeyemi appeared to be a little distant. He gave up on his lecture about halfway through and informed his students that he had been feeling sick. He leaned against a desk and asked if there was anything anyone wanted to talk about.

The young woman who had recited the Emily Dickinson poem a couple of weeks before turned sideways in her chair to face more of the class and asked if anyone had a great poem that they wanted to share. She was met with nervous laughter. Nobody was willing.

Opeyemi perked up at this and said, "This is a wonderful idea! Is there anybody brave enough to share their words with us?"

A small troubadour in the back of my head started whispering, *This is your chance . . . This is the way to win her back. Profess your feelings, and your message of love will take flight and wind its way through the open window and find her on the breeze.*

The class was silent, and against every logical impulse in my brain, I spoke abruptly before reason could stop my words. "I'll go."

All eyes in the room jumped to me. Can began snapping. My pulse quickened, and I felt the same thumping in my chest I had experienced in Dara's apartment so many nights ago. This was okay, though. I was safe. I was in a room full of poets and was potentially going to receive some meaningful feedback about both my writing and my feelings. I figured it was a good time to jump from the safety of the dock anyway. I opened my notebook to the page with the messily scribbled entry and cleared my throat.

"No no no!" the professor called. "This is a *great* poem, is it not? And a great poem should be orated from the front of the class. Should it not?"

The class released a collective gasp. Every one of them was happy and relieved that they had not been the literary sacrificial lamb to have spoken up so recklessly. My knees were a little weak as I made my way to the lectern. I felt my cheeks grow flush, and the saliva in my mouth grew thick and slimy. I swallowed hard to relieve the unwelcome sensation. The entire class was staring back at me.

Opeyemi encouraged me, saying, "These are *your* words. Never be ashamed of *your* words."

"This is called 'With Your Body between Me and the Candle,'" I announced.

*With your body between me and the candle*
*I watched your silhouette*
*Flickering on my bare skin*
*As I lay awake*
*As you feigned sleep*

*Your dancing shadow made violent, passionate love to me*

151

*I felt it then*
*As I feel you now*
*In time the flame faltered*
*And turned to*
*Darkness*

*I wondered where your shadow would hide*
*In that quiet darkness*
*In time*
*I felt it creeping into me*
*Entering me*
*In the stillness and the darkness of the room*

*You may have gone*
*But the part of you that only appears*
*In candlelight*
*Is with me still*
*Makes love to me still*
*Hides within me*
*Still*

A huge rush of adrenaline surged through my body as I completed the final stanza, and I became light-headed as a result. I steadied myself with both hands on the wooden lectern in front of me to keep from getting too wobbly. The room was completely silent. I noticed a few classmates exchanging glances with each other. Another moment of silence passed, and Opeyemi asked me if I could read it one more time. I didn't want to, but I felt like there was no way I could refuse him.

I read the words for a second time. The class responded with a small offering of clapping hands. From the reaction and the smattering of applause, I couldn't say if the class liked it or disliked it. As with most things, it was probably somewhere in the middle.

"I applaud you for doing that." The professor smiled. "I applaud you, and I *hear* your words. I understand what you have written. Would you mind if we ask the class for their feedback?"

I raised one open palm upward toward the class and said under my breath, "Go ahead."

The Dickinson fan spoke first. "I liked it."

"Why?" our professor probed.

"I don't know. I like the way it made me feel."

I saw something genuine in her as she made the comment and realized that she was being honest. I felt good and nodded in her direction to offer a subtle thank-you.

I saw Anson raise his hand in the back of the room. Opeyemi's palms were pressed together in front of him. He extended his arms and pointed at Anson with all ten fingertips.

"I hate to be critical, but I didn't like it. I don't think it's a poem. I think it's more of a love letter."

"Can't love letters be poetry?" Opeyemi pressed.

"Sure," Anson agreed. "But not this one. This is more like a boy with a broken heart. Not a great poet. I'm sorry." He directed this to me. "I'm not talking about you. I'm just critiquing the voice in this poem."

I raised my hands in a surrender of sorts to demonstrate that I understood and respected his opinion. I didn't want to explain that I *was* the voice in this poem, so he kind of *was* talking about me. I just let it go.

Can, only one seat away from Anson, turned to him. "I disagree."

"Of course you do." Anson dismissed her words under his breath. Some of the class laughed.

"Well, I do disagree. I agree that it's a love letter, but it's also a poem." She looked right at me. "I like that you said that there's a part of us that exists only in candlelight. I think that's . . . I agree with that."

I appreciated Can's praise of the work and especially liked that she had addressed Anson's critique head-on.

"I want somebody to write this poem about me," another female voice from the side of the class announced. The room responded with light laughter.

"What did you think?" Anson called out, addressing Opeyemi.

The class was silent as our professor considered the question. "I'd say that was a successful effort."

He then looked out the window. I had now grown accustomed to him doing this whenever he was thinking deeply. "I would warn the person who wrote these words," he continued, "that when you turn love into a candle, you are destined to be burned or to watch that love drift away like smoke. Or both."

The comment was both interesting and thoughtful, and the class collectively processed the professor's wisdom. Anson couldn't leave well enough alone, and he pressed further. "But did you think it was a *great* poem?"

"What does it matter?" Opeyemi answered immediately, his eyes still fixed on a point outside of the window and far off.

"It doesn't, but what about the challenge?" Anson reminded him. "Does he get automatic A's in all of your classes now?"

The comment came off as a little facetious, and I was beginning to resent that he was talking about me like I wasn't there.

The professor laughed and turned to face the class. "You heard that poem. Do you believe that the poet is so preoccupied about whatever meaningless grade he earns in any of my meaningless poetry classes?"

154

Opeyemi turned his eyes to me as he finished his question. I shook my head no. My action was barely perceptible. But the professor had received it, and he nodded at me ever so slightly in response.

His words replayed in my mind. He had just referred to me as a "poet." Was it that easy to become a poet? Was writing a poem and then reciting it in front of a room full of peers enough to join the ranks of Keats and Cisneros and Bukowski and Creeley? I doubted it. But still, he had just called me a "poet."

For anyone who's curious, I still can't say if my poem was good or not—and I don't know if Opeyemi liked it or not. I gathered from the class discussion that at least three of my classmates thought it was pretty good. I'll leave the final verdict to you.

# Chapter 26

I wasn't cured, but in a strange way, the impromptu recital in poetry class was good for me. I wasn't overwhelmed by the reaction from my fellow students, but I had received an encouraging message from Opeyemi about writing my truth, and that felt liberating.

So what if I'd said stupid things to Dara? So what if I wrote silly poems? I was just being me. At some point, I had to stop worrying about what anyone else thought and just get comfortable with who I was. Right? Eventually, someone would meet me and love exactly who I was. Some other girl in a plaid hat would walk up to me and hand me her phone number.

Friday afternoon on campus was pleasant. After a couple of gray, drizzly days, the sun had returned, which made me glad. We were scheduled to play our show the next night, and that was set to take place in a huge outdoor courtyard behind the fraternity house. I was ready. In a strange way, the nearly two weeks of pining for Dara had helped my nerves. With my mind so wrapped up in thoughts of her, I'd had no time for stage fright. Besides, we had overrehearsed at this point and were ready to blow everyone away. I gave full credit to Dylan for putting everything together and leading us through all the prep.

My last class ended. I packed my bag and emerged from the dark classroom into the bright world beyond the door. I began a slow march past the brick buildings and bustling campus to my apartment. I had the entire evening wide open and wasn't in any hurry to get anywhere. While walking, I constructed a list, in my head, of some friends that I wanted to call and invite to the following night's show. I was thinking of Dan Dan, my old roommate from the dorms, and a few other people. It was probably too late in the week, and they likely had plans, but I figured I would give it a shot anyway.

My train of thought was derailed by a familiar voice.

"Jeff?"

I almost bumped into her while walking down Bruin Walk. She had just descended the steps from Ackerman Union. I had been sidetracked by my thoughts and an expert game of hacky sack, which demanded my attention at the side of the walkway, so I didn't see her until she was right in front of me.

"Hey," I greeted Dara.

"Hey."

I knew just by the way she said that single word that she was *back* and that the cold girl who had blockaded me from her doorway was nowhere to be found. At least for right now.

"How are you?" I asked.

"Good." She was warm, but a little tentative. "I'm just about to walk home."

A muscled boy in a tank top walked past us in a small group. He turned his head brazenly and gawked at Dara. "Hellooo, legs!"

The guys walking with him laughed aloud as they all jogged their way up the stairs to the doors leading to the large student union.

I felt sorry for Dara and couldn't imagine what that must have felt like. She pretended not to hear anything and asked, "Do you want to walk with me?"

"Sure."

The walk back to her place was a strange game of chess. I wanted to ask her what had happened in the last couple of weeks to better understand why she had cut me off. For my simple life, this was about the most traumatic thing that had ever happened to me. Every mild remark I made to her in the mere direction of that topic was expertly deflected. After about ten minutes, I realized that if I wanted to spend any time with her, I was going to have to ignore the fact that she had gone completely dark on me. We were going to pretend it didn't happen.

Her apartment complex came into view. By this point, we had settled into her desired pattern of inane and meaningless discussions about the weather and an article she had happened to find on the Supreme Court justices that she thought could help me with my American politics paper.

I was annoyed. I resented that she thought she could find me on campus, ask me to walk her home, and expect everything to go back to the way it was before she'd run out on me after we'd slept together. She only liked the version of our relationship where I would tell her what was on my mind and she would find me the perfectly curated book or song or movie to complete my education on the subject.

Well, that wasn't good enough for me. "Dara," I finally said, "what the hell happened?"

"What do you mean?"

"Come on, you know what I mean. What happened with *us*?"

She looked uncomfortable. "Can't we just have a nice afternoon walk?"

"We can. But don't you think it's all a little odd?" I meant it as a question for her to answer, but I suppose she took it as rhetorical and said nothing. I was exasperated. "It doesn't make any sense to me."

"It makes perfect sense." She dug immediately into her purse. I recognized that she was looking for cigarettes. "You just don't understand." Her tone struck a familiar balance between frustration and condescension. "There's a lot you don't understand."

Her words hurt, and I reacted. "Oh, I understand. I get it. I get that you don't see us ever being together, and that's why you ran out on me and never called me back. I get that you can do better. I get all that. It's fine with me—it really is. But aren't you at least my friend? Can't you at least be honest with me about what's going on?"

Dara looked up from her purse. Her expression darkened. "I am honest with you, more honest with you than anyone else I have ever known. Just because I don't tell you everything doesn't mean I'm lying. Just because we don't talk doesn't mean I'm not thinking about you. You think I am doing better than you? You don't know anything!"

We stood facing each other. There was something deep in the molten core of this girl; and she could shift, tremor, or erupt at any moment. She was right: I didn't understand. I didn't understand any of it.

She broke the silence. "I need cigarettes."

Dara crossed the street abruptly and entered the small convenience store attached to the gas station across from her building. Not having much of a choice, I followed behind her. She placed her bag on the counter and spoke to the attendant, who had been jarred from a waking sleep when she walked in.

"Reds," she said without looking at him.

He reached back and retrieved the box off the shelf without taking his eyes off her. "You have ID?"

Dara rolled her eyes and produced a blue passport with a circular insignia and three variations of the word "passport" scrawled across the cover. I glanced at the open page as she flashed her picture and official details. In the picture, she looked much younger and wore a hard expression. The writing was in both English and maybe Russian or Belarusian. I saw her name was spelled "Darya" and not "Dara." I recalled the scrap of paper she had handed me weeks ago with her name and phone number written on it. She had spelled her name "Dara" on it.

The spelling of her name was the only coherent thing I could see before she quickly flipped her passport closed. I wanted to ask her if I could take a closer look before she tucked it away in her bag, but it was not the right time.

She paid the man, rushed outside to a trash receptacle, and hastily removed the cellophane wrapper from the pack. Owing to static electricity, her attempts to place the refuse into the large circular opening were unsuccessful. The wrapper eventually came to rest on the asphalt below her feet.

"Do you want one?"

I didn't smoke, and Dara knew that. "No thanks."

She took the first long drag of her cigarette. She looked back at it in disgust. "This is wrong."

Apparently, the clerk had handed her the wrong brand. Dara crushed her cigarette underfoot, threw her remaining pack in the trash, and walked back inside the convenience store.

"Hey, Jeff."

I heard another female voice behind me and turned to see Naomi in her car rolling to a slow stop. Carey was in the passenger seat next to her. I could only see her through the distortion of the angled windshield, but her expression conveyed something like discomfort. "We just pulled in to get some gas and saw you standing there."

The comment came off as overexplained, which called its credibility into question. I assumed she must have seen us from the street and pulled into the station to be nosy.

"Who's your friend?" Naomi asked with a hint of teasing in her voice.

"You know who it is."

"Is it Dara?" she asked with a wicked smile.

I didn't say anything. A moment passed before I spoke. "Well, I need to get going. It was nice to see you guys." Then I headed into the convenience store.

"Hey, wait!" Naomi called. "Is she coming to the show tomorrow?"

"I don't think so, no."

"But you've worked so hard. Isn't she going to come and support you? *We'll* both be there," she declared, motioning to her passenger and herself.

"See you guys later," I offered in retreat.

Dara had just paid for the second pack of cigarettes. "Those were your friends?"

"Kind of," I admitted.

"Was that Naomi? The driver?"

"How'd you know?"

"You told me about her." She unwrapped the pack and handed the cellophane to the clerk. He took it and threw it away in an unseen garbage can. Dara removed a cigarette and lit it in the store where she stood.

"You can't smoke in here," the clerk cautioned as Dara released an enormous plume of smoke in his direction before turning to walk out.

"You must have been watching them pretty closely," I noted, glancing over and realizing that the shop's tinted windows provided a clear view onto the lot.

"Yes," she confessed. "I think she acts very much like an American."

I knew she was using the term "American" as an insult, but I didn't care enough to argue with her. "Well, she *is* American, so . . ."

"The quiet girl likes you very much, I think." Dara said the words without emotion as we exited the store and stepped back outside.

"What makes you say that?"

"I can just tell. You learn about people if you look closely." She took a long drag on her cigarette.

Dara was closing off. All the warmth I had felt when we'd bumped into each other on campus was now gone completely. Her guard was back up.

"So what did they want?" she asked as we crossed traffic to the opposite sidewalk.

Out of the corner of my eye, I saw Naomi's car exiting the gas station lot and cruising away. *So much for needing gas.*

"Nothing. Although she did ask if you were going to be at our show tomorrow. She wanted to put you on the guest list." I overembellished the point because I wanted to see if Dara had remembered the show and if she would come.

"I don't think I can. You know Saturday is a busy night for me. I'm bartending, and it's always crazy."

I sensed that it wasn't a good time to broach any sensitive topics, but that last comment gnawed at me a little. "Bartending? I thought you told me you were a waitress. A couple of times."

Dara crushed her cigarette and pulled her pack out of her bag. "Same thing."

"Is it really?" I said, mild disbelief coloring my words.

"Yes. At a restaurant. I serve food, and I serve drinks. Same thing." She was doing the thing where she would make her accent thicker during a tense part of the conversation. "You don't believe?"

I was resigned at this point. "I mean, if that's what you're telling me to believe, then that's what I believe."

She abruptly changed the subject, lighting herself another Marlboro Red. "So you don't smoke cigarettes at all?"

"No, I never have."

"Where I am from, this is strange. All boys, from a young age, will try cigarettes and drinking. It's very different here." She seemed to be insulting me. "Where I am from, boys must be more like men at a very young age."

I knew she wasn't talking about cigarettes, but beyond that, I had no idea what she was getting at. I wanted to stay with her and follow her up to her apartment, but I feared that we were heading for a contentious place. Dara was trying to pick a fight with me, and I wanted no part of it. I decided to cut my losses and find an exit. At least we had spoken, and at least the silent treatment was over. I thought it was time to head back to my corner and figure out what I should do in the next round—if there *was* a next round.

"I'm going to head back to my place now. It was nice seeing you."

"Okay," she said as she stared out into the street and smoked, completely uninterested.

I turned on my heel and walked off in the direction of my apartment.

She called softly, "JA nie viedaju, što ja rabić!"

I heard it. It was probably an insult, but I didn't care. I just kept walking.

# Chapter 27

Francis came out of his room in tight jeans, a T-shirt with the sleeves cut off, red wristbands, a red headband tied off and hanging loosely in the back, and a generous application of eyeliner. He looked like a rock star. Wearing only black jeans and a black T-shirt, I felt a slight pang of jealousy. "Impressive."

"You like it?" he asked, wondering if he had missed the mark.

"I love it!" I assured him. "You look like you're ready to set the stage on fire."

"I am," he said to his reflection, admiring himself in the mirror.

I decided to apply a little eyeliner as well but didn't quite have Francis's nerve, so I put on a small amount. I was surprised by how much I enjoyed the transformation. "Dude, I can see why women wake up an hour early and put this on every day."

"I have some gel," Francis offered. "You can try to spike your hair up a little."

"Okay," I agreed.

Dylan walked into the room while Francis and I were admiring ourselves in the mirror. "What are you two idiots doing?"

"We're getting ready for the show," I replied, laughing at his unfiltered disgust.

"A rock show or a runway show?"

Dylan opted to take his normal day-to-day look onstage. He wore baggy brown corduroys, a white V-neck T-shirt, and a John Deere trucker hat. If I wasn't mistaken, it was the exact same thing he had worn to his classes the day before.

We walked to the fraternity house early. We were going to settle in and party a bit before people started showing up. Two guys in a jeep rolled by us and yelled, "Headband!"

Francis smiled at this. "See that, guys? The women want us, and the men want to *be* us."

Dylan threw up his hands in unintentionally comical exasperation. "How do get that from a couple of guys shouting 'Headband!' at us from a moving car?"

"It's all part of the plan," Francis said confidently. "Just let it play out."

Dylan dismissed our drummer's newfound wisdom. "You're crazy."

I didn't say anything but laughed inaudibly to myself. I liked this new side of Francis. Being a pretend rock star agreed with him.

About one minute later, a car full of girls drove by and catcalled us. "Ow ow owwww!"

Dylan shook his head a little. "Jesus Christ."

# Chapter 28

Apparently, our band name had been included on a bunch of flyers posted around Westwood. We hadn't heard about this, but many people had seen the adverts and were anticipating this "new band" that would be opening for the more recognizable headlining act, the Alfemales. A BBX brother who was working "security" at the door of their house told us that several folks had shown up asking if this was the place where they could see Dutch Candy.

Some people in the audience had even recognized us from our small sampling of shows the prior year. One girl, whom we didn't know, showed up in full-on punk rock regalia. She had stylishly emblazoned the words "Dutch Candy" in thick black letters across the back of her heavily studded denim jacket. Dylan, Francis, and I were all surprised to see it; and we asked if we could take a picture with her.

She stood with her back facing the camera and her head in profile, mischievously eyeing the lens like a badass. I could still smell the permanent marker fumes on her jacket as we crowded around her for the photo. She was attractive, in a "nose ring and heavy eyeliner" way. She had come with a couple of girlfriends who were less enthusiastic about the band, but no less friendly. They were all students at UCLA.

Francis told her, "We're going to make you proud of that jacket tonight."

She squealed, "You guys are so cute! Can I get a picture too?" She handed her camera to Naomi, who had shown up early with her friends to preparty and help us get set up.

"The really cute one is mine," Naomi playfully warned her when she handed back the camera. "I don't care what you do with the other two."

The venue was small, but it was packed. I'd say they'd jammed in about three hundred people into a space that could comfortably hold maybe two hundred. The stage was nothing more than an elevated plywood platform that butted against the back of the fraternity house.

Dylan looked at me. "You want to kick us off?"

I didn't know what he meant. "What?"

"You want to tell them who we are?"

I gave him a thumbs-up and turned to my microphone. I hadn't thought about this moment at all, and I just said the first stupid thing that came to mind: "If we're Dutch Candy, then why are *you* so fucking sweet?"

The entire mass of three hundred souls screamed at me and put their hands and red Solo cups in the air. The fraternity had tapped several kegs almost two hours earlier, with many more waiting on ice. I had no doubt that the spontaneous and grateful applause was more about the free beer and less about the band, but I didn't care. I was about to blast off into outer space just the same.

Francis counted off, "One, two, three, four!"

Then he began assaulting the drums for a couple of beats before Dylan came in with the unmistakable opening riff, which sent a roar through the crowd. I came in playing chords as meaty as I could to make up for the missing bass line. This was my song to sing. So I stepped up to the mic and, in my most dangerous Billy Idol affectation, let the crowd absolutely *have* it.

"On the floors of Tokyo-o . . ."

Another roar rose up in appreciation of my passable impression.

Dylan, Francis, and I couldn't stop smiling at one another. We were giddy and having a great time. And if I might say, the two of them were playing brilliantly. I was holding my own, but that was enough. Francis blew my mind with his drumming. He was excellent and added a layer of depth that was undeniable. I had to give Dylan credit too. This was the perfect song to open with. It was catchy as hell—punk rock enough for the guys and romantic enough for the ladies. Think about it . . . what woman doesn't love a lonely guy who asks the world to dance?

The song ended, and the masses showed us much love and ample applause. We hadn't thought to rehearse the transitions, so there was a moment of silence between the songs where some asshole shouted, "Where's your bass player?" There was laughter, but it was only a light dusting.

I'd wondered if anyone would mention our lack of a bass player and felt a slight tinge of inadequacy. The thought was immediately cured by Francis's aggressive and immediate response to the heckler: "He's upstairs with your mother!"

The crowd went absolutely crazy. I used the jolt of momentum and started attacking the chord progression for Dramarama's "Anything Anything." Apparently, I got it right because another roar rose up from the crowd.

Our number one fan in the Dutch Candy denim jacket had worked her way to the front of the stage with two of her girlfriends. She shouted, "I love this song!"

"And we love you!" I assured her.

Francis came in right on time with the drums, and Dylan expertly layered in the telltale riff that gave the song its signature sound. We knew this was a bass-heavy song in parts, so Dylan and I planned to switch off a couple of times and let him take over the rhythm so he could play the lower strings and fake a couple of low notes. We achieved the effect adequately, and although I was a little stiff, I was able to layer the signature riff in a couple of parts without drawing any boos.

Our thirty minutes flew by. Almost as soon as we had stepped on the stage, we found ourselves wrapping up our punk cover of Bruce Springsteen's "Atlantic City." I loved this song so much. It had held a lot of promise in rehearsal, but it was clear that it wasn't as much of a crowd-pleaser as the others, and it proved to be a poor song choice to end the show on. We struck the final chord, and the audience applauded us just the same.

"Thank you, guys! You've been great!" I screamed, and we all planned to unceremoniously walk offstage.

No sooner had I uttered the words than the shouts for "More!" began to rain down on us. We stood there and watched in amazement.

I looked to Dylan. "What do we do?"

He shrugged. "I don't know."

Eventually, the random shouts morphed into an organized chant. "One more song! One more song! One more song!"

Denim Jacket was going crazy, and her two friends had begun to match her zeal. Naomi, Maya, Carey, and Keisha—who had been standing in a cluster with a couple of other friends at the side of the stage for the entire show—were screaming louder than anyone.

A fraternity brother from BBX who had been helping us to get set up approached the stage and shouted over the din, "Can you do one more?"

Damn right we could! I once again had to thank Dylan for preparing us well. We huddled for a moment and decided on "Sweat" by Inner Circle. This was the perfect song to end on, and I was glad to stay onstage for a couple more minutes. Dylan sang lead and was able to affect the perfect reggae vibe without overdoing it. He sounded great from the first note.

I don't know why, but from the time I had peeked over and saw her chanting for "one more song," I'd found myself unable to take my eyes off Carey. I had never found her that attractive, but I kept glancing over to the side of the stage. She was swaying side to side with her head down and her beer in the air.

She was typically a modest dresser, but that night, she was wearing a fitted crop top and low-cut jeans. With her new wardrobe and her arm in the air, I could see the more pronounced outline of her figure. I stared for a moment, and she caught me. She stared back at me with her heavy-lidded eyes. Holding my gaze, she took a sip from her red Solo cup and smiled as she pulled the drink away from her lips. I finally understood why they called her the Look. Unfortunately, I had to break the spell and rush to my microphone for some harmonies.

We looped the song around two times and stretched the four-minute play time to about eight minutes before finally winding it down. The crowd was amazing. I felt like a rock star. Before walking off the stage, I repeated the dumb line that I had opened the show with: "If we're Dutch Candy, then why are *you* so fucking sweet?"

Our superfan was still in the front row. Francis called to her, "Did we make you proud?"

"You know it!" she shouted back at him.

Carey greeted me with a congratulatory hug as I walked offstage. "You guys were great!"

"Thank you. I saw you guys by the stage the whole time. I didn't realize you were such fans."

She smiled mischievously, slurring her words a bit. "You saw all of us, or were you looking at one of us in particular?"

This was a side of Carey I had not seen before. I decided to play along. "I know . . . You caught me looking at you, didn't you?"

She laughed, "I did."

"I hope you weren't offended."

"Why would I be offended by that?" Her words were still slurred, but her tone was sincere. "I've been waiting for you to look at me."

Of course, Dylan and Naomi picked that exact moment to crash our party.

"So . . . what are you two talking about?" Naomi teased.

"Dude, how awesome was that?" Dylan exclaimed, practically jumping on me.

"It was incredible!" I offered, matching his enthusiasm. "How much fun was that?" Then the real question popped into my head. "How incredible is our drummer?"

"So incredible!" Dylan agreed. "He was on a whole other level tonight."

"Hey, where is he?" I picked my head up and craned my neck to find Francis in front of the stage, speaking to the girl in the denim jacket and both of her friends.

"Look," I instructed Dylan. We both watched for a moment until Francis peeked over in our direction. We waved them all over.

Francis reintroduced our superfan, whose name was Espy, and her two friends Sammy and Jes.

"What did you think?" Dylan asked the trio of newcomers.

Espy spoke first. "Amazing! But I wish you guys would play a couple of your own songs. I came here to hear Dutch Candy."

"Next time," Dylan assured her.

"When is the next show?"

"Francis handles all of that," I said, directing her to him. "Give him your number."

"Who's Francis?" she asked, looking at our drummer. "You told me your name was Rocket!"

Dylan and I exploded with laughter, and Francis turned red, fastening an "I'm going to kill you guys" look on his face.

"So your real name is Francis, and your stage name is Rocket?" Espy asked. She was laughing but still trying to get to the bottom of it.

"He's lying!" Dylan cut in. "He likes to be called Francey. That's his stage name. Or you can call him Francey Pants—he loves that!"

Espy couldn't hide her enthusiasm. "Ooh, I like that . . . *Francey Pants.*"

Francis turned to Dylan and mouthed, "Why?"

I had not yet realized, but Naomi and Carey had slipped away. I asked Dylan as an aside, "Where'd the girls go?"

"I think Carey was feeling sick, so Naomi took her to get some air or something."

"Oh, she seemed a little tipsy when I was talking to her." I wondered if she'd known what she was saying to me. "I hope she's okay."

"I'm sure she's fine," Dylan mused. "She's not a big drinker. They started early, and she probably went a little too hard."

"That's the downside of a free keg." I looked down and realized I was the only one here without a drink. "Hey, speaking of a free keg, I'm going to get a beer. You want anything?"

"No, I'm good."

"I'll be right back." I headed off in the direction of the keg. As I ambled away, I could hear Dylan joining the conversation with Espy, Sammy, Jes, and Francis—I mean, Francey Pants.

# Chapter 29

I didn't expect to see Dara standing in the corner of the courtyard. She was dressed for a casual evening out, wearing black capris, a black three-quarter-sleeved jersey, and black ballet flats. As simply as she was dressed, she was still breathtaking. I watched her for a moment. I found myself staring at the gentle slope down the nape of her neck. I remembered how I'd pressed myself tightly against her from behind and nuzzled that very spot on her neck during the night I'd spent with her in her bedroom.

She stood with her back to the larger crowd, comfortably navigating a conversation with a guy wearing a trucker hat and a girl with pink hair. They appeared to be a couple based on the way he was standing with his arm draped over her.

Dara held a red plastic cup in her right hand, and I wondered if she was slumming it with cheap beer or if she had talked one of the fraternity brothers into finding her a bottle of red wine. Nothing could escape her feminine charms. If she wanted pinot noir, she was *getting* pinot noir.

She spoke with her hands and bobbed the plastic cup in front of her as she made a point that brought smiles to her new friends' faces. I recalled how she spoke more freely with her hands when she was excited; and I wondered if that was a result of their conversation, the contents of her cup, or seeing a great show.

Dara looked happy. I recalled our last moment together on the sidewalk in front of her apartment when she did not look so happy. I diverted myself from the course I had set for the keg and walked in her direction instead. I got maybe ten feet away from her when our eyes met.

Trucker Hat followed her line of sight and saw me approaching. "Dutch Candy! Dude, that was so awesome!"

He offered a high five, which I returned.

"Whoa!" Pink Hair spoke out in reverence. "It's you! I loved your show. You guys were amazing!"

"Thanks."

We all shared an awkward moment of silence where nobody knew what else to say. I looked directly at Dara, and she looked at me.

"Hey," I said.

"Hey," she replied. I noticed then she had worn her hair a little differently in sideswept bangs, which she had tucked behind her ear.

Pink Hair finally caught on. "Oh . . . You guys know each other?"

"We do," Dara confirmed without looking away from me.

The couple politely excused themselves and shuffled over to another group of cheerful friends. The Alfemales were doing a sound check and addressing the crowd. They gave a fifteen-minute warning for their set to begin.

It was just Dara and me in the darkest corner of the courtyard, standing face-to-face. She looked at me without turning away, and we said nothing for several seconds.

I felt something coming off her. Tension? Maybe sexual tension? I'd never gotten that feeling from her before—*ever*. I liked it, but I was on such a high, and I wanted to enjoy the moment. I didn't want tension—of any kind. I felt like being happy and celebrating.

I finally broke the silence. "Thanks for coming."

"I wanted to. I was curious."

"*Curious*? About what?"

"The show." She motioned to the packed courtyard. "All of *this*." A smile crossed her lips.

"Well, now that you saw it, what do you think?"

"I don't know if I should say."

There was something behind her words. I couldn't tell if she was teasing me or truly hiding something.

"Really?" I smiled. "You can't even give me a hint?"

"I think . . ." She caught herself.

"Yeah?"

"I think . . . you looked like you were having a lot of fun up there."

"I was."

"Well, I'm glad. It is nice. I've never been to anything like this."

"You've never been to a college party?"

She shook her head. "No."

"You live two streets away . . ."

Dara waved the comment off. Her tone was flat. "Let's not talk about it."

I decided to make a joke and break the tension. "Well, thank you very much for coming. I know it must have been hard to get out of *both* of your shifts tonight as a bartender *and* a waitress."

She laughed loudly. "Well, it was worth it to see you wearing makeup." It was the most effortlessly playful thing Dara had ever said to me.

I couldn't hide my dopey grin. "Do you like it?"

She smirked, "It's growing on me."

"Let me guess, the boys in Belarus don't wear makeup either?"

In the dim light, I could see her embarrassed expression. "Jeff, I'm sorry about how I acted yesterday. I was having a bad day."

I was shocked. I couldn't believe she was apologizing to me. Don't get me wrong—I appreciated it. But yesterday had just been a small disagreement. If she'd wanted to apologize for something, she should have apologized for completely ignoring me for more than a week. She should have apologized for kicking me out of her apartment the morning after we had slept together. Even so, I accepted the small reconciliation that she was willing to offer.

"It's okay." I couldn't tell if it was the right time to get into a deeper conversation. "You know . . ."

"What?"

I realized we didn't have time for it right now. I needed to grab my guitar and a few other items off the stage before the next band began. I had a safe place in the fraternity house where I could stash everything. I offered only this much to Dara: "If you need to talk to me about something, you know you can, right?"

"I know," she replied even though she didn't sound convinced.

"Hey, I have to go and get my things off the stage. Will you be around for a while?"

She looked down and pursed her lips. "I am probably going to leave."

"What? You're leaving?" My words were playful. "Don't tell me you skipped work tonight and got all dressed up just so you could go home early."

Dara smiled. "You're probably right." She paused. "But I think I should go."

I knew there was no changing her mind. "Can you wait for me? I'll walk you back."

"No," she said immediately. "This is your night to be with your friends and celebrate."

"Can't you just wait for a few minutes?"

"I saw you with the girl from the gas station."

I thought that was an odd thing for her to say. "Yeah, she's here to see Dylan."

"Not her. The other girl."

I was surprised that she'd even recognized Carey. She probably only caught a glimpse of her through the open car window. I downplayed the connection. "She's just a friend."

"I saw her hug you when you walked offstage."

"She's never done that before . . ." I didn't know why I got defensive.

"I don't mind." Dara smiled. "She's pretty."

"Don't tell me you're jealous," I teased.

"Of course I'm not jealous." Her voice got more serious. "I said she's pretty because she's pretty and for no other reason at all."

I threw up my hands in surrender. "Okay, she's pretty."

"I don't want to keep you. You can walk me out now, but I want you to stay here with your friends."

I didn't disagree with her logic. As much as I wanted to follow her home, tonight really *was* about celebrating with Dylan and Francis. "Okay. But can we go have lunch or something next week?"

"We can," Dara promised weakly.

I walked her to the curb outside the fraternity house. I had been hoping for a kiss or at least a hug. She offered me only a smile and a simple "Good night" and started walking off in the direction of her apartment.

"Dara."

She turned to look at me. "What?"

"Thanks for coming tonight."

She smiled. "It was fun. You have a great life, Jeff. You should go spend time with your friends."

She turned and walked away. I stared after her for a moment, hoping she would look back at me. She didn't.

# Chapter 30

I woke up early the next morning and spent about twenty minutes trying to wipe away the remnants of my eyeliner. I was sure my father would have been embarrassed to witness his son waking up with makeup smeared around his eyes. I couldn't imagine what Francis was going to do. He had gone full Cleopatra and would probably require a gasoline-soaked rag to wipe away the evidence.

I was still buzzing from the night before and decided to spend my residual adrenaline on a ride out to the Santa Monica cliffs. I needed a little time by myself to clear my mind. I rode down to Wilshire, around and past the Los Angeles National Cemetery, eventually turning left on San Vicente. I followed the long boulevard past the Sunday-morning coffee drinkers in Brentwood and out to sea.

San Vicente was long and flat. I was free to pedal at a relaxed pace, letting the wind whip through my mind. The night before had revealed a couple of new feelings while, at the same time, reaffirming some existing emotions.

I had seen Carey in a new light. My roommate's incessant, but amusing, girlfriend had been subtly trying to foist her friend into my life for several weeks. But I wasn't interested. Carey had never really been attractive to me, but maybe that was beginning to change. The memory of her dancing at the side of the stage was still playing on a loop in my mind. She had made herself up a little differently than I was used to, and I'd thought she looked sexy. I also recalled the last thing she'd said to me before we were interrupted: "I've been waiting for you to look at me."

But the real issue on my mind was Dara. Complicated, mesmerizing, unforgettable Dara. In the last couple of days, I had seen a new side of her. She was usually so in control and so reserved, but during our walk home on Friday, she had broken down. And last night, she'd been harder to read than usual. I was happy to see her at the show and then sad to see her go. She'd talked about Carey, but I couldn't imagine that Dara was jealous of Carey. What was really on her mind last night?

Despite my plodding pace, time seemed to fly, and I was turning left onto Ocean Avenue before I knew it. I crossed without a car in sight and dismounted my bike to walk the rest of the way to my usual bench in the quaint strip of grass known as Palisades Park. I caught my breath and stared out over the ocean, hypnotized by the whitecaps rising and falling at random and frantic intervals.

# Chapter 31

Francis, Todd, Yuri, and I skipped our Tuesday classes to play golf at the Riviera Country Club. In truth, I would have skipped a final exam for a chance to play Riviera. This was one of the most exclusive clubs in Southern California, but through Todd's uncle and his Hollywood connections, we were able to score a 10:15 a.m. tee time for our foursome.

Todd made Francis and me change our clothes before he would even let us into his SUV. Still unsatisfied with our look, he ended up buying us new polo shirts at the club so we wouldn't stand out and embarrass him. He was good-natured about it, as was his typical state, but you could see he was taking it seriously.

I didn't care about the dress codes or the heightened sense of decorum. I was just happy to play some golf—and I was crushing the ball. It was another idyllic day in Los Angeles, and the vibrant blue sky cut a gorgeous contrast against the perfectly manicured green fairways.

Francis and Yuri were not the greatest golfers. For those of us keeping score, it was only a two-man race between Todd and me. By the ninth hole, I had a four-stroke lead.

"I should get a few strokes deducted because those are my old clubs,"

Todd teased as we packed into the cart.

"You should get a few penalty strokes for swinging a driver the size of a Volkswagen Bug," I retorted.

Yuri was stopped on the path ahead of us. He was superhigh. He had shown up to play in an old-timey pair of plaid knickerbockers and knee-high socks. By my math, he was more suited for playing in the 1890s instead of the 1990s. I'd assumed Todd would be annoyed by the clownish attire, but he was fully supportive and had bought him a classic newsboy cap along with our shirts at the pro shop. He'd even found a similar plaid design to match the silly pants.

Looking off into a cluster of trees, Yuri extended his arm to point. "Doesn't that dark shape look like a giant?"

"You're like Don Quixote of the Links," Todd quipped. "Let's stop for a drink before the tenth."

"Roger that." Yuri stepped on the gas and motored ahead on the golf course.

Todd and I had a long time to catch up as we wound our way through the course, so I gave him a full update on my dilemma with Dara and Carey. At this point, he had heard me talking about Dara for a while, and he was one of the few people who knew the complete details of our relationship. He also knew Carey—and he probably would never admit to it, but he had tried his hand at wooing her on many different occasions. Carey had always politely avoided his advances. I had never made any mention of it to him, and I assumed that his history with her would not cloud his ability to dispense advice.

We rolled up to the sixteenth tee box. At this point, he had reduced my once-formidable lead to a single stroke. "As far as I can see, Jeff, you really don't have a dilemma."

"Why do you say that?"

"What is this hole, 180 yards?" he asked.

I peeked at the scorecard. "Hmm . . . 166 from the blue tees."

"Okay. So can you reach back and hand me my driver?"

I shot him a puzzled look. "Driver? For this hole? Are you sure you wouldn't rather swing one of your irons?"

"Looks like I have a bit of a *dilemma*, doesn't it?"

Todd had used the term "dilemma" a couple of times during the conversation, and his overstressing of the word was a clear indication that he was trying to make a point. I assumed he was drawing an analogy. The 7 iron was an appropriate club for a 170-yard shot, whereas the driver was more suited for a 240-yard drive.

"Are you saying that Dara is the driver, and Carey is the 7 iron?"

"No, there's no analogy here," he said, playing dumb. "I just asked for the driver. You're the one who suggested it was the wrong club."

"Okay, I know you're making an analogy." A spike of irritation flared, but I pushed it back down. "I'm just not sure what you're getting at."

Todd's tone softened. "I love swinging my biggest club. I do, I really love it. But I can't use it in every situation." He looked at me as if to say "Do you get it?"

I felt stupid, like I should have understood the meaning. "I'm still not sure what this has to do with Dara or Carey."

"Where are you on the course right now? You're in college, right?"

"Right," I agreed.

"Look at your scorecard of life. Check out your hole." He motioned for me to look at the Riviera scorecard, and I played along. "Look at what hole you're on. See?"

He pointed to the card. "It says that you're going to parties and hanging out with friends. You're sneaking into the pool after dark and playing in a garage band, right?"

"Okay, all that's true."

"You have to know where you are on the course." Todd tapped the card again with his index finger. "You may love swinging the big club, but sometimes you gotta slide that back into your golf bag and pick the right club."

I got the analogy at that point, and it was surprisingly appropriate and useful. I was sure Carey and Dara would have been offended to have been compared to golf clubs, but I realized the comparison was not only for them—it was for *all* relationships. I had only one problem with what Todd was saying. "Yeah, but I hate the idea of settling for a lesser club."

"That's my point." He perked up. "You're *not* settling for a lesser club. You are *wisely* choosing the right club for wherever you are on the course. Now hand me my driver."

"*Your* driver?" I questioned.

Todd didn't hesitate. "Yeah."

"You serious?"

"Yeah, give it to me."

I reached back and slid the club out of the bag. "Here you go."

He strode to the tee box and jabbed a ball-topped tee into the turf. Francis shot him a look from his position in the other cart and shook his head slightly to object to the club selection. Todd ignored the silent protest, reared back, and let her rip. Without a doubt, this was his best swing of the entire round. He connected solidly and drove the ball straight at the flag. Predictably, it sailed high and far over the green and well out of sight.

"Man!" Todd exclaimed. "That felt good!"

Yuri stood next to his cart, admiring the impressive flight path. "That was awesome. Part of my soul was on that ball."

"I'm counting that," I said to Todd as he walked back to the cart.

"I expect you to."

"You know you're probably going to lose the round because of that."

Todd slid the club back into its position in his golf bag and sat back behind the wheel, looking straight ahead. "You're up. Which club are *you* going to use?"

I thought to myself, *Maybe I'll just throw my ball as far as I can out over the ocean and let the waves carry it out to sea.*

I ended up winning the round by four strokes. As a part of our bet, Todd had to buy everyone lunch at the nineteenth hole. He would have paid anyway. He didn't always have to be so generous, but he always was, and we all appreciated him for it. We were halfway through the second round of beers when our sandwiches finally made it to the table.

# Chapter 32

Dara hadn't returned any of my calls since Sunday, and she was absent from class on Wednesday. A few more brave students took their turn at reading their "great poem" to the class. For the most part, the subject matter was both dark and abstract. Most of the students who had decided to share their work were broadcasting from a similar emotional frequency, and I didn't completely understand it. I said nothing, but Anson was unsurprisingly vocal and offered at least one biting criticism of each recited verse.

It was only a matter of time before one of the offended poets called him out and demanded that he should read his own original poem and show the fakers what a true artist's work should be like. After claiming he didn't have any of his greatest poetry with him, Anson eventually agreed to read a "minor work" from his "collection."

I must confess, I was impressed with his swagger and self-confidence. He was arrogant and preening, but he had a certain something that you had to admire. He removed his round-rim glasses and wiped them with the loose flap of his shirt. "This poem is called 'Sips and Kisses.'"

He began:

*I wrestle with the meaning of poetry*

*I wonder what it is*
*And my friend of seven years*
*Tells me an old story about his grandfather*
*Age 94 at the time*
*Slipping in and out of consciousness*
*On his deathbed*
*Waking every so often*
*Long enough to make two small requests*
*Repeatedly*
*At every conscious opportunity*
*"A sip of bourbon, please*
*And a kiss from my wife"*

*He took a sip*
*And stole a kiss*
*His eyes opened wider*
*Long enough to say "Woohoo"*
*And then back to sleep*
*Back to a state of unconsciousness*
*Gone*
*Until the next round of*
*"Woohoo"*

*I no longer have to wonder . . .*
*Poetry is the sip and the kiss*
*That we steal*
*When we are momentarily conscious*

*Age 94*
*He should know a thing or two*

I'll admit it—I wanted to hate it, but I liked it. The meaning was clear, and the message was positive. Nobody spoke up, and I got the sense that the class was searching for something negative or critical to say.

Finally, a boy in the front asked, "Why did you include such precise numbers? I was a little distracted by that. Why did you mention your friend was your 'friend of *seven* years'? And why did you repeat that the man was *ninety-four* years old? I was distracted by that."

Anson looked at him calmly, waited a beat, and then recited a children's limerick, presumably from a first-grade creative writing lesson. "Details, details are the *thing* to make your writing interes*ting*." He heavily stressed the rhyming syllables for some unknown reason. His extra flourish didn't help to make the message any more meaningful, but it did make his tone much more condescending—and I think that was the effect he was going for.

No other students were willing to comment. Silently, Anson folded his paper and walked back to his seat slowly. I regretted not speaking up and announcing my favorable opinion of the poem. I have grown to realize that the appreciation of art sometimes requires a detachment from how you feel about the artist or the author. It would have been good for the class to hear my point of view, especially given that Anson had been critical of my work the week before. There would have been a valuable lesson in that, but I stayed quiet.

I walked back to my apartment, half hoping Dara would jump out of a bush and surprise me. She did not. However, two random strangers about five minutes apart called out "Dutch Candy!" while walking past me on campus. You'd have thought that would have put me in a good mood. It did not.

I saw Keisha exiting the John Wooden Center. Apparently, she had just worked out. I flagged her down. "Hey, Keisha!"

"Hey, Jeff!"

"I didn't get to talk to you at the show, but I wanted to thank you for coming."

She displayed her trademark smile. "That was so much fun! When are you guys playing again?"

"Nothing planned," I was disappointed to report.

She had a conspirator's look in her eye. "Hmm . . ."

"What?" I wondered aloud.

"Nothing yet, but I *may* have something for you."

I was surprised at this. I didn't know what she could possibly have in mind, but I was intrigued. "Okay, let me know. But I wanted to talk to you about something else."

She scrunched her nose into an expression of caution. "About Carey?"

I was taken aback. "No, not about her. I saw your mask exhibit in Fowler, and I wanted to tell you how great it was."

Keisha looked relieved. "Oh, okay. Thank you! So you liked it?"

"Liked it? I loved it," I answered truthfully. "Very clever and *very* relevant for today. I loved the use of photography to set context too. It was well done."

"Aww . . ." She beamed brightly. "Now you're going to make me blush."

Her comment about Carey was still giving me pause. "But I do feel like I should ask . . . What did you think I was going to say about Carey?"

"Um . . . That was a mistake." Keisha withdrew a little. "Can you pretend I didn't mention her?"

I let her off the hook. "Mention who?"

She smiled again. "Okay, thanks."

I turned the conversation back to her exhibit, and we discussed her art for a little while longer before walking off in separate directions.

# Chapter 33

A couple more days passed, and I still had not heard from Dara. I had stopped leaving her messages but was calling frequently and trying to catch her live on the phone. I always hung up before the machine turned on, but I suspected she was home, and I was sure she knew it was me. I was slipping into the same lovesick and depressed prison that I had occupied during the first bout of Dara's inexplicably imposed exile.

I hid it a little bit better this time, and my roommates didn't suspect anything. I left the apartment frequently on bike rides to the cliff and for midterm study groups, and they always assumed I was on an exciting adventure with my international companion. I never said anything to contradict their assumptions and met most of their questions regarding my whereabouts with a "cat that ate the canary" smile.

In subtle ways, Dylan and Francis started treating me differently. I realized that dating such a mysterious and sophisticated figure had afforded me a couple of extra status points in my peer group. I knew it was a meaningless currency, but I played along. I played along because I liked the attention and because I didn't want to face what was *really* going on.

Another week went by. I snuck out of town to visit a friend in Santa

Barbara, hitching a ride from a weird dude I met on a UCLA rideshare board. I went on the trip both to get away from Dara (and the source of my heartache) and also because I knew everyone would assume that I was spending the weekend with her—and I wanted that. The latter effect was indeed achieved, and I let the speculation spread without correcting anyone. Pathetic, I know.

I skipped all my Wednesday classes because I couldn't bear the thought of sitting in that room again, constantly gazing at the door and waiting for Dara to walk in. My plan backfired somewhat. The hour I spent in my apartment staring at the clock between 11:00 a.m. and noon was torture. I kept asking myself, *What if she* had *gone to class?* I could have been sitting next to her, striking up a conversation and having lunch and then . . . Who knew? I left the apartment, hopped on my bike, and rode as fast as I could in the direction of the ocean just to clear my mind.

I had also begun routinely using the alternative route into Westwood through the back alley behind Dara's apartment. Sometimes her balcony door was open with music pouring out, and sometimes it was closed. So many times, I wanted to run up her stairs and knock on her door, but I couldn't stand facing another encounter like the last.

# Chapter 34

Finally, after another weekend of listening to sad songs, turning down invitations to parties, and hiding in my room, the phone finally rang. I had just gotten home from classes on Monday afternoon. Francis answered with his newly adopted greeting: "Dutch Candy World Headquarters." Then he proceeded to have a friendly conversation, so I gave up hope that it could be Dara. He didn't know her, and besides, what could they have to talk about? After about five minutes, he finally said, "Jeff, it's for you."

I picked up the phone in my room.

"Jeff."

Her unmistakable voice gave me chills. "Hey."

"How have you been?" she asked cautiously.

"Good. How about you?"

"I've been okay." She was silent for a moment. "What have you been doing?"

"Nothing. Just school, and that's it. I haven't seen you in poetry class."

"Oh . . ." Dara paused. "I had to drop it."

I thought that was strange. Everyone knew that class was an automatic A on their transcript. "Why?" I asked.

"I just didn't have the time."

I knew that had to be a lie and wanted to understand the real reason. I figured I should leave it alone, but I couldn't help myself. "You didn't have time for an hour every Wednesday?"

"Jeff . . . ," she pleaded. "I didn't call to talk about poetry class."

"What did you call to talk about?"

"I called to see how you are."

"I told you I'm good."

After a short silence, she asked, "Did you ever go out with the girl from the party?"

Why was she talking about Carey? I responded truthfully to the question. "I haven't seen her since that night."

"Why not?" Dara spoke calmly, like a therapist probing a patient.

"To be honest," I said, "I've had someone else on my mind."

She was silent for another moment. "Jeff, I think you should go out with her."

"And you know what's best for me?" My words were sharp.

"I don't know what's best." She spoke flatly, refusing to match my level of emotion. "And I'm not trying to tell you what's best for you."

"Then what *are* you telling me?"

Dara collected herself and changed the subject. "I have something for you. That's actually why I called."

"Okay."

"I already told Francis. He's excited, so I hope you will accept it."

She had my full attention. "What is it?"

"I know you all love Blues Traveler."

Dylan, Francis, and I were huge fans; and I'd spoken about their music many times with Dara. I had even mentioned a time when we'd all traveled up to San Luis Obispo to see a show and couldn't get in because we'd lost our tickets on the way. "Okay, that's true. What about them?"

"I have tickets for a show this week, but I can't use them. So I want you to have them."

"You can't use them? You aren't coming?"

"I have to work," she said, using her standby excuse. "Will you take them? Francis already said yes."

I was annoyed because I knew she had already spoken to Francis and gotten him excited about the tickets as a way of controlling the situation. I wanted to play hard to get and say no, but I also wanted to go. "I guess so. How many tickets are there?"

"How many do you need?"

"You don't have them already?" I asked.

"It's not like that. I've been offered VIP passes," she explained. "And they asked how many I need. I can call them and give them your name, and you can take your friends if you want."

I wondered what Dara was up to, but at the same time, I was also blinded by the chance to see one of my favorite bands live. I said, "Can you get me three? Can I get one for Dylan too?"

"Can I give you six?" she asked right away.

"Six?"

"Yeah, and you can all take dates?" She gave me a moment to let her request sink in. "I think it would be nice if you asked that girl to go with you. Aren't you all friends?"

I felt like I had been punched in the stomach. I had waited silently for weeks for Dara to come to her senses and find her way back to me. But when she finally did, she was going out of her way to set me up on a date with another woman. I was heartbroken.

We were both quiet for a moment, and eventually, I spoke. "Why are you doing this for me?"

"I just wanted to do something nice for you. You're a good person and a good friend. That's all."

"Can I see you?"

"I don't have time, but I think you should take that other girl out."

She still wouldn't say Carey's name.

# Chapter 35

"VIP passes?" Dylan repeated when he heard the news. "What does that mean?"

In the end, I'd accepted everything that Dara had to offer. I'd accepted six free VIP passes with all access to a hospitality suite, unlimited free drinks from the bar, and seating in the orchestra, which was just a fancy way of saying the first few rows. I'd stopped myself from asking her for a parking pass. I had a little bit of pride.

Dylan was the biggest fan among the three of us, and he had to sit down to take it all in. I explained everything that was included, and he asked me many times over if this was a prank. I didn't blame him because we had a none-too-glorious history of playing pranks on one another. I assured him that it was all legit this time.

"So how did you even get these?"

I had just asked Dara a similar question on the phone. She'd told me that her friend had connections at the Westshire and he could get her VIP passes whenever she wanted them. I felt a dull pain deep inside upon hearing this. I assumed that this "friend" was much more than a friend. When I passed the answer along to my roommates, I modified it a little and said, "Dara has some connections through her work at the

198

Westshire, and they offered her VIP passes for this show."

Francis asked, "Are we finally going to get to hang out with your Russian concubine?"

Based on his question, I realized that he didn't know Dara wouldn't be coming with us. I'd assumed she had told him when they were on the phone. I knew both Dylan and Francis believed I was dating Dara in some form or another. I decided it was probably a good time to tell them the truth. I wasn't going to tell them the complete truth—that I had been posturing for over a month and telling white lies on a daily basis to make my relationship with Dara seem more advanced than it was. But I could at least tell them we weren't a couple.

"The thing is," I began tentatively, "I'm not currently *together* with Dara. We're not dating right now. We're just friends at this point."

I realized that I'd phrased it in such a way to suggest that we *had* been dating. I just couldn't let go of the deception.

Dylan was trying to make sense of what I was telling them. "Wait, so you guys aren't together?"

"No, but we're still good friends."

"Has this been like an on-again, off-again thing for you guys?"

He had probably assumed that because of my horrible mood swings from the last several weeks.

"Something like that, but it's definitely *off* right now." I felt a slight relief at admitting that, but I felt sadness too. The only realm where Dara and I had ever been together was in the illusion I had created for my roommates, and at that moment, even that was being shattered.

"She's not even your girlfriend, but she's giving you six VIP passes?" Dylan laughed a little despite the touchy subject. "That's amazing!"

"I already told you," I started, trying to explain again, "we're still friends."

"So . . ." Francis had been formulating a different question in his head. "If she's not coming to the show, are you still taking a date?"

"I was hoping to," I confessed.

"Who?"

Dylan spoke before I could say a word. "You want me to have Naomi ask Carey to come?"

"You think she'd want to?" I asked.

"I'll call her right now." Without any further prompting, he went into his room to make the call and invite both girls.

Francis and I were left behind in the living room. "So it's the three of us, Naomi, and Carey. Who's getting the sixth ticket?"

"I'm not sure," I admitted. "I guess I assumed that we would make it a triple date, and maybe we could ask Maya. But to be honest, I hadn't thought about it. Who do *you* want to invite?"

Francis responded without missing a beat, "I was thinking we could ask Espy, from the show. She seems cool."

The concert was on Saturday. I had called the venue and confirmed our six spots on the VIP list. I was a little curious and asked if there were any outstanding charges on the reservation. After a moment of faint typing through the phone, the attendant informed me that the entire package had been comped and there would be no charges at all. The same dull heartache set in as I realized that when she wasn't slumming it with me, Dara was mixing with a significantly more advantaged crowd.

I pushed that realization down as far as it would go. I wanted to enjoy the show and the time with my friends. I didn't want to make all of this about Dara.

The woman on the phone explained that I could bring my car right up the valet and they would take care of that for me. I only needed to give them my name. My roommates and I had already decided to splurge on a limo for the event. We were all broke but thought we should go the extra mile since everything else was paid for.

She also advised me that John Popper and the boys would be taking the stage at 8:30 p.m. and that Rusted Root, the opening act, was expected to take the stage at 7:30 p.m. I was only vaguely aware of Rusted Root but was still excited to watch them perform. The woman made a point to stress that the Westshire shows typically ran on schedule, so we would be well-advised to be punctual.

"Besides," she explained with a hint of envy, "the hospitality suite is really nice. You should come early and have dinner and drinks."

# Chapter 36

We planned to have a few drinks and snacks and listen to the Blues Traveler albums in preparation for the show. Although we were a little concerned if Espy would hit it off with Naomi and Carey and vice versa, they all got along like best friends from the first "hello." I was impressed with how warm Naomi was to the group's new addition. She could sometimes mark her territory, but she went out of her way to accommodate without overdoing it.

Besides, Espy was very likable, so she had no problem getting along at all. She had once again worn her Dutch Candy jacket, and she'd added a few more flourishes. As we got to know her better, we learned she was a math major, but she said most of her close friends were either theater majors or art majors. That didn't surprise me, given her flair for the dramatic. Espy was also frickin' hysterical and would say anything to anybody at any time. You had to be on your toes with her.

She got to our place about ten minutes earlier than Naomi and Carey, and as the two other girls walked up to the door, Espy watched them through the window and mock berated her date. "Francis, what is this shit? What's with all these white people? You didn't tell me I was going to be on a goddamn episode of *Friends* tonight!"

"Espy," I protested, "I'm a quarter Colombian. On my mother's side."

"Please!" she scoffed and dismissed me with a wave. "You a cracka-ass cracka."

I could only laugh.

Naomi had gotten into the rock 'n' roll spirit as well. She'd always been a good dresser and had put together a worn black motorcycle jacket over a skintight olive maxi dress. By far, my favorite part of her outfit was a set of dangling earrings with the letters *DC* embossed on a lightning bolt design. The tribute to our band was an excellent touch, and of course, Espy vowed to find her own pair for our next show.

The single best outfit of the night belonged to Francis. He surprised us with a more extreme version of his Dutch Candy punk rock ensemble. He'd gone heavier than usual on the makeup and buzzed the top and sides of his hair, giving himself something that resembled a flattop mullet. It might not sound too appealing, but he was able to pull it off in a big way.

With black boots and a new pair of jeans that fit him like tights, he looked like a complete badass. He later admitted to getting both of those items from a girl in his study group. Apparently, they were about the same size.

When Francis revealed the unexpected source of these new outfit features, Espy didn't hold back. "Whoa whoa whoa . . . Just so we're clear . . . Your plan is, at some point this evening, to ease yourself out of another woman's pants and *then* get into mine?"

The room erupted into laughter. Francis let it die down a bit and then deadpanned, "That's the plan."

Espy nodded. "All right, works for me."

Prior to that evening, I'd been worried about what it might be like to spend so much time with Carey. Our last meeting had been less than ideal, and I was still a little concerned about the offhand remark Keisha had made when we'd bumped into each other on campus.

But my apprehensions dissipated the second I saw her. She was standing next to Naomi outside of our front door. She was smiling warmly, like she hadn't a single care in the entire world. She wasn't giving off the same sexy and alluring vibes as she had from the side of the stage during our show. Instead, she opted to return to her more typical dressed-down state. She was holding a wrapped box and looking comfortable in blue jeans and a red T-shirt bearing the message "Have a Coke and a Smile" in bold white letters.

As soon as she walked in, I joked, "Can I get you anything? A Coke, perhaps?"

Carey replied without hesitation, "No, I'm good for now. Maybe just a smile?"

*Okay, point for Carey.*

She handed me the small wrapped package. "This is for all you guys from Naomi and me, as a thank-you for inviting us to the show."

"You didn't have to do that," I said, taking the gift.

Dylan and Francis joined me as I tore through the paper to reveal a plain white box about the same size as a coffee cup. The gift inside was a set of six customized drink coasters depicting an absurd picture that we had taken last year in front of Oro's Gym in Venice Beach. We had dreamed up this stupid idea after a long night of partying and decided to drive ninety minutes to the famed gym the next morning just to stage this photograph. I am embarrassed to admit we often spent our weekends running ridiculous stunts like this one.

We positioned ourselves at the entrance of the gym and leaned against three motorcycles that had been parked in front of their trademark deadlifting cartoon signage. Being idiots, we had removed our shirts to reveal our barely passable physiques and flexed feebly, just enough to relay mockery (and jealousy, if I'm finally being honest) of the weight lifters in the gym behind us.

The photo itself would have been good enough with only the three of us as subjects, but two of the gym's profoundly muscled staffers were also captured storming out of the front doors behind us, their faces twisted into reprimand as they pointed toward us. You couldn't have staged the moment any better. It was clear that we were being jackasses and these two meatheads weren't having any of it.

We ran and left our camera in the hands of the stranger we had asked to take the picture. In a stroke of pure luck, we bumped into her again about an hour later while browsing the shops on Ocean Front Walk. We loved the picture so much that we'd blown it up to poster size and hung it as the centerpiece in our apartment.

"I'm always complaining to Carey that you guys never use coasters." Naomi motioned to the wall-mounted art in all its glory. "She got the idea to make these when she came over and saw that picture hanging on the wall."

"How did you get the copies done?" I asked.

Naomi laughed. "Dylan has the original picture in his room. I used that." She immediately went to work wedging coasters under everyone's drink. "Now I can breathe a little, although we should have gotten you four more."

Carey approached me separately. "Do you like them?"

"Are you kidding? These are awesome!"

"Good, I'm glad." She had something else on her mind. "Hey, um . . . Do you remember the last time we were together?"

"At the BBX show?" I asked.

"Yeah, I think I may have been a little out of it. I usually don't drink a lot . . ."

"No, you were fine. I was happy we got to talk a little bit."

Carey's eyebrows shot up. "You were?"

"Yeah, and we haven't spoken since then. That's why I wanted you to come tonight."

She had something else on her mind. I saw her trying to formulate the thought. Finally, she just blurted it out. "Don't you have a girlfriend? *That girl*, from the gas station and the show?"

This must have been on Carey's mind since she'd gotten the invitation to come to the concert with me. I'd been so wrapped up in my own point of view that I had completely overlooked how confusing this must have been for her. She had undoubtedly been hearing from Naomi that I was in a relationship.

"Dara and I are just friends," I reassured her. "There was something between us, but it's not a thing anymore. We're just friends—that's it."

She narrowed her eyes a bit and tilted her head, studying me. "Didn't I see you with her after your show?"

"She just came to the show as a friend. She left right after the set, and that's when I came back to look for you. You'd already gone home."

From her expression, I could tell this was new information for her. "You were looking for me that night?"

"Yes, Carey. I wanted to hang out." I wasn't exactly telling the truth, but I just went with it. "That's why I asked you to come with us tonight."

Carey smiled and blushed. She drew a sharp breath and began what seemed to be shaping up as a question but abandoned it before getting the words out. Finally, she exhaled and settled on a simple "Okay."

"Anyway," I continued with a smile, "let's just have a great time tonight. No pressure, no expectations. Let's just spend time with our friends and watch a great show. Does that sound like a plan?"

I sensed the tension leaving her as she smiled. "It does. It's not as good as Francey's plan, but it'll work."

We wasted no time joining the larger conversation and catching right up to speed on the great time everyone was having. Espy was sitting comfortably close to Francis and was matching Dylan's irreverent beer-fuel comedy stride for stride.

At some point, Dylan turned to Espy and asked, "Wait a minute, where did you even come from? Did Francey's parents call and pay you to be his friend? How did you *really* hear about us?"

She spoke easily through a pleasant laugh. "I saw you guys last year at the Northwest Campus Auditorium by the dorms."

"You were at the dorms show?" Francis asked.

"Yep!" Espy explained, "You played 'Wild Child' and 'What's Gone Wrong' by the Untouchables. It was the three of you and some guy in a dress playing bass and . . ." She swooned melodramatically like a Southern belle. "Well, I guess I just fell in love with you vagabonds on the spot."

She had described the second show that we had ever played. We'd joined a small showcase of bands for a concert at the dorms. Dylan had grown up listening to the Untouchables and already knew all the guitar leads, so we'd built a set list of songs that he knew well. I was impressed that Espy had gone to the show and was even more impressed that she'd remembered us when she'd seen our band name on the BBX flyer.

Dylan was smiling. "So you saw us play four songs, and you ruined a perfectly good jacket for a crappy cover band?"

"I didn't ruin my jacket." She extended her arms, offering a better view of the article of clothing in question. "I've transformed it into a priceless work of art!"

Naomi agreed, "True, I love that jacket."

Espy continued, "Anyway, I can't believe you just called the Francey Pants Band a 'crappy cover band'!"

"What do you mean 'the Francey Pants Band'?" Dylan feigned outrage. "What the hell kind of name is that? If anything, we should call the band Dylo Beats."

"Oh, good one," Naomi said in support of her beau, snapping her fingers in approval. "Jeff, what would you call it if you had to change the name?"

"Well, I wouldn't change the name," I asserted. "But if I absolutely had to, I would smash those two names together for Francey Pants & Dylo Beats."

Carey jumped in, saying, "Maybe they can use that name when you start your solo career, baby."

She was met by a chorus of "oohs" in response to her one-liner. She had used the term "baby" for comedic effect, but I was a young man sipping on my second beer, so of course I was slightly turned on.

Francis couldn't resist a playful jab at my lacking abilities. "Or we'll use the name when you get kicked out because you can't actually play guitar . . . baby."

"Or sing . . . baby," Dylan added quickly.

Everyone shared an uproarious laugh at my expense, and I was okay with it.

The limo arrived at around six forty-five, and we piled in. I can't stress enough how much fun that moment was. We weren't drinking that much, but everybody was loose and laughing. We were all excited about the show. But more than anything, we were just happy to be young and together, riding in a limo with our heads peeking out of the sunroof.

I thought about Todd's golf club metaphor, and in that moment, I understood what he'd been trying to say. *Where am I on the course at this moment?* I asked myself. I was sipping a cheap beer in a limo that I had I split three ways because I had no money. I was sitting in jeans and a T-shirt next to a cute and unassuming girl who was also wearing jeans and a T-shirt. And we were all about to watch a jam band play happy music for a couple of hours.

Dylan, who was a couple of drinks ahead of everyone else, shushed us all and demanded the attention of the entire limo. We all complied, eager to hear whatever amusing commentary he thought needed to be shared at that specific moment. "Everybody, look at my girlfriend!"

Naomi's eyes widened. "Be nice."

"This is nice," Dylan promised. He had everyone's attention at this point. "I just want everyone to look at how beautiful my girlfriend is."

That was it. That was all he'd wanted to say. I respected that move. It was a classic, and I had seen him do the same thing for his ex-girlfriend—the one he'd thrown the chili cheese fries at. But I wasn't about to tell anyone that. I just let him bask in the power of his perfectly landed flattery.

Naomi blushed. "Thank you, baby. That was really sweet."

Espy took full advantage of the opening and asked in a loud voice with precise comic timing, "Why are *you* so fucking sweet?"

The whole car erupted in laughter for the millionth time on the thirty-minute limo ride.

# Chapter 37

As promised, the Westshire Theater rolled out the red carpet for us. I had no idea who had pulled the strings to get us these passes, but if you had told me it was a member of the royal family, I would have believed you. As soon as we were dropped off, we were greeted at the door of our limo and escorted through our own entrance past every other patiently waiting concertgoer. The young man escorting us must have thought that Francis was a visiting rock star because he gravitated right to him and started subtly addressing him as the leader of our group.

Who could blame him anyway? Francis looked the part, and the fact that he was with Espy only validated him even further. She was riotously telling everyone in a played-up adoring voice, "Oh, I'm with the drummer. I carry his sticks when he lets me. He's in the band Dutch Candy. Maybe you've heard of them. I'm sure you will."

On one particularly comical occasion, we were all standing in a loose group with a few others in the hospitality suite. Espy was speaking with another guest and was bragging about Francis, telling the stranger that the heavily made-up drummer was the leader of the band Dutch Candy.

The gentleman she was speaking with was dressed nicely in a sleek black-on-black suit. He was taking her very seriously. He nodded his head earnestly and said, "Now that's interesting . . . I don't think I've heard of this band before. Yet tonight, I hear you talking about them. And earlier outside, I saw a girl with a Dutch Candy jacket on."

He hadn't realized that Espy was that same girl. Of course, she didn't miss a beat. "I think I saw her too! She was outside, right? She had incredible tits!"

The man excused himself politely.

Dylan shook his head. "Damn, Espy, I really thought Naomi was going to be our Yoko Ono. But you're kind of a wrecking ball, aren't you?"

She winked. "When I need to be."

Naomi punched Dylan in the arm. "What's that supposed to mean? You think I'm Yoko Ono?"

Everyone was having a good time and starting to mingle. I snuck out of the hospitality suite a little early so I could see Rusted Root. I didn't know much about them, but I was curious. Carey caught me on the way out and wondered where I was going. I told her, and she asked if she could join me.

Our seats were wonderful. We were in the second row of some hastily assembled banquet chairs. The stage was maybe ten feet away. The chairs were marked only by numbered badges that had been clipped on to the back. There was no real security to speak of. We could have chosen any spot we liked.

The band nodded slightly to us as we took our seats. Not because we recognized each other, but because we were so close in such an intimate space that it would have been weird not to offer some form of greeting. I was mesmerized by their music, and we ended up staying for the balance of their set. I thought they were fantastic. They were promoting a new album that was, in my mind, destined to be a classic.

Later that night, Carey surprised me by buying me a CD from their merch booth in the front lobby. There were a few songs that I thought would earn them a lot of radio play. I was excited to go home and dissect the entire album.

The connection between Carey and me was comfortable. The rest of our group had left us alone, and we felt like the only two people in the room. I felt some of the affection from the last time we were together returning. Encouraged by a few drinks and both the intimacy and uniqueness of the moment, I put my arm around her. She leaned against me, and we sat like that for a long time, enjoying the music and the experience itself. We untangled every now and again to clap for the various songs but always found ourselves nestled back together by the time the first verse of the next song began.

Rusted Root finished their set, and the houselights came up slightly. The audience applauded; and the stagehands quickly got to work switching instruments, equipment, and cables. Carey turned to me and smiled with her inimitable eyes. "I like them."

"Me too," I agreed. "Wanna try to find our friends and see what they're up to?"

"Not really." She grinned at me. "I'm good right here."

We stared at each other, both waiting for the other person to make the first move. The moment got the better of me, and I had to kiss her. So I did, and she kissed me back. We remained like that for quite some time, oblivious to the world around us. If we had any intention to be subtle or to keep the moment hidden from view, we had picked a horrible spot. We were sitting in front of an auditorium with the houselights turned up.

No sooner had we pulled away from each other and resumed a more civilized form of communication than Naomi stumbled into the orchestra section. "There you guys are!" She sat in the chair directly in front of us and turned back to face us. "You look comfortable."

"We watched the first band," I offered, hoping to avoid any discussion about how "comfortable" we looked.

I realized that Naomi's unannounced visit had startled Carey and caused her to blush uncontrollably. Naomi recognized that the seats behind us were filling up and the houselights were coming back down. She stood. "I'm going to go get everybody."

Carey looked at me. "That was close."

"You didn't want her to see us?"

"Not really, no." Noticing the quizzical look on my face, she added, "She still thinks you're dating someone else."

"I see." I sounded standoffish, but really, I just couldn't think of anything else to say to her.

"She thinks you have secrets that you're hiding." She squinted playfully, as if to search my face for a clue. "Is that true?"

I laughed. "That's pretty funny. I am the least mysterious person you'll ever meet."

"Aha!" She pointed at me. "Isn't that *exactly* what a person with secrets would say?"

Our section was starting to fill up too, and well-dressed music fans were taking their seats all around us. An older couple sat in front of us. They were on the shorter side, and Carey and I gave each other a playful high five to celebrate that we wouldn't have to crane to see the stage over anyone else's big head.

Our group of friends filed in shortly and took their seats. Our dates conspired for a moment and decided that they should all go use the bathroom one more time before the band got started. They left Dylan,

Francis, and me to save their seats.

Dylan asked me right away, "How's it going with you and Carey tonight?"

"It's good."

"Just 'good'? Not 'great'? It seems like you guys are already a couple."

"Who? Carey and me? How can you even think about us?" I replied, trying to deflect the attention. "Francey and Espy are the breakout couple of the night—maybe the whole year!"

Francis wasn't one to overstate these things. "She's cool. I like her."

"Any girl that can go out on a first date like this, with you dressed up like that," I reasoned aloud, "she must be pretty cool."

"Who said this was our first date?" Francis deadpanned.

Dylan's reaction was knee-jerk. "You been holding out on us?"

He shot us both a sideways look through his rock star eyeliner. "Maybe."

Dylan just shook his head. He turned to me. "Hey, next time you see Dara, you have to thank her for me."

I didn't want to hear her name at that moment. "Okay, I will."

He laughed a little at the thought of his next question. "Does she even know you brought a date? What do you think she'd say If she found out that you used her ticket to take another girl out? She'd probably flip out!"

"She'd bring out the Bear," Francis added, in what I believed was yet another silly Soviet reference.

"Probably," I lied.

When the girls returned, they all sat together. I wondered if that was Naomi's idea so she could keep Carey away from me since she still believed I was dating Dara. I laughed to myself about that.

I hated to admit it, but Dylan's comment kind of got to me. He'd asked me what I thought Dara would say if she saw me with another girl. I wasn't about to tell anyone this, but she wouldn't have even cared. Dara was the one who'd made this date possible. She was the unseen puppet master, and everything was working out exactly as she had planned. The thought was bringing me back down to earth, and I pushed aside the feelings I had for Dara, trying to stay focused on the incredible evening that was unfolding before me.

On the plus side, the concert was amazing. I had already loved this band, but the live show was even better than I had imagined. I was astounded by how the live performance sounded exactly like the recorded album. Outside of their many tangential jams, the songs were pitch-perfect copies of what they had recorded in the studio. This, to me, was a hallmark of great musicianship. A few songs into the set, their front man announced they were going to play a new track that was scheduled for release in a couple of months. I thought he might have been joking when he rattled off the name "The Poignant and Epic Saga of Featherhead and Lucky Lack."

I turned to Dylan and asked, "You think he's serious?"

He shrugged his shoulders. "We're about to find out."

A shrill harmonica played for a couple of bars, paving the way for the first verse: "I remember hearing a story about a girl who wanted to fly . . ."

As best I could tell from the rapid-fire and mind-blowing lyrics, the story was about a girl who wanted to fly and a boy in a wheelchair. By the end of the song, she had joined NASA, and he had sprouted wings (you read that correctly). They often met high up in the sky to celebrate how

216

awesome their lives had become. The lead singer then observed, in perfect meter and rhyme, that "tax dollars and miracles can let the weirdest people date."

Dylan jerked his head to me and shouted above the song, "Did he just say, 'Tax dollars and miracles can let the weirdest people date'?"

I turned to him and shouted back in reply, "I think he did! And you know what? This is my new favorite song!"

I wished Opeyemi could have been in the crowd that night. John Popper was a poet of the highest order, and this bizarre song was unquestionably a sample of the great poetry that my quirky professor had been trying to teach me about for the last several weeks.

The show continued. The band was flawless. They played two encores, and "Run-Around" was predictably their last song of the night. The auditorium cleared out, and the hospitality suite was a bit of a ghost town afterward, so we couldn't linger. We had heard whispers of a band meet and greet, but try as we might, we weren't able to figure out where to go. We had the limo for only another hour, so we decided it was time to go home. The energy was still very high, and Naomi knew of a couple of parties. We set a course back to Westwood.

Carey had to leave us early because she was working the next morning for a nonprofit, where she donated her time on the weekends. We dropped her off at the ΔΔΓ house, and she gave me a friendly hug goodbye before crawling out the limousine door. I had expected someone to make a comment or tease us about our first date—if that was what it'd been—but nobody said anything. I did, however, catch a slight glare from Naomi.

We drove past a few of the places where we expected to find the remains of a party, but the revelers were nowhere to be seen. Ultimately, the driver dropped us off at our apartment, and the five of us headed back inside to resume the round of drinks we had started earlier that evening. Espy, who lived a ten-minute walk away, joined us for the nightcap. She and Francis had become very well acquainted through the course of the evening. I didn't see when, but at some point, they slipped out of the living room and presumably headed back to Francis's bedroom.

Dylan and I occupied ourselves with a few more drinks and an enthusiastic recounting of the entire concert while Naomi took out her contact lenses, brushed her teeth, and did all the responsible things an adult would do before going to bed. I knew it was only a matter of time before she would join us on the couch and turn the discussion to *other* topics. I suspected what those other topics would be and didn't feel like having that conversation.

When she finally settled in next to my roommate, I saw a glint in her eye and assumed she was about to begin playing twenty questions about my dating life. Before that could get underway, I excused myself politely and said I didn't want to be a third wheel.

# Chapter 38

I ignored the first set of rings, but when the phone blasted off on its second course of sonic expletives, I realized I was already a part of whatever conversation was waiting for me on the other end. I had to pick up.

A high-pitched voice spoke up from the other end of the line. "Is this Jeff?"

"Yeah."

"You got a pen?"

"I do," I said, blinking up at the darkened ceiling. There was a pen and a notepad on the end table next to my bed. I kept them there to write down my dreams and make little notes throughout the night whenever I couldn't sleep. I'd had some strange dreams in the last few months.

"Write this down: 823 Branson Canyon. You got it?"

"Yeah, I got it."

"Good. Come get your friend."

"Get my friend?" My voice was hoarse from the night of drinking and singing along with the band. "What are you talking about? Who is this?"

"Are you coming or not?"

I had already dropped off Carey at her house, and I knew Naomi was sleeping in Dylan's room down the hall. There was only one person he could be talking about. "Dara? Is this about her? Can you put her on the phone?"

"She won't come to the phone. She gave me your number. Are you going to come get her?"

"I'll come as soon as I can. Is she okay?"

"She's a crazy bitch."

I wanted to say something heroic to defend her and tell him she was neither "crazy" nor a "bitch." But I knew that would only force me further down whatever social structure had just turned me into a middle-of-the-night errand boy.

I lay there, wondering what the hell was happening and how the hell I was supposed to get a car. And where the hell was Branson Canyon? Something told me that Dara was in trouble, and I knew it was real trouble.

In my mind, Dara had always been hovering over me, just out of reach. I saw her in real life all the time, but if I were honest, I'd seen only her hologram. I believed the real Dara was miles away from me, broadcasting an image from a world where I would never belong. I'd known this for a while, but I was only now starting to admit it to myself. I got the strange sense that tonight I would finally get a glimpse into her world. Her *real* world. Based on that phone call, I already hated it. Or maybe it was more accurate to say that I hated *myself* for being so outmatched by whatever was waiting for me.

I rose reluctantly and pulled on a pair of jeans and a white T-shirt that hung haphazardly on the back of my desk chair.

A few minutes later, I rapped on Yuri and Todd's door with my knuckles. Despite the hour, Yuri opened quickly, looking wide-awake and superhigh. "Hey, Jeff, come on in. Everyone's gone, but you can hang out if you like."

"Yuri, I hate to do this, but is Todd here?"

"Yeah, he's sleeping. Is it something I can help with?"

"I think Dara might be in trouble, and I need to borrow his car."

Yuri's eyes widened. "What kind of trouble?"

"I got a call five minutes ago from a man I don't know, and he gave me an address. I need to go pick her up."

"A call? Just out of the blue? At this hour?"

"Yeah, I have no idea what's going on, but I need to get her."

Yuri regarded me carefully. "Are you in trouble?"

"Me? No."

He thought for a moment. "You need to borrow Todd's car?"

"Yeah."

"I'll go get you the keys." He left me in the hallway standing at the open door. This was not a social call, so I did not follow him in. He returned only moments later. "I got you the SUV."

"You think Todd will be okay if I take this without asking him?"

Yuri nodded his head resolutely. "It's fine."

"Thank you."

He turned serious. "Do you need me to come with you?"

"I think I'm okay on my own."

"Be safe. Don't worry about getting the truck back anytime soon. Do whatever you need."

I was certain I'd find a Thomas Guide located within arm's reach of the driver's seat, and my spirits spiked ever so slightly when I reached into the seatback compartment of the passenger side and felt the spiral-bound spine.

Branson Canyon was actually Branson Canyon *Drive*, and it was located up in the Hollywood Hills. I kept one eye on the road and one eye on the pages of the guide. I followed Wilshire to Santa Monica Boulevard before eventually winding my way up a labyrinth of steep hillside streets. I knew I was getting close as the houses became more and more opulent.

The gate to 823 Branson Canyon Drive was wide open, inviting me in. I pulled in slowly over the crunch of the pea-gravel driveway. The property was a little larger than I'd imagined. Most of the homes were nestled into little hillside crannies, but this was more of a hilltop estate. The landscaping was verdant and tastefully overgrown—lots of ivy on walls, hedges, and several thickly leaved trees. I caught a glimpse of a breathtaking twinkling cityscape between the hedges as I pulled forward. Advancing as far as I could behind a row of nice cars, I pulled in behind a black Mercedes-Benz. I put the transmission into park and killed the engine.

Before I could open the driver's-side door completely, I saw the figure of a man moving on the unlit landing in front of what appeared to be the dark outline of a towering front door. With my door ajar, my cab light was on. He could see me, but I could not see him clearly. I could tell he was a bit on the short and pudgy side. I figured he was much taller when standing on his money. I was committed and exposed, so I got out of the SUV and walked to him.

"Jeff?"

"Yeah, I'm Jeff," I answered, trying to sound tougher than I was.

"Come get this crazy bitch and get her out of here."

I got close to him, and he looked so plain and soft all over until you got to his eyes. He had the eyes of a man who didn't give a damn about anyone else.

"She's in the bathroom in my room up the stairs."

He turned his back and pushed open one of the two ten-foot doors. The room was lit by the ambient glow of the city's lights visible through a wall of windows opposite the entryway. Just past a short foyer, the stairs curled over to the right. I caught sight of a well-dressed larger man sitting on a stool at the oversized island, which separated the living area from the kitchen. The room was dark, but I noticed a severely bent nose in the center of his face. He kept his eyes on me the entire time.

As if following my line of sight, the mysterious host saw fit to introduce me. "He works for me. He was going to drop your friend off at a bus stop down the hill if you didn't get here when you did."

The bedroom was open. I entered and was treated to another mind-blowing view of the city through the floor-to-ceiling windows. I noticed a bed facing the view and took inventory of the severely disheveled bedding. The floor was covered in blankets and pillows, and a nightstand was knocked over. My heart sank.

I saw light framing the closed bathroom door and knew that was where I would find my friend. Approaching quickly, I called, "Dara!" No response came, so I tried again. "Hey, Dara! It's me!"

I pressed my cheek against the flat surface of the door. "Let's go. I'm going to take you home."

A moment passed. Without a sound, the door pulled inward, and a flood of light entered the room. She looked at me. She was embarrassed, and she looked much younger somehow. There was a small cut on the bottom right corner of her lip, and a blue bruise was forming under her right eye.

I smiled. Maybe I was trying to comfort her. Maybe I was the happiest man in the world because I was her hero. "Let's go," I said it again, trying to sound like the hero at the end of a movie.

I tried to put an arm around her, but she shrugged it off. Dara was wearing men's pajamas and clutched a full-size brown paper bag to her chest. I assumed the bag contained her clothes and maybe her purse.

We walked out of the room and down the stairs. Both men were seated at the marble island, and our presence interrupted their hushed conversation. I felt them staring at us in the dimly lit room as we walked out the front door.

Dara said nothing as I navigated an awkward five-point turn so that I could drive straight out the gate and leave all of this behind us. I crossed the small break in the hedge, stealing one last view of the sprawling city. The lights were less magnificent now, and the rising sun began lending its first few fiery colors to the morning horizon.

A similar inferno rose up in Dara, and her own colors came to the surface. She let out a bloodcurdling scream. I slammed the brakes. The moment was surreal. She stared straight ahead and screamed viciously again into the space right in front of her.

"Dara, are you—"

She jerked the door open and stormed out to the overlook I had been admiring moments before. She screamed again and threw the paper bag far off into the direction of the city below. Picking up some large flat foreign object off the ground, she set off back in the direction of the house. I exited and made my way to the rear of Todd's SUV just in time to see her throw what I realized was a large paving stone into the back window of the Mercedes-Benz. Predictably, the alarm responded as every light on the exterior of the car began blinking.

I stood in awe. Dara walked calmly past me and said, "Let's go."

In the rearview mirror, I saw both men running out of the house as we drove away. *Well, she got them back. Now they're even. Now it's over.*

Well, it wasn't over.

# Chapter 39

I knew Dara didn't want to talk about any of the last several hours of her life. I knew that, and as curious as I was about what circumstances had led her to accompany a strange man to his home in the Hollywood Hills and lock herself in his bathroom while apparently wearing his pajamas, I didn't ask her about it.

Dara was conspicuously quiet next to me. My mind raced for the right conversation starter. I felt like I might have been her hero, and I wanted to push the conversation in that direction. I wanted her to say something about how I had dropped everything and "saved" her. I wanted us to talk about *that*; and I wanted her to realize that the secret life that had blackened her eye, bloodied her lip, and forced her into locked bathrooms in the middle of the night would be a million miles away from her when she was with me.

She finally perked up. I saw her formulating a thought. "Turn here."

"Turn?"

"Yeah, turn left at the next street."

I merged over a lane and made the turn with little incident. There were very few other cars on the road. Dara instructed me like that, curtly

226

offering driving instructions in a manner that said "I am giving directions only, and this doesn't mean we're having a conversation."

I followed her cues and didn't say anything else.

She instructed me to come to a stop. "Pull in behind this red car."

I was unfamiliar with this neighborhood. The buildings looked like old warehouses, and only a smattering of cars occupied the curbside parking spaces. I reasoned that we were in the Hollywood area, but geographically speaking, I was unaware of anything more than that.

"Here? Are you sure?"

"Yeah, my car is around here."

I looked around. "Your car? I can take you to it."

"This is close enough."

"Are you sure?" I asked the question again, pretending to be helpful and chivalrous. In truth, I simply didn't want her to leave. I was basking in the glow of having pulled off the most daring rescue of my life, and I wanted to continue living in that moment with my damsel.

Dara opened the door before I came to a full stop and jumped out. The scene was ridiculous. She crossed around the front of the SUV and began walking across the four-lane city street in a pair of oversized men's pajamas. I noticed a bulge in the front waistband and realized that although she had jettisoned the large paper bag off the cliff at her assailant's house, she had retained a small bag or purse. I assumed at least her keys and personal items were with her and she would find her way home.

I rolled down the window. "Dara!"

She spun around, annoyed. "What?"

I wasn't even sure what I wanted to ask. "Are you okay?"

"Of course I am. I'm always okay. This is nothing to me. Are you okay?"

I knew the emotions in her reply were not meant for me. I just stared at her.

Dara stared back at me and then offered, "Head straight down this street. Eventually, you'll hit the 10."

"Can I call you later?"

"Do whatever you want." And with that, she turned and continued walking up the street.

There was nothing left for me here. The sky was completely lit up. The illusion of mystery and romance had been shattered by Dara and burned off by the rising sun. Morning was in full view, and the more respectable inhabitants of this marginally unrespectable place started working their way into sight. I was no longer a clandestine denizen of the night. I was now a sleepy-eyed whipping boy, navigating his way home on unfamiliar streets. *Damn.*

Yuri and Todd's lights were off as I crept up the stairs. They didn't seem to be up, and I didn't want to wake them and go through the whole story. I left the keys behind the large potted palm, as Todd had instructed me to do on prior occasions when I had borrowed one of his cars.

I entered my apartment at around six thirty in the morning to find Naomi sitting on our living room couch. Her presence startled me. "Hey."

"Hey," she returned.

"What are you doing?" I asked, more out of surprise than curiosity.

"I couldn't sleep, so . . . What are *you* doing?" she asked in a dry, but curious, tone.

"You wouldn't believe me if I told you."

"You weren't with Carey, were you?"

"Carey? No," I replied, perhaps a bit too forcefully.

Naomi looked at me for a moment. "Were you at Dara's?"

"No." That was an honest answer, for the most part.

"I saw you go to bed at about 1:00 a.m. I'm just curious what you do from one until six in the morning."

I wasn't sure if she really wanted an answer. "I just had some things I needed to do."

She sat holding my gaze for an uncomfortable moment. "I'm not going to say anything to her. Just promise me you won't hurt my friend."

"I'll do my best."

I then made my way down the hall leading to my bedroom. I needed to sleep.

# Chapter 40

I wasn't exactly sure when I fell asleep. I recalled lying down with a lot on my mind, then reaching over and slipping the Rusted Root album into my CD player. I pressed a square button emblazoned with a red right-facing triangle. The last song I recalled hearing before drifting off to sleep was the haunting ballad "Beautiful People."

I met up with Dara at about noon. I gauged the time because the sun was high up in the sky. I had ridden my bike to the end of San Vicente Boulevard and turned left on Ocean Avenue to assume a seat on my favorite bench. We sat together, overlooking the Pacific Ocean and facing the blue horizon in silence. Out of the corner of my eye, I saw Dara and sensed her uneasiness, but I let more time pass without saying anything.

As usual, my mind was racing. I was fidgeting, and she sat like a statue. More time passed, and I couldn't bear the silence. I had to say something. "I love the way the light dances off the whitecaps and sparkles when you squint."

"It's peaceful."

Two young men were walking down a small path in our general direction. They must have been in college or, at most, a couple of years out of school. They had that fraternity house look about them. They were both well-built and good-looking. I immediately felt an emotion resembling both jealousy and intimidation. One wore a UCLA tank top, and the other held his shirt bunched up in his hand. They had headphones on, and I reasoned that they had just completed a run. They were now walking to cool down and enjoy the view off the cliff.

Of course, they noticed Dara, and I could see them slyly shifting their eyes to alert each other of her presence. They were subtle enough, but I had become sensitive to it. The taller boy in the tank top turned slightly and walked in our direction. The other followed.

Dara and I were just far enough from each other on the bench that no reasonable person would assume we were a couple, and our current body language might have even suggested she was either unaware of my presence or simply ignoring me. In any event, the pair of young bucks read into those cues and decided they should try their luck with my friend. I kept my gaze focused forward but tracked Dara with the corner of my eye. If she had noticed the two of them approaching, she neither showed it nor reacted to it.

Tank Top smiled. "Hey, haven't I seen you on campus?"

She ignored the question. At this point, I was now looking up at the two young men. From their facial expressions, they *might* have finally caught on that I was here *with* this beautiful woman and not simply sitting on the same bench.

Tank Top was polite, but undeterred. "Excuse me," he offered more firmly in her direction.

She looked up at him.

"I've seen you before, right?" he continued effortlessly in a voice that suggested he had every right to command Dara's attention and start an important conversation with her based on the possibility that he had *seen* her before. He continued, "At the sculpture garden? On campus, right?"

Shirtless interjected awkwardly, "UCLA." He was in marginally better shape and better-looking than his companion, but in his single off-key utterance, he had revealed he was the lesser communicator and the beta in their social strata.

Dara's voice was flat. "I go there sometimes."

"Me too." Tank Top smiled warmly. "I always go there between classes. I just love it. What are you doing out here today? Are you guys together?"

I had been through these types of scenarios many times before when out with Dara. I was starting to learn how it all worked. Usually, she made just enough of a reference to me to fend off her pursuers while not filling me with any false hope. She might say something like "Sorry, guys. There is only one person I want to spend my day with, and he's right here next to me."

Dara took a similar tact on this occasion. "We're enjoying the view." Her voice was still flat. "Yes, we are together."

A peculiar moment passed, and Shirtless piped up. "*Together* together?"

Dara turned to him. Her lips curled up slightly in bemusement. She laid her accent on a little more thickly. "What is meaning for this, 'together together'?"

Shirtless turned a faint shade of crimson at her question but wanted to save face, so without losing any of the bass from his voice, he answered, "Are you together as friends or as a couple?"

Dara was still looking right at him. She let his question and its childish absurdity hang in the air. "Funny, I was going to ask you the same thing.

You are a cute couple."

Tank Top immediately smirked and nodded, acknowledging her flawless defense to their advances. A skilled communicator himself, he recognized she was toying with them and realized that no matter what angle he was prepared to take, the ultimate answer was a hard and fast "no." He accepted that and knew it was time to move on. There would surely be other women crossing his path that day, and he could strike up a new conversation with one of them.

Shirtless went the other route. Knitting his eyebrows, he snorted in derisive denial. "What? You think we're a couple?"

Tank Top smirked, "Let's go, Brent."

"Dude, she thinks we're gay."

Tank Top grabbed his friend by the shoulders and turned him back to the path in a familiar manner. "No, she doesn't. She's just asking us to leave."

He then offered a polite salutation to us to help erase the messy exchange. "Have a nice day, you guys. Sorry to bother you."

A more naïve observer might have thought he was just being nice, but a skilled cynic like me recognized that he was leaving the bridge unburned for the next time he saw Dara on campus.

Shirtless was still negotiating internally with his pride and didn't see the humor or meaninglessness in the exchange. In a final verbal shotgun blast, he called over his shoulder to no one in particular, "I'm not gay! I fucked a real Russian girl last year! She was hotter than that bitch!"

Dara stared after the two idiots. Her expression was frozen, unreadable. She turned to me and asked, "Does he think I'm Russian? I'm insulted."

"Want me to kick his ass?" I joked, hoping to lighten the mood.

"Waste of your time."

"Yeah, I'd rather sit here with you in awkward silence."

"Silence is never awkward. Only people are awkward. If you knew these things, we'd get along better."

I was facing her and thinking of the next thing to say. I hadn't noticed to that point, but she was still wearing the men's pajamas from our morning drop-off. The cut on her lip was still visible, and the shadow under her eye had bloomed into an undeniable black eye. I couldn't keep my thoughts to myself. "You look tired, Dara."

"I am a little tired," she admitted. "I think I will take a short nap."

"Here?"

She motioned widely to the Pacific. "Out there."

"What?"

Dara rose and began walking toward the railing. "I'm going to jump."

I sprang up to follow her, playing along with her implausible declaration. "You'll never make it. You need to cross six lanes of PCH and about a quarter mile of beach."

A sandy landscape came into view in the distance below the cliff as we neared the railing. The angular perspective revealed a long expanse of land extending from the base of the cliff to the ocean. The Pacific Coast Highway remained out of view, but the sounds of zooming autos made their way more readily to our ears as we approached the ledge.

"You don't think I can make it?"

"Not unless you can fly," I said.

"I flew to Los Angeles."

"That's true, but you were on a plane, right?"

"How would you feel if I left?"

"Sad," I answered honestly. "I'd miss you."

"I wouldn't miss you."

"Gee, thanks," I said sarcastically. Her comment hurt me immediately.

"Don't take it personally. I wouldn't miss anybody."

"I think you act tougher than you are," I said, unable to hide my frustration with her cryptic comments.

She looked out to the horizon. "Maybe."

"I think there is a heart in you somewhere, Dara. It probably won't ever be mine, but it's in there."

"Somewhere. Maybe. But it's completely broken."

"If it's broken, maybe it can be fixed," I suggested.

"I doubt it."

I lost my patience. "Dara, I don't even know what we're talking about. Sometimes you can be so exhausting! It's a beautiful day. Can you just smile and be happy and spend time with your friend? Can you stop the 'mysterious, tortured girl' act for one day?"

As soon as the words left my mouth, I felt regret. True, she was being self-absorbed and dramatic, but I didn't need to say all that. Obviously, she had been through something horrible last night.

She offered no discernible reaction. "You're right."

And with that response, she crouched slightly and sprang upward, propelling herself high into the air. Up, up, up, Dara rose as her figure became smaller in the sky. Her upward trajectory tilted out toward the ocean, and her rapidly decreasing size became a small speck in the distant sky that barreled at an incredibly high speed toward the horizon.

"Jeff! Jeff, get up. Get up. You have a visitor."

I woke from a deep sleep. "What?"

# Chapter 41

Dylan was crouching over my bed, shaking me by the shoulder. "Jeff, get up. Get up! Some guy came to the door." His voice was panicked. "You have to talk to him. He said he knows you. He knows your name, and he knows our phone number."

Blinking myself awake, I saw a blurry figure filling the doorway behind Dylan. He was huge, and he did not look like the kind of person I wanted to upset.

"Nice to see you again, Jeff." His voice was neither angry nor happy, just loud. "I need you to come out here." He beckoned me with a finger and turned, heading back to the living room.

I had no choice in the matter. I jumped out of bed, pulled on some clothes, and joined my visitor. My mind raced as I struggled to recall where I had seen him before. I thought for a moment that this might have been another one of Dylan's performance art pranks. The previous year, he had asked me to dress up like a gangster and burst into his art class during his final presentation.

He'd wanted me to confront him, in character, in front of his entire class about a fictitious drug deal that had gone bad and then storm out of the classroom. I did as I was instructed, and the prank went off exceedingly well. Dylan was slotted to deliver his final presentation only minutes after my tirade ended, and rather than presenting to the class, he got up from his desk and said, "Fuck this shit. I gotta get out of here!"

Somehow, his professor understood that this ridiculous skit was, in fact, his final presentation. Dylan received a perfect score and passed the class. I hoped that this morning's visitor was more of the same nonsense. But deep down, I knew better.

I turned the corner at the end of the hall and looked past the living room through our front window. Where I was typically treated to a wide-open view of the street, there was now a large black sedan at rest in the no-parking zone right in front of our apartment. It was facing the wrong way. The sedan had been driven up onto the sidewalk. It had a huge gash on the trunk, and the back window was completely blown out.

Dylan was behind me, explaining, "He drove up here like that and jumped the curb."

Our large visitor could see the wheels turning in my head as I took notice of his severely bent nose and registered where I had seen him and that car before. "You starting to get the picture?" he asked.

"Yeah, I got it."

"My friend asked me to drop off his car, and he said you were going to fix it for him."

"I didn't do this!" I protested.

"Not my problem."

"Where am I going to get the money to—"

He stopped me in midsentence. "*How* you pay for the repair is not my problem either." He walked to the door and paused to speak. "I know you got pulled into all this by that crazy bitch. Sorry about that. That's just bad luck for you, but it's also not my problem. We'll be back in a week for the car. It better look brand-new. Understood?"

I looked the large man right in the eye. "This is so fucked-up."

"Look, fella," he continued sincerely, "pulling the money together, as difficult as that seems, is going to be much less of a problem for you than *not* pulling the money together. Does that make sense?"

He was threatening me with bodily harm if I didn't pay for the repair. "It makes sense."

And just like that, he was gone. I stood staring straight ahead through the window in disbelief. Dylan advanced closer to the window to watch him leave. "He's getting into a truck. There's another guy."

We both heard the tires screech as they drove away.

"Dude, I'm sorry!" Dylan blurted. "He just came to the door and asked if Jeff Newcastle lived here."

"Don't worry about that. It's not your fault."

I walked out of the apartment and down onto the curb, surveying all the damage on the back of the car. "How am I going to pay for this?" I said to no one in particular.

The top of the trunk was dented and severely scratched. The back window had been completely shattered and blown out. Tiny shards of glass were spread across the back seat and floor. Much of the upholstery had been sliced in different places. A paving stone shaped like a diamond, roughly two feet by three feet in size, was wedged behind the driver's seat.

Dylan remarked, "Did you throw that through the back window?"

I managed a slight laugh at his question. "No."

"Who could even lift that?" he wondered aloud.

It took us a while to notice, but they had left the keys on the roof of the car above the driver's-side door. I jumped into the driver's seat, and Dylan joined me in the passenger seat. If I kept my eyes fixed forward, this was the nicest car I had ever been in by a wide margin, but a simple peek over my shoulder changed that perception completely. I backed off the sidewalk slowly but still managed to slam the underside of the front bumper on the top of the curb. I pulled onto the street and began looking for a legal space to park that was close to the apartment.

Dylan had so many questions. He knew I was a little shaken up, so he proceeded tentatively. "Who was that guy? Why did he leave you this car?"

Starting with the 3:00 a.m. phone call and the trip up to Branson Canyon Drive, I told him most of the story. I explained that I didn't know everything, but from what I understood, there had been a fight, and Dara had locked herself in the bathroom to get away and called me to come get her. There were a few details that I couldn't share, such as the disheveled bed, the bloody lip, the black eye, and the men's pajamas. It painted such a horrible picture, and I couldn't talk about it. I also made it seem like there'd been many other people in the house, like at a party.

He listened and asked a couple of brief questions. He asked specifically about that car. He wanted to know how it'd gotten smashed. I lied to him about that and told him I didn't know. I didn't want to make Dara out to be crazed and destructive, so I told him I didn't have all the details but would talk to her later and ask her about what had happened.

"Why did he bring the car here?" Dylan asked.

"Dara called me from his phone, so I guess he looked me up." That was kind of true. She had given him my name and number, so I was sure it *had* been an easy lookup.

"But if you didn't do it . . ." Dylan was trying to understand. He knew something didn't sound quite right, but the morning had already been stressful enough, so he didn't press that issue any further and opted to change his line of questioning.

He softened his tone all the way down. "Why do you think she called you? She knows you don't have a car, right?"

That was a question that I had already given some thought to and would continue to think about. "She knows that I care about her. She knows I wouldn't let anything bad happen to her."

"Are you going to ask her to pay for this?"

"I don't know. I haven't thought about it."

In my mind, I wanted to take care of it for Dara. I hated to acknowledge it, but I strongly suspected that the soft man I had seen in the doorway was her rich boyfriend. He was the reason she would go dark on me from time to time. I assumed that she had finally broken free of him and I was there to help her. I assumed he sent me the car because he wanted it fixed and figured I was the errand boy. He didn't know who'd thrown the slab of concrete through the back window, and he didn't care. I realized that I needed to take care of the car myself and leave Dara out of it. I didn't want to give her any reason to see him again.

"I'm sure you don't want to hear this, but . . ." Dylan paused. "I don't think you're all the way over this girl. I think it's much better that you're not dating her."

"Can we not talk about this?"

I found an open spot on the street near the apartment and pulled up alongside the curb. We got out of the car and walked back to the apartment in complete silence.

Dylan was late for his shift at work, so he had to leave right away. I had the afternoon open but needed time to find a solution for my new five-thousand-pound problem. Before he ran out, Dylan promised to keep the details of the morning to himself, although we agreed that we would tell Francis. Francis had left the apartment with Espy before any of the craziness ensued, and he still needed to be brought up to speed.

# Chapter 42

I looked through the yellow pages and was surprised at how easy it was to find body shops in the area. In a few of the ads, the businesses specifically mentioned their expertise on windows, paint scratches, and dents. That sounded like a perfect match for my needs. Two of those shops claimed to specialize in Mercedes-Benzes. I called them both, and based on the communication skills of the phone operator, I settled on a garage that was less than five miles away from me on Pico Boulevard. I realized quickly that I was not going to get an estimate over the phone and that I needed to bring the car in as soon as possible.

I was alone, so I would have to throw my bike in the back of the Mercedes and pedal my way back home. That seemed simple enough.

Before I could leave the apartment, the phone rang, and Carey's kind voice greeted me on the other side. The feeling was so strange. Only last night I was sitting wrapped up in this girl's arms and having an amazing evening with her. But somehow, after everything I had been through in the last twelve hours, all that emotion had, for the most part, dissipated.

Against the irrationally blinding brightness of Dara, Carey had just faded from view. I felt bad, but there was nothing I could do about it. That experience from this morning was just way too intense, and whether I liked it or not, Dara had crawled her way back under my skin.

I wasn't dumb. I knew that the other man was her boyfriend. But she had finally left him and come running to me. Why else had she called *me* at three in the morning? I couldn't get her out of my mind.

"Jeff?"

I tried to sound present. "Hey, Carey, what's up?"

"Just finished my volunteer work. What are you up to?"

I wasn't sure what to say. "I got dragged into some crazy thing. I have to run an errand."

"You need help?" she offered graciously.

I thought for a moment about asking her to drive me but decided against it. "That's sweet of you, but no."

There was a slight pause. "So I was calling for a couple of reasons."

"Okay, what's up?"

"Well, first, thanks again for such a great time last night."

"Good, I'm glad you enjoyed it," I replied honestly. "I had a great time too."

"Did you really?" Carey almost sounded surprised.

"Of course I did."

"Good, I'm glad."

I was still preoccupied about getting the car to the shop, so I moved the conversation along a little more quickly. "You mentioned you were calling for a couple of reasons?"

"Oh, right." She collected herself. "You know how I'm in Delta Delta Gamma, and we have these silly events all the time?"

I understood exactly where she was going with this. "I'm aware, yeah."

"So we have this big party every year, and it's later this month, and . . ." Her voice shook ever so slightly. "You probably think it's stupid, but we have to bring a date. Naomi is going with Dylan, and um . . ." She paused for a moment. "I thought maybe you and I could go with them."

I wish she hadn't asked me, but there was no way I could say no. "When is it?"

"End of this month, the twenty-fourth."

"Okay." I was quiet for a moment and wondered if that date was significant and if I could use it to manufacture an excuse not to go.

She sensed something. "Is that a bad day?"

I realized I wasn't going to get out of this. "No, it's fine. I think that'll work."

"Yeah?"

"Yeah, I'm sure it'll work."

"So you can go?"

"Yes," I assured her. "I can definitely go."

"Yay! I'm so happy! All my sorority sisters are going to be so jealous."

"Jealous?" I laughed a little. "I think you have me mistaken for someone else."

I could sense Carey smile on the other end. "I don't think so."

I wanted to change the topic, so I thought of an inane segue. "What's

245

the dress code?"

"Not sure yet . . ." Her mood dropped. "We're supposed to have this dumb theme, but we're still deciding."

"You don't seem like a big fan."

"It's just a silly thing we do every year . . . Anyway, some of the house wants to do it, and some of us want to do formal dress instead. You can just wear a suit if you want. Do you have a suit?"

"Yeah, I think I can pull one together."

We locked in the date, and Carey thanked me again for the night before and for agreeing to escort her to her upcoming event. She couldn't hide her excitement. I was flattered, of course, that a girl could be so happy about going on a date with me.

But my mind was about a million miles away.

# Chapter 43

I was not ready for the confusing bullshit associated with dropping a car off at a repair shop, especially considering that this was not my car and I knew nothing about it. I didn't know the model or the year or even what type of fuel it took. I didn't have the paperwork or the registration or anything. The receptionist, who was named Matt, was also the phone operator and one of the mechanics. He regarded me cautiously at first, trying to understand why I had shown up at this run-down location with a car that cost more than all the other cars in his garage put together.

I realized Matt would never go for the real story, so I had to modify the details a bit. I told him it was my dad's car and I'd gotten into some trouble and needed to fix it as fast as possible. Eventually, I was able to fumble my way through all the paperwork by pulling the year and model off an owner's manual and a VIN off a small metal plate on the inside edge of the driver's side door. In the process, I'd learned that the car was a 1994 Mercedes-Benz S600 Lorinser edition with a V12 engine. Apparently, that was a pretty nice car. I didn't know much more than that.

The shop was going to clean out the back seat for me and repair a couple of deep gouges and rips in the leather upholstery. They would also repair, buff, and paint the severely dented trunk as well as replace and reseal the rear window. Matt said he would need a little more time to finalize the pricing, but he estimated that the total bill would come in between $4,500 and $5,500. I felt sick to my stomach. I had only about $1,300 to my name. The idea of spending three or four times my life savings to fix a problem that I didn't create was nauseating and infuriating. But what could I do? I had to take care of this.

Fortunately, I had a credit card, which I rarely ever used, in my wallet. At that point, I had a zero balance and a $5,800 limit. At least I could live through this ordeal and figure the rest out later. I had no choice but to move forward. Every moment I wasted was working against me. I told Matt I needed to get the repairs done by the following Saturday, and he genuinely laughed. He squinted at the ceiling, doing a few calculations in his mind, and reasoned that at the very best, they could be done in three weeks. He circled the twenty-fourth on a dirty desktop calendar in front of him.

Strange, I had just been asked out on a date for the twenty-fourth. I smiled to myself at the random symmetry of life.

I had just spent an hour with Matt discussing what he had to do and how complicated it was to order a rear window from Germany. I knew his time estimate was reasonable and maybe even ambitious. I made peace with the unavoidable reality that I would not have the car ready by next weekend as instructed. *Damn.* If the big guy with the bent nose from this morning came back to my apartment, I'd have to cross that bridge when I got to it.

To get the repairs started and the window ordered, I needed to put down a $2,500 deposit on my credit card. I let Matt imprint my card on to a carbon receipt. He stapled a copy of the receipt and several other documents at their upper left corners and handed them to me so I would have my own record of the transaction. I folded the bundle of papers and tucked it all into my backpack.

I rode my bike east on Pico as far as Veteran Avenue and followed that back to Westwood. In total, the trip took me only forty-five minutes. Soon, I was back in my apartment, sitting on the couch with my feet up on the coffee table, wondering what the hell had just happened and what the hell would happen next.

I called Dara, but she didn't answer.

# Chapter 44

Dylan and Francis got home around the same time that evening. They were both alone; and we, just the three of us, had some time to discuss the events from earlier that day. Francis was shocked, and it took him a while to get his mind around what we were telling him.

I explained the whole story to Francis and again to Dylan—starting from the early-morning phone call. I retold the same version I had already shared with Dylan and withheld the same key details so as not to incriminate Dara. I had spent that whole day thinking about her and was even more resolved to protect her at this point. I told them both a little bit about the body shop and the work that needed to be done and showed them the receipt. Dylan noticed immediately that the estimated delivery date was several weeks away.

"What are you going to do?" he asked solemnly. "Didn't that guy say he wanted it back in perfect condition by next weekend?"

"I don't know what I'm going to do. I'll just tell him the truth."

"You think . . . You think that guy . . ." Dylan started his question twice but didn't have the heart to say what was on his mind.

"Do I think that scary fucker will accept a three-week repair?" I finished the question for him. "Or do I think he'll just beat my ass?"

Dylan nodded stiffly. "Yeah, something like that."

"I don't know." Their grave expressions were bringing me further down than I already was. "I saw everything they have to do to fix the car. There's no way they can get it done in a week."

"You're just going to roll the dice?" Francis asked.

"I guess so," I admitted. "I may try to find the number and call them."

"You think Dara knows how to contact them?" Dylan asked tentatively.

I was sure that she did. "Maybe. I don't know."

Dylan was insistent. "You have to call her and tell her about all this shit."

"I will."

Francis was fixated on the danger. "Are you worried?"

"I don't know. Maybe. But I have to believe these guys will be reasonable. You think they'd rather have their car two weeks later or mess up some kid who they don't even know?" I offered my logic.

"That's a good point," Dylan conceded.

The conversation continued like that for a while. We discussed our visitor from that morning for quite some time and my crazy trip up to the Hollywood Hills. We even discussed Carey's phone call and her invite to the ΔΔΓ party. Dylan was pleased to hear I would be joining him. He usually hated those parties and thought we could make it fun. I didn't know how I was going to make anything fun anymore.

# Chapter 45

Carey and I spoke on the phone on Monday night and met up on campus on Tuesday at the Kerckhoff Coffee House. I couldn't deny it. She was great. She was interesting, ambitious, and funny; and I genuinely liked getting to know her. But I was still blinded by someone else, and as a result, I couldn't see myself with Carey in that way. More than that, I just couldn't *feel* it. That part of me was reserved for another girl.

I felt like Carey and I could be good friends. I could tell she wanted more, but I kept a little distance. I was sure she was bewildered because we'd had such an intimate moment together at the Blues Traveler show, and now I was apparently going back to zero. I just thought it would be better if I didn't send her any more of the wrong signals.

She spent many of her evenings serving ice cream and other treats at a funky little dessert shop on Sawtelle, about a block from the Nuart Theatre on Santa Monica Boulevard. I had been to the Nuart on a prior occasion to watch a midnight showing of *The Rocky Horror Picture Show*. This area was within reasonable proximity to campus and defined by a tiny, but interesting, strip of shops and restaurants.

On Tuesday night, Carey called our apartment and left a message asking if I would like her to bring over some ice cream after her shift ended. I ignored the call. She called again on Wednesday, and again, I just let the call go to the answering machine. About ten minutes later, Dylan came through the door and played the message while I lay on the couch watching TV.

"Hey, this message is from tonight." He pointed this out to me after listening to the time stamp.

"Yeah," I acknowledged.

"Are you going to call her back and tell her to come by?" he asked. "I'll take some ice cream."

"No, I have a few other things I need to do."

"Like what, watch TV?"

"No," I insisted. "I'm just relaxing. I picked up a bunch of early shifts at work to pay for this stupid car, and I just want to relax some nights."

Dylan was genuinely shocked. "You're paying for the car?"

I got up and went to my room. "Can you just stay out of it?"

# Chapter 46

A few nights later, Carey called from work again. Francis answered, and without asking me, he invited her over to join us all for movie night. Then he proceeded to put in an order for four pints of ice cream: one for himself, one for Espy (who was now coming by our apartment quite frequently), one for Dylan, and one for me. Thankfully, Naomi was busy and wouldn't be joining us that evening.

He hung up and announced to the room, "Sorry, bro! Somebody had to do it!"

"Preach!" Espy said. "Mama needs some cookies and cream!"

As promised, Carey arrived a while later and joined us for the evening, carrying a large box with ice cream containers in it. I was happy to eat it, but I felt bad to think she was spending her money on us. She insisted that it was all heavily discounted and she didn't mind doing it.

We all decided to watch *Bad Lieutenant*. Dylan, Francis, and I offered a ridiculous and sarcastic running commentary reminiscent of a crude and more sophomoric *Mystery Science Theater 3000*. This was our typical mode when watching a film together, and it usually drove everyone around us crazy. But the girls didn't seem to mind on this night, and there was a lot of laughter to go around. Espy caught on quickly and jumped headfirst into the fracas. Despite the deeply unsettling nature of the film, the overall experience was much like watching a comedy.

Espy had the best line of the night when, upon viewing a particularly bizarre and disgusting scene in which Harvey Keitel pulls over two teenage girls and performs a lewd act on the side of their car, she deadpanned, "I know that move—it's called a 'Simi Valley car wash.' You guys have never done that?"

As the evening wore down, Carey lingered for a while and eventually said her goodbyes and left. I didn't feel like making a dramatic scene, so I remained on the couch as she got up and showed herself out.

Francis was the first to speak. "What was that?"

I wasn't sure what he meant. "What?"

He continued, "You couldn't walk her out?" Francis was not usually so vocal about such things.

Dylan joined the critique of my poor behavior. "Dude, that girl is so into you and so nice! You need to make more of an effort."

I tried to play it down. "We're just friends."

"She likes you and cares about you!" He had moved beyond playful banter. He was scolding me.

Espy got up. She was uncomfortable, and you could see it in her face. "Guys, I'm just going to leave."

Francis spoke up. "No, you don't have to go."

"I do." Espy picked up her jacket and book bag. "This is important, and it's between you guys." She beelined for the door. Pausing for a moment, she turned to me, "Jeff, these two guys care about you so much."

She was about to say something else, but she left instead.

A moment passed while we processed Espy's parting words. Dylan picked up where the conversation had left off. He spoke softly, attempting to diffuse any tension. "We think you're overlooking Carey because you're still thinking about Dara."

"You guys have talked about this?" I asked, wondering if I should feel betrayed.

Dylan continued, "Of course we have! We see you every day. I know you said you're not dating her, but it's clear you're still thinking about her. You're not yourself. It's starting again."

"What's starting again?"

"The moping," Dylan answered. "Ever since you had to go and save her last weekend . . ."

"I wasn't moping tonight."

"No shit." Dylan seized on the point. "That's because you're happy around Carey."

"I've known you for two years, Jeff," Francis began. He continued to surprise me by how much he was willing to open up. "When you first started seeing Dara, you changed. You were sneaking around, and you got so quiet all the time . . . But when we see you with Carey, you're happy, and you always seem to be having fun."

I was annoyed. "You guys never saw me when I was around Dara."

"Don't you think that's weird?" Dylan questioned. "She's never come around. She's never tried to meet your best friends. She practically ran out of the show after we played. Why didn't she just come up and introduce herself? She had you sneaking around to see her."

"Stop saying that. I never snuck around."

"That's what it seemed like," Dylan retorted. "The point is you have to move on. You have this amazing girl who's so into you, and you're being kind of a jerk to her."

I was still annoyed. "Guys, I know you're trying to help, but I'm not going to discuss this. It's my own business." I got up and retreated to my room. They didn't know what was really going on. They didn't know that Dara was trying to break out of a bad relationship, and I had to help her through it. She wasn't calling me, but she would soon. Everything would work out soon.

I lifted the handset from the phone on my desk. I stared down at the number grid and fought the desire to punch in the familiar seven-digit pattern. I felt a rush of sadness followed by anger; and in an aggressive move, I reared the phone over my head and slammed it down on the ground, breaking it into many pieces.

I heard footsteps shuffling to my door. It was Dylan. "Jeff, you okay?"

"I'm fine."

"You sure?"

"Yeah, I'm fine."

# Chapter 47

On Friday, I was in a bad place mentally. I hadn't been sleeping well, and I was getting up early for work, so I was exhausted. I was also tense with the realization that at any point, some hulking bent-nosed goon would come crashing through my front door and demand from me a car that I did not have. I sleepwalked through my day of classes and sat in on a late-afternoon study group in preparation for a midterm exam scheduled for the following week.

I wasn't much help to the rest of the group, and I cut out early to get something to eat at a burger shack on campus. I sat out in an open-air courtyard and watched the blue sky take on the first subtle hints of twilight. A stranger walked by my table and shouted, "Dutch Candy!"

I smiled. I'd needed that.

Finishing my meal, I bussed my table and set off on the thirty-minute walk back to my apartment. Campus was sparsely peopled, as was typically the case on Friday afternoons and certainly on Friday evenings. I had no plans for the rest of the night except to lie in bed and wonder how the whole car fiasco would play out.

I neared the long alley where I could either stay straight and proceed home or make a hard left and walk down a long hill to Dara's apartment. What did I have to lose at this point? Dara had already let go of the rope. What difference would it make if I stopped in and forced a conversation? How could it hurt? There's a point where you're falling, and it won't matter if you fall any faster. Your next stop is the ground. But maybe, just maybe, there was a chance I could grab a tree branch and save myself.

Getting closer to the stairway leading to her place, I swore I heard the same Piano Sonata no. 14 from the last time I was with her in the apartment. I jogged up the stairs, clinging to the side of her building. As I crested her landing, the music evaporated. I listened carefully and thought I heard, at one moment, a faint and fleeting piano note. But I reasoned that it was just a ghost of the song replaying in my mind—a trick of my subconscious and nothing more. *Was the song really playing at all?* I wondered.

No answer came after I knocked loudly on her front door and waited. I knocked again and rang her bell. Again, no answer. I wasn't proud of it, but I placed my ear tightly against the door and listened for a moment. I heard nothing—just the rhythmic pulsing of the blood in the side of my face playing against the cold-painted surface of the purple door.

Of course, I should have just left her apartment and walked back to my place. Either she wasn't home, or maybe there was a small chance that she *was* home and chose not to answer the door. If the latter were true, I didn't yet take offense because she had not seen or heard me, so it was not personal against me.

"Dara!" I called out. "It's me, Jeff!"

Again, I paused and listened. Nothing. Not a sound. A moment passed.

"Dara, you there?"

I conjured an image in my mind of her standing with her forehead pressed to the other side of the door. In my daydream, we stood in dramatic symmetry, facing each other with our heads bowed in mutual amorous reverence. She was crying softly, and though she might have wanted to, she was reluctant to let me in because she was embarrassed from last weekend's episode. How could she face me after I had found her in such a compromised state?

*Poof!* The bubble burst. I wasn't sure what to do with the dispersing mist of that momentary image, so I sent it to the same dreamlike reservoir where the piano sonata had floated off to.

Damn, I didn't want to leave. I took a seat in one of the patio chairs in the small alcove by her front door. The acrid smell of stale stubbed cigarette butts greeted me from a stone ashtray on the matching end table next to me. I hoped against hope that she could have been sitting in the other chair next to me and condescendingly telling me about her superior view of the world.

The sky was growing dark, and I could imagine the streetscape below me. I could imagine the familiar gas station, restaurants, and shops. In my mind, the small village was beginning to buzz. Happy people filled the streets. I leaned back in the comfortable chair; and somewhere, intertwined in the pungent odors emanating from the ashtray, I picked up delicate notes of Dara's pleasant scent all around me.

# Chapter 48

I heard footsteps coming up the stairs, and I froze. There were only two other apartments accessible from this staircase, so there was a reasonable chance that this was Dara arriving home. I could hear quite clearly when the footfalls changed in pitch from the boxier echo of the staircase to the solid thud of the outside hallway. The individual had indeed reached the landing and turned in the direction of Dara's doorway.

I was shielded by the alcove and could only sit and wait for the figure to come into view. There was no apartment beyond hers, and I couldn't think of a plausible reason for somebody else to be approaching. The cadence of her steps was slower than I expected. I heard, or maybe sensed, that her feet were dragging. Perhaps she was tired or maybe hurt.

I was nervous about how she would react. The last time I'd stopped by unannounced had not gone so well. I didn't want to come off as a stalker who was leaving too many messages and lying in wait at her door. I could play this off as an uncomplicated social visit from an old friend who was eager to catch up after going incommunicado for a small spell. I could say I'd been on the way home from campus and had decided to stop by and take a seat to rest my legs. Basically, that was true. I could say that I'd come up from Westwood. That would mean I didn't even have to go out of my way to pass her apartment. I would just play it off.

The footsteps became more labored. The dragging that I had heard was now more of a scraping sound. The short walk from the staircase to the door, which should have taken no more than a couple of seconds, had gone on for a minute at least. I heard heavy breathing, as if Dara or maybe some other person was struggling to make the short journey. I heard the sounds growing closer and sensed that they were immediately around the corner of the alcove. I knew that the physical form of this person would become visible imminently, and I braced for the impact.

A woman. An old woman, whom I had never seen before, turned the corner. She looked at me and was not startled to see me sitting in the chair. I wondered if she was a maid, or maybe she was delivering something to the apartment. She carried nothing with her—no bag, no purse, nothing. She was dressed up in a style that could possibly have passed for a current fashion among the elderly but, based on my knowledge of old Bogart films, would have been a little more in place in the 1940s. That was my guess anyway. I didn't know for sure.

She sidestepped by me and produced an old-fashioned key from her pocket. I realized that she was walking just fine and tried to understand what the source of the dragging feet and labored breath was.

Placing the key in the door, she looked back at me over her shoulder and uttered something in a language I did not recognize. "Vy zhubilisia?"

"What?"

She entered the apartment and left the door open behind her. Against my better judgment, I followed her in. The apartment was completely empty. All of the furniture, the books, the entertainment center, the

262

colorful walls, the appliances, and the window coverings—all of it was all gone.

"Did Dara leave?"

The woman could only stare at me.

"The girl that used to live here, did she go?"

Again, she spoke in a language I didn't understand. "Nie tut."

"Nie tut?" I repeated the phrase. "What does that mean?"

She looked at me with sadness in her eyes.

I ran to the bedroom. The room was empty. A vision of the night we had spent together in each other's arms swept across my mind. I wondered if it was real or imagined or dreamed.

I stepped in farther and smelled the lingering flowery scent of Dara in the air. There was a pile of books on the ground where the bed used to be. I saw a flash of the name Yakub Kolas on one. Nothing was clear. Everything was out of focus.

"Što vy bačycie?"

"I don't know what you're saying."

"Nikoli tut."

"Can you speak English? Can you tell me anything?" I pleaded.

She offered no answer and walked silently out of the room. I remained for a moment longer, grasping one final memory of the space before walking out into the living room. The strange woman was gone. The apartment was small. I peeked into the bathroom and onto the balcony. She had vanished. There was no other place she could be. I remembered her entrance and thought she might be gathering the equipment from the outside hallway.

I walked out through the door and turned the corner of the alcove, hoping to find some common words that I could use to get some answers. The old woman was not there. There was no equipment. The hallway stretched out as usual, granting access to a staircase and a couple of other apartments. I could see no one else. *So strange*, I thought to myself.

Dara was gone. I felt sadness and maybe even a little relief at this. I wasn't sure how I felt, and I reasoned that I needed a little time to collect my thoughts. It was best to leave, but I figured that I should grab the books from her bedroom floor. They were the last token I had to remember her by, and it wouldn't hurt to keep them and read through them from time to time.

Stepping back into her alcove, I was shocked to see that the door had been closed behind me. I was sure I had not closed it when I'd walked out. I was even more surprised to see myself still reclining in the cushions of the patio chair, where I was sleeping peacefully.

# Chapter 49

I was not sure how much time had passed by the time I woke up. I estimated it was a couple of hours at least. From what I could tell, my head had not moved. It remained propped completely upright against the chair's back, numbing the back of my skull as a result.

The dream came flooding back. The image of myself sleeping in this chair came flooding back. The interior of Dara's vacant apartment and the strange woman and her foreign words all came flooding back.

I felt a sense of shame for having fallen asleep. Prior to drifting off, I'd wondered if Dara was inside and avoiding me; and I'd thought that sitting outside of her front door, in vigil, would somehow make her realize how dedicated to her I had been all along. I thought, maybe, that level of dedication would compel her to open the door to her apartment and possibly more. With even just a little rest to clear my head, I saw the situation more clearly and regretted my decision.

But buried in my shame was a small spark of excitement. I had just seen a vision of my world without Dara, and although I didn't want it to be true and I didn't want her to leave me, I realized that I would be okay without her. I realized that, at some point, the furniture would be removed and the walls would be painted beige. At that point, I would just have to move forward. I didn't like the notion of facing these facts, but after my dream, I realized I could live with them.

Intent on leaving, I rose quickly. In my haste, I bumped the small end table, both knocking the ashtray to the ground and sending a sharp pain into the side of my knee. *Damn.* I looked at the mess I had created in the faint glow of a nearby bulb and realized it would be pointless to try to clean that up. The mess was exactly as you would expect from dropping a full ashtray onto a hard surface from a height of three feet.

There was no way I could clean that without better lighting and with neither a broom nor a dustpan. So much for a stealthy exit. I smiled ironically at the only bit of symmetry that my relationship with Dara had ever offered to me. I would go home and sift through the ashes of my broken heart, and she could come home and sift through the remnants of a broken ashtray.

# Chapter 50

The night air had turned cool, and I was starting to feel a chill as I neared my apartment. All the lights were on, and I saw the outline of several people moving around through our large street-facing front window.

I got to the top of our stoop and heard laughing and shouting through the door. In the background, there was the undeniable jangle of Dylan's brand-new CD, which we had been playing on repeat in our apartment for the last week. Dylan had lived in Sacramento and grew up with a couple of the guys who were gaining traction as an indie band. Their first album was called *Motorcade of Generosity*, which had been released earlier in the year. He played the CD often, and this week, it had seen particularly heavy rotation. It was great from beginning to end and sounded like nothing else I had ever heard.

Dylan had explained that their name, Cake, had nothing to do with food and was more about how things built up as a result of time or overuse. He assured us the band would be touring in California to promote the album and that he could get us backstage passes whenever we wanted. Since the Blues Traveler show, our expectations for concerts had spiked considerably.

I paused for a moment and considered going somewhere else. I wasn't sure I was ready to walk in and deal with the barrage of curious eyes that would no doubt be asking me where I had been.

An unmistakable guitar started and stopped and started again for a couple of bars. Dylan's voice boomed through the door. "Listen! Listen to this one. This one's called 'Jolene.' This is about . . . This is about . . . You just gotta listen to it . . ."

His voice was earnest. It was a tone I recognized from many prior conversations. This was his "drunk, but serious" voice. He was both inebriated and sincere. He wanted everyone to hear the song but couldn't quite articulate more than that.

The room quieted down at his prompting. Of course, Naomi called out, sounding slightly annoyed, "We *are* listening! How can we *not* listen? You have the music up so loud we can't even talk!"

Dylan only retorted, "Just listen! This is about us." As if on perfect cue, the intro swelled and gave way to the first verse. "Well, Jolene unlocked the thick breezeway door . . ."

The lyrics grew more and more poetic and specific, and I was dying to see how Naomi would react to Dylan's comment that this song was somehow related to their relationship. There was a slight record-scratch moment when I broke the seal of our front door, which caused a few heads to jerk in my direction, but that was short-lived. I'd been worried I might be met by prying eyes, but in truth, I was barely acknowledged at all. There were about fifteen people in the living room, mostly Naomi's girlfriends, and I recognized many of them. I saw Maya right away, and then there was Keisha, who smiled brightly and held up one of our new coasters with a proud look. I wondered if she had helped put that gift together.

Francis was standing with his arm around Espy, who had added red streaks to her black hair. I loved the new look. *And* I loved that Maya could see my roommate with his new girlfriend.

Before I could take further inventory, Dylan greeted me, "Jeff, where you been?"

"Just out. I didn't know we were having a party."

"This is the postparty. We went to a huge Sigma Rho party, but they wouldn't let Francey in."

Francis had rushed Sigma Rho and gotten only about halfway through a quarter as a member. This was intended to be the infamous first quarter, where the brothers put the new initiates through a hazing period. After a couple of run-ins with some of the more antagonistic members of the fraternity, he decided the system wasn't for him.

I'd never gotten many details. But I had heard the "last straw" story, where one of the bros wanted him to hold a hot dog in his asshole as a rite of initiation, and Francis thought that was ridiculous. The story goes that he was given an ultimatum to either put the hot dog in his ass or leave the house and, thus, forfeit his candidacy to become a brother. To his credit, Francis walked right out. As he did so with both his pride and sphincter fully intact, one of the bros went after him and tried to plead with him to stay. As I understood it, he told Francis, "Dude, I'll talk to the guys . . . You don't have to put the thing up your ass, okay? You can just pinch it between your butt cheeks. We'll make an exception for you."

Incredibly, the generous concession was not enough to change my roommate's mind. Francis just kept on walking. The next day, several members of Sigma Rho came over and told him they were sorry. They said things had gotten out of hand and that they didn't blame him for walking out. They told him he was always welcome at the house and he should feel free to stop by anytime. I'd been there when they'd come by and had been impressed with the way they'd handled it. I knew Francis had been over to the house a few times since then. But I suppose on

269

that night, either the invitation had expired, or the wrong guys were watching the door.

"So you all came back here after that?" I asked.

"Not exactly. Naomi and a few of her sisters went in, and we stood around for a while on the street like idiots wondering what to do. Eventually, we went to Harrington's and then just came back here."

"How long were you at Harrington's?"

"Couple of hours, I think," Dylan estimated.

"Wait . . . What time is it now?"

"It's like maybe twelve."

"Twelve?"

I was surprised I had slept that long in front of Dara's door.

Dylan saw that something was calculating behind my eyes and cocked his head slightly. "Dude, what's up? Where were you? Don't tell me you were with—"

"No," I said, reading his mind. "I was *not* with Dara."

He stared at me. "Okay." I recognized that a new thought was occurring to him. He lowered his voice. "Is everything cool with the whole car thing?"

He knew that the next day was supposed to be the "pickup," and he knew the car wasn't ready. I didn't have any new information to share, and I had already resolved to just *deal with it* as it happened. There was nothing I could do until I saw these people again or got the car. "Definitely, everything's cool."

I scrambled to think of a question to change the subject. "Hey, um . . .

So what time did everyone get here? Looks like Naomi brought half her sorority."

"What? I heard my name. What are you guys talking about? It better be nice!" Naomi walked up to us and poked Dylan in the side playfully.

"I was just asking when everyone got here."

"Too bad you weren't here thirty minutes ago. Carey came with us, but she decided to go home early."

"I thought she was working tonight."

"She was, but she got off work and came over. She told me you didn't have any plans tonight, so she was wondering where you were. So, mysterious boy, where were you?"

I twisted so she could see my backpack. "I had a late study group."

Naomi pinched her chin in a mock thinking pose. "Are you sure you were at a study group? It's kind of late on a Friday for that, don't you think?"

"We got dinner afterward," I lied.

"We?" Naomi smiled. "Who's 'we'?"

"The whole study group," I lied again.

She looked at Dylan as if she was asking for his opinion. "I don't know . . . It sounds fishy."

Dylan came to my defense, kinda. "I believe it. He's a nerd."

She remained playful but got a touch more serious. "Can I ask you a question?"

"Sure."

"Will you answer honestly?" she persisted.

"Maybe. It depends on the question."

"Are you dating anyone else? Like, *seeing* anyone else?"

"I'm not dating *anyone*. How can I be dating anyone *else*?"

Naomi regarded me for a moment. "You should call Carey. I know she'd like to hear from you."

"It's kind of late," I protested.

"She's probably still up. Call her and ask her on a date for tomorrow."

Maybe it was Naomi's power of persuasion. Maybe it was the beige walls and the missing furniture in my dream. But I felt like it was a good idea.

# Chapter 51

*To the owner of the black Mercedes and his discount goon,*

*I am having the car fixed. It will be as good as new, and I am spending a small fortune on it. You're rich and I am broke, and I am spending ALL my money on the damage I didn't even create because that makes a lot of fucking sense. (that was sarcasm)*

*I spoke with the mechanics at the garage and they said that based on the damage to the leather and the trunk, and the special order of a rear window from Germany, there is no way they can complete the repair up to your standards in only one week. So . . . no car today.*

*I have been told the car will be ready by the 24th of this month. I spoke with them again today; they said the window was being shipped and they confirmed the date. You can see a copy of the estimate and receipt (with the delivery date) in this envelope. I purposely blacked-out the address of the shop because I don't want to get anyone else involved.*

*You guys have my phone number. If you need to call me, you can do that any time. Just leave a message because I am usually out. I'll probably be working extra shifts to pay for this bullshit.*

*If this isn't good enough for you and you need to come and kick my ass or worse to prove a point, then fuck you!*

*And while you're at it, go fuck yourself!*

*Jeff*

"I like it." Francis's eyes darted back up to the top of the page. After a long moment of rereading, he repeated himself. "I like it." And then once more for emphasis. "I like it a lot."

Dylan was incredulous. "You like that shit? You don't think that's ridiculous? You don't think he's just asking for it? You don't know what these guys are capable of!"

Francis handed the note back to me. "It's good. Don't change a thing. I like the part about the sarcasm, and telling them to fuck off is a nice touch too."

"I can't believe this . . ." Dylan was talking to me and himself. "Okay, but if they come here and start beating you up, I'm *not* jumping in."

"Oh, I'm not jumping in either." Francis wanted to make that clear. "I don't have anything to do with it. I just like the letter. It's well written."

Despite the protests, Dylan agreed to leave the note pinned to the door for the rest of the day or until it was opened. He promised not to move it or replace my message with a more neutered and placating version.

# Chapter 52

I held a container in each hand and walked over to Carey. "I'm surprised. You serve ice cream every night, and you chose this place. I figured you'd be sick of it by now."

"No, it's just the opposite. I love ice cream! But I can't eat a lot of it because I'm lactose intolerant."

"Oh . . . So you come here for sorbet?"

"Yep!" she said, pulling the white Styrofoam cylinder from my outstretched hand. She held it to her chest with both hands, closed her eyes, and smiled a smile of ecstasy. "I love it so much, and this place makes the best!"

"Nice to know that a pint of ice cream can make you that happy."

"Sorbet," she corrected.

"Right, sorbet," I chuckled. "I won't forget again."

"So . . ." Carey smiled. "I'm excited to see the surprise. Last big surprise, you took me to the Westshire, so I'm curious to see what you have in store this time."

"Don't get your hopes too far up."

She beamed. "I'm sure it'll be great."

"All right, follow me. It's a little bit of a walk."

Carey and I walked down Westwood Boulevard, left onto Kinross Avenue, and ran across Glendon.

"What's this? An office building?" she asked, observing a tall building in front of us.

"Something like that," I explained. "I came here about a year ago for a party. There's an open space on the top floor with nice views."

By her expression, Carey was intrigued and possibly impressed. I had been wanting to take Dara here for the last few weeks, but it had never happened. I thought it would be a nice place to eat ice cream with Carey. I recalled there was a quaint spot in the northwestern corner of the top floor that offered a great view of the mountains beyond Westwood, as well as a more distant view of the Pacific Ocean.

We entered a nondescript lobby and pressed a round button on the wall near the elevator. The doors slid open immediately, and I followed Carey into the boxy compartment. As I suspected, the uppermost level was completely vacant, and we advanced around a barrier wall into the large space I had recalled from my previous visit. The room was wide open and lined with floor-to-ceiling windows.

"This is really nice!" Carey said, marveling at the sight.

"Is your sorbet still frozen?"

She squeezed her container and gauged that the contents were still solid. "Yes."

I produced two spoons and a wad of napkins that I had been clutching to the side of my own frozen container.

"So what is this place?"

"To be honest, I don't know. I've only been here once, but I've wanted to come back ever since."

She was genuinely appreciative. "That's nice, and you brought me!"

The northwest corner was wide open except for a red couch that had been backed up against the window, partially blocking the view.

"Hey, help me turn this around," I asked. "We can eat facing the window."

Carey and I made quick work of spinning the bulky piece of furniture and creating the ideal seating arrangement. We both plopped down and began digging into our frozen treats.

"You know . . ." She paused briefly. "I was a little bit surprised that you called last night. I was glad, but I didn't expect it."

"I know. It was late. Naomi told me—"

"It's not that," she said, cutting me off. "When I went to your place and you weren't there, I just assumed you were *out* for the evening."

She had placed extra emphasis on the word "out." She was implying I was "out" on a date, presumably with Dara.

"Sorry about that. I didn't realize you guys were coming over. I guess I got there right after you left, and there was a party going on. I would have come back sooner if I had known."

"Well, I'm glad you finally called, and I'm glad we could go on this date."

"*Is* this a date?" I asked the question in an attempt to be playful, but it came off as more of a rebuke to her innocent advances. I tried to think of something to say to make light of my careless comment, but no words came. My cheeks flushed slightly.

277

I saw a momentary flicker of disappointment on Carey's face, but she quickly replaced it with a smile. I knew she wanted this to be something more than just two friends hanging out and eating ice cream or sorbet or whatever. I still wasn't sure how I felt about her. She was sweet, and I knew there were a lot of guys who found her attractive. Maybe I was comparing her with Dara too much.

We sat quietly, and I sensed the onset of an awkward moment. But Carey was a skilled communicator and quickly guided me through a comfortable conversation about our families to help lighten the mood.

There was no denying it—Carey was interesting. She shared a couple of stories about her young life traveling with her parents through South and Central America. Her parents were missionaries, and they frequently went abroad to build schools and homes for disadvantaged families in impoverished areas while spreading the Gospel to nonbelievers.

I learned that Carey was born two months early in Ecuador, the day before her parents were supposed to fly back to the States and finally settle down for a prolonged period to raise their infant daughter. So instead of in a cushy American hospital, Carey was born, less than five pounds, in a village with no running water. She was more susceptible to sickness and contracted a fever that her parents believed was well over one hundred degrees. They couldn't know for sure because they had no access to a thermometer. One of the older women in the village took them into her home so the premature baby could rest more comfortably with her mother in a bed. She covered Carey completely in wet leaves from some tree or plant that was native to the area. Carey remained like that for days.

One of the most incredible parts of the story was that, fifty years prior, the woman who cared for Carey lost a child to a fever in the days immediately following birth. The woman had never forgiven herself for the little girl's death. She believed that Carey was sent from God as a way for her to atone for the mistake and make her way back into heaven. Carey got her real name from the deceased infant, who was known by her mother for only three days in the living world as Carina—a word that translates into English as "dear" or "beloved."

Eventually, Carey got better, but her family missed their flight home. They were also out of money, so it took another couple of months before they could find a phone and arrange a loan to buy tickets and come home.

When Carey turned five, she went on her first missionary trip with her parents to Guatemala. She estimated that she had been to at least ten countries by age twenty. But now she just wanted to stay in LA and be a college kid for a while. Her parents had just returned with her two younger brothers from a trip to Mexico. Carey had skipped the trip and spent her summer in Los Angeles, reading scripts and interning for a writing agency.

Her story kept unfolding, and I kept on asking questions. She stopped herself several times, insisting that she was talking too much and trying to turn the subject to me. But I was enjoying her stories and was happy to give my mind a break. I sat reveling in the view and listening to her talk about her fascinating life.

"What agency are you working for? Is it connected to a big studio?"

"I'm not actually working there. It's more like volunteer work."

"You said you're reading scripts? Are you like an editor?"

"Oh, no." Carey shook her head. "Studios get scripts all the time, and they will often ask a few different people to read them and make notes or recommend them to another reader."

"Scripts for movies?" I was genuinely curious.

"Yeah . . ." She said it like it was obvious.

"I assumed that a producer or a director would read them," I said, trying to understand how it worked.

"Oh, of course they do," she clarified. "This is like low-level screening to make notes only. Like I might read a script and answer questions like 'What genre is this?' 'Is there a lot of bad language?' 'Are there guns?' I just make basic notes. Sometimes one of the agents will ask me questions, or they'll ask what I thought."

"That sounds great! Have you ever read anything that got famous?"

"I started only this last summer, so nothing I've read has even been made. But I think two of the scripts I've read will be produced." She remembered something. "Oh yeah, I read one script that was like a scene for a rip-off of *Pretty Woman*, and I let the agent know."

"I feel like I am more excited by this than you are."

"You know, I have a couple of scripts I am reading now. I can let you read one."

"Sure, I would love to," I admitted. "Is that the work you had to do today?"

"What do you mean?"

"Last night, when I asked what you were doing today, you said you had to work."

"Oh, that? That's for PETS." She said the word as if I would know what she was talking about. "I can do that a little later today."

"What's PETS?"

"We didn't already talk about this?"

I went through the catalog of our past discussions. "No, I don't think so."

"PETS, it's a nonprofit in West Hollywood. It stands for Providing Emotional Therapy and Support. I thought we'd spoken about this before."

"Sorry, must have been some other dude. Is it like an animal shelter?"

"It's food and supply delivery for pets. Sometimes it's animal care, but I just do deliveries. We help take care of pets for HIV and AIDS patients in the area. They can't always . . ." She trailed off, but I understood the point she was making.

"That's amazing! I'm so impressed. How did you find that?"

"One of my bosses at the agency heads it up in West Hollywood. He was a TV producer for a long time and made a fortune, so I guess he just wants to give back. He still works with writers and producers, but he spends most of his time on this."

"And you have a bunch of deliveries today?"

"Well, I have a car, so I volunteer to drop off food and medicine and supplies. I have about seven drop-offs today."

"Am I keeping you from it?"

"I have time. I can do it after this. I told Nathan already—he's the guy who runs it. And he said it was more important to go on a . . ." She was about to say the word "date" again but stopped herself. "He said it was more important to go out and have fun. He's like my life coach."

I doubted that Carey needed a life coach and genuinely felt bad that I had made her second-guess if this was a date. After talking with her and getting to know her, I realized that she was interesting and smart and had high integrity. I was enjoying my time with her.

"Can't we go now? Can I go with you and help?"

"You want to deliver dog food?"

"Hell yeah!"

"Okay, let's go. I have to stop at the warehouse and pick one more thing up, so you may actually get to meet Nathan."

# Chapter 53

The walk from Westwood to the Delta Delta Gamma house on Hilgard Avenue, where Carey lived, took us about thirty minutes. She retrieved her key from her room while I waited in a foyer of sorts. She told me I could wait in a small space adjacent to the entryway called the Kissing Room.

I was amused to no end by the name of the room. "Why do you call it that?"

Carey grinned slyly. "I'll show you later."

I had gotten the gist, but I would be up for a more formal demonstration when we returned. I poked my head into the doorway of the famed chamber and observed a space about fifteen feet by twenty feet. The room was tastefully decorated with a bay window seat, several couches, and a few fancy chairs. It boasted elaborate curtains, rugs, and wallpaper. Had I not known better, I would have assumed I was getting a glimpse at a historical replica of a Victorian sitting room. I could see where the room would elicit just the right amount of classy romance while keeping the baser instincts of any visiting males at bay.

A thought struck me. I wondered how frequently two or more couples had found themselves tucked away in the Kissing Room, frantically pawing and gnawing at each other. I wondered if these couples ever caught sideways glimpses of each other in the throes of similar passion. On more than one of these occasions, I imagined a competition of sorts would break out. The thought amused me, and I reasoned that there were no losers in competitions like that.

I heard a familiar rhythmic drumming like sneakered footsteps bounding down a stairway and turned to see Carey taking the final steps. She had changed her clothes to a considerably more casual ensemble consisting of jeans, Chucks, and a pale-yellow woman's V-neck T-shirt that sported a faded tropical design emblazoned with the words "Hawaii Is for Loafers" in a fancy curlicued script.

"You changed," I noticed aloud.

"I did. We're going to be carrying bags, so . . ."

Carey and I illegally crossed Hilgard Avenue in a slight jog to avoid any crossing traffic. Somehow, she had scored a permanent parking spot in the visitors parking garage directly across from her sorority house. Her car was baking in the sun on the top level. We got in, and I recognized the smell of dry dog food right away.

She looked at me and scrunched her face apologetically. "Sorry about the smell."

"No problem," I assured her.

Carey set off north, and we navigated back onto Hilgard for a slight jog up the avenue until making an easy right onto the famed Sunset Boulevard. Nathan's warehouse wasn't a warehouse at all. From what I could tell, he was operating out of a decommissioned West Hollywood hotel. The entire complex had been converted into apartments. The grounds were perfectly manicured in what I can best describe as "old Hollywood and palm tree" motif. The exterior walls of the various buildings were painted in a pastel blue with darker shades of the same color to make the art deco accents and trim pop.

# Chapter 54

As if by telepathy, Nathan had anticipated our exact arrival time and was waiting with his toy dog in his arms, directing Carey to pull off and continue onto a long horseshoe driveway, which was hidden almost entirely from passing traffic by thick and well-groomed vegetation.

Nathan was a dead ringer for the actor Nathan Lane, with slightly sharper features. He greeted Carey warmly through the window. "Hello, darling!" His energy was apparent in just these two words. He continued emphatically, but sincerely, "Thank you so much. I don't know what I would do without you! I have everything ready for you inside."

We both got out of the car, and Nathan took a quick inventory of me. "And you're Jeff." He said it *and* kind of asked it, but he mostly said it. I saw him glance at Carey, who blushed immediately. "Are you still on your date?"

His question hung in the air for a moment, and neither she nor I did anything with it, so Nathan resolved it for himself. "Well, no matter! You're here, and I appreciate that."

"Jeff heard what I was doing this afternoon," Carey informed him. "And he asked if he could come with me and help with the deliveries."

"Did he?" Nathan smiled warmly at me. "Well, that was nice of you. Our customers will love meeting a new person. They don't get many visitors. And you're in luck because I have two more drop-offs, if you think you can handle it."

"No problem," I answered promptly and then realized that I should have checked with Carey first. Turning to her, I added, "If you have the time."

"Of course."

"Come on in." Nathan walked back to the old front door of the hotel and held it open for us. "I have some medicine in the refrigerator. Carina sweetie"—he used her real name—"I need you to drop this off first because we can't let it get too warm. And I have a few more large bags in the warehouse."

Apparently, Nathan had commandeered the converted hotel lobby (which was now serving as a large main office for PETS) and a few of the spacious carports. The various and plentiful PETS supplies were stored meticulously on shelves lining the walls of the office and throughout the carports.

"Jeff . . . ," Nathan began and paused. "Come here, let me show you."

I followed him into a small room behind a counter and through a door leading to the closest carport. "I need you to put four more of these bags in Carina's car. Can you do that for me?"

"I can."

"I left it open!" Carey called to us, referring to her car.

"And you," Nathan said, turning back to her, "my sweet angel, let me get you the two additional addresses and some instructions for the insulin."

Carey was delighted by the news. "You got it?"

"I did."

"How?"

"Mexico." Nathan's voice remained audible as he walked behind her back into his office. "I had a friend bring it up from Mexico. I can get all I need, and it's so much more affordable."

"That's such great news!"

I picked up the first forty-pound bag of dog food and showed myself out of the carport in the direction of the car. Unbeknownst to me, Carey had already opened the trunk. I realized I could get one or maybe two more bags into the trunk before I would be forced to wedge the final bags into the back seat. This was going to be a packed car.

I heard them speaking faintly as I deadlifted the next forty-pounder. Carey was insisting, "It's good. He asks a lot of questions, and he listens."

"That's sweet. That's not like most guys his age."

"Tell me about it! But he doesn't share a lot."

"Well . . . At least he doesn't sell drugs."

"Nathan!" she reprimanded.

I decided quickly that I didn't want to hear them talk about me and drug dealers. I went about completing the task at hand before noisily entering the office from the front door.

"All done?" Nathan asked.

"I am."

"Excellent! Can I offer you something to drink before you leave? I have bottled water and juice."

"Sure, I'll have any juice you have," I requested.

Carey was sitting at a table to the side with a Thomas Guide open. She was academically running her index finger down a page. She spoke in my direction without looking at me. "How well do you know this area?"

"Not at all, but I can read the Thomas Guide if you need me to play copilot."

"Okay, I'll take you up on that. I am just plotting one more address. I have all the drop-offs marked with a sticky note. You'll have to help me navigate."

Nathan reentered with two bottles of apple juice. He spoke as he placed one on the table next to Carey. "Jeff, do you like theater?"

"I do. I haven't seen much of it, but I like what I have seen."

"Good, then you're in luck! My friend wrote a superb play, and it's beginning a run at the Village Playhouse on Wednesday night in Westwood. I have two tickets for the opening, but unfortunately, I will not be able to attend. Can I give you the tickets and trust you to escort the lovely Ms. Carina safely to and from the show?"

As he finished the question, he offered me the drink with an outstretched hand. Carey looked up at me, apparently wondering how I would respond. There was no way I could say no.

I accepted the drink and met her eyes. "Thanks," I said instinctively to Nathan, still looking toward my "date" and trying to read her expression. "What do you think? You want to join me for a play on Wednesday night?"

"Of course." Her answer was honest and uncomplicated. "I'd love to."

Nathan was already walking to his desk. Upon reaching it, he slid open the top drawer and retrieved two stiff strips of paper. "Thank you, guys.

You're doing me a favor because I'd hate to think these tickets were going to waste."

# Chapter 55

Carey and I finally got our bearings and were confident we knew exactly where we were headed for the first and most crucial drop-off of the day. With that concern behind us, we were able to discuss other matters.

"That was nice of Nathan. Did you see the prices on those tickets? They're $108 each!"

Carey smiled and glanced up at the rearview in anticipation of a lane change. "He's always doing stuff like that. He doesn't pay me, so he's always giving me gifts."

"It's nice of you to do all this work for him."

"I like doing it. I'm happy to do it for free. It's such a simple thing, and we make these patients feel better." She paused to think about it. "We make them feel a *little* better."

"It's amazing . . . what you guys do."

"Thanks, Jeff." The use of my name caught me by surprise. "It is nice, but I think most people are nice. We all have a little extra to give. We should give it freely—without expecting anything. The world would be better."

Carey and I sat in the car for several moments, enjoying the silence. My mind was spinning a bit. This girl was quite different from most of the people I spent my time with. She was kind and selfless. The more I got to know her, the more I was impressed by her approach to life.

After a few more moments of staring straight ahead through the windshield, she finally broke the quiet. "What do you like to do in your free time?"

The question caught me off guard, and I struggled to think of a good answer. "Lots of stuff."

"But what do you *really* like to do? If you had a whole day to yourself, what would you do?"

When she put it like that, the answer was easy for me. "I'd ride my bike out to the cliff at the end of San Vicente Boulevard."

She perked up at this. "Where's that?"

"You know Brentwood, right?"

"Yeah."

"Just jump on the main boulevard and ride west all the way to the end," I explained. "I go there and read sometimes and just look out at the water. Sometimes I'll ride down to Pacific Palisades or back all the way up to Will Rogers State Historic Park and ride up the fire trails as high as I can go for the view."

"I didn't know you were such a fan of biking."

"I'm not really an avid biker. I'm not fast or competitive. I just like to cruise and be out on my own."

Carey reacted genuinely, taking it all in. "Cool."

"Do you have a bike?"

"I don't, but there are a couple at the house. I'm sure I could borrow one if I needed to." She caught herself. "But . . . I don't ride a lot. I don't know if I could make it all the way to the ocean."

"You could. You only need to cruise. It's not about getting there fast—it's just about getting there."

She smiled. "You should put that on a T-shirt."

"What, 'Biking Is for Loafers'?"

We spent the rest of the day delivering forty-pound bags of dog food, medicine, and other supplies to various homes and apartments throughout West Hollywood and Hollywood. The process was both sad and uplifting at the same time. Most of the patients we visited were in bad shape.

When we'd left PETS, I'd had no idea what to expect. I hadn't even considered it and was not mentally prepared to see, firsthand, what an awful toll AIDS took on its victims. Many of the patients were severely emaciated and displayed a bouquet of open sores ranging in color from pink to red to purple to black on their faces, arms, hands, necks, and foreheads—pretty much anywhere we could see. Every one of them, without exception, smiled broadly when Carey arrived at their door with their goodies.

Carey was amazing. She knew everyone's name and details about their lives. She hugged everyone and got down on the floor to greet all the animals. While in the patients' homes, she gave all of her attention to the individuals we were serving and regarded me only to give instructions about how to store food and how to make the pets' environments more sanitary and comfortable. I did everything as I was told. I was impressed by how immediately and naturally this sweet girl had transformed into my boss without giving it a second thought.

293

My interactions with the patients were quite awkward. I was polite but said as little as possible. In almost every instance, my timidity was returned with the same look of slight shame. AIDS creeps up on people quickly, and victims do not need to think back very far to a time when they were not treated as pariahs. My averted eyes and minimal conversation were nothing new to anyone I encountered, and my discomfort was a reminder of the world's discomfort. I did the best I could, but it wasn't that good.

After four stops, Carey turned to me in the car and squeezed my hand. She looked at me seriously and said, "This isn't easy, Jeff. It's not for everyone, but you're doing great. You want to keep going?"

"Yeah, let's finish. I'll loosen up. I just . . ." I couldn't finish the thought.

She started the car. "Don't worry. You're doing great."

Other than the hugs and kisses received from their pets, it dawned on me that most of the individuals we were serving had been cut off from the world. The efforts of PETS to help AIDS victims adopt and care for cuddly pets gave those sick individuals access to consistent emotional support. In my opinion, the genuine interest and affection that Carey displayed during her drop-offs were almost as important. Nathan knew what she was all about, and his comments about her being an angel hadn't been just playful rhetoric. He knew she was special.

Carey and I arrived at her sorority house after dark. We had dropped off her car in the parking garage, darted back across Hilgard Avenue, and walked up the steps toward her front door. I had no idea what the night had in store. We had talked about maybe getting dinner or going to a movie, and although I was still a little pensive from the day's activities, the general buzz of Westwood and all the people milling about on the streets were improving my state of mind. As we neared the front entry, the thoughts of the Kissing Room came to mind, and my mood improved significantly.

"She's here!" I heard a girl's voice call through the door. Then another muffled voice came in response.

Naomi stepped out of the door and snapped, "Carey, where have you been?"

"With Jeff. Why?"

"We have the chancellor's banquet tonight."

"That's tonight?" she said to Naomi but looked over at me.

"Yes, and we're all leaving in fifteen minutes. You *have* to get changed."

Naomi was dressed formally. Several other girls stood behind her in similar attire. They all looked very nice.

Carey shot me an "I'm sorry" look and explained, "I really have to do this."

"It's no problem." I smiled. "We'll hang out another night. Wednesday, we'll see the play."

"Thank you. Thanks for everything today." She gave me an endearing look. We had spent a nice day together and had gotten to know each other well. Now would have been a perfect time to lean over and give her a kiss. We hadn't kissed since the Blues Traveler show. She wanted me to, and I wanted to. But neither of us was willing to make such a bold move with so many watchful eyes upon us.

"Go," I insisted. "Get ready, or you'll be late."

Carey darted up the stairs, calling to no one in particular, "Don't leave without me! I only need two minutes!"

Naomi spoke under her breath to no one in particular. "Please tell me she's going to spend more than two minutes getting ready for this."

I was left alone in the foyer with a dozen or so formally dressed sorority girls. Predictably, Naomi spoke first. "How was the date?"

Offering the least possible information, I exchanged a few words with her about my day with Carey and excused myself so they could "all focus on getting ready to go."

I felt like a horrible person because I had to admit that Naomi and her sorority sisters all looked so damn sexy when they dressed up. I wished that Carey could have adopted a similar style. I didn't expect her to look like Dara, but at a minimum, she could take a few beauty tips from her roommates. I knew I was taking a shallow position, but I couldn't help it. Carey was revealing herself as an exceptional person, but there was a lingering physical part of the equation that I just couldn't get over.

Cutting through campus, the walk home was about thirty minutes door to door. Upon reaching my place, I noticed a white rectangle hanging on the door in the exact place where I had left it this morning. Apparently, I had not received any unwanted visitors.

# Chapter 56

Monday and Tuesday were relatively uneventful. The envelope remained frozen in place on the outside of our door, and there were even moments when I had completely forgotten about the issue.

Carey came over on Tuesday night to drop off ice cream, and as promised, she brought me one of the scripts she had read for Nathan. "I thought you would love it, and I asked Nathan, and he said you could borrow it. But please don't lose it. I'll need it back."

"Cool!" I looked at the title and read it aloud. "*Nice Is Nice.*"

Francis was already digging into his pint of ice cream. "What's it about?"

"It's about a love triangle," she launched in. "It's about a boy who meets a beautiful Russian spy, and he falls in love. But the spy is actually a horrible person, and she's trying to kill his whole family and two goofy roommates. And in the end, he should have just dated the sweet girl from his hometown . . ."

Francis and I looked at each other. I spoke first. "You're kidding, right?"

Carey smiled and pointed at me. "Gotcha!"

Now I was the one blushing. "Good one, you did get me."

"It's actually pronounced '*Neese' Is Nice*, as in Nice, France. It's about some college friends that go on a backpacking adventure across Europe," she clarified. "It's good. It's funny. I think you'll like it."

She didn't want to tell me too much about the script so as not to give it away. But she said the characters reminded her of Dylan, Francis, and me. I put the manuscript in my room on my bookshelf for safekeeping.

When I returned, Francis and Carey were talking about how successful the chancellor's banquet had been for her. She was buzzing. She had gone to the event that night with an important agenda: she was trying to sponsor an outreach day for at-risk youth in the local area, and part of her master plan was to receive an official school sponsorship. The chancellor—who rarely, if ever, showed up at these events—had been at the banquet. Since none of the other attendees had anything to discuss with him, Carey approached him straightaway and spent ten minutes selling him the idea. She said he liked "the direction she was heading" and could see that this was "something the university could be interested in exploring further."

The chancellor had encouraged her to put together a formal proposal and offered her an hour-long meeting at some undetermined point in the future for her to present her ideas for a sorority-led curriculum. He asked her to assemble a group and set the plan in motion. He was confident that he would like the ideas and assumed there was "something they could do."

Carey asked me no less than five times what I thought he'd meant by the phrase "something they could do."

I assured her she would get all the sponsorship and funding she needed. She simply had to come up with a great idea. Francis, who was reclining on the sofa next to us and nearly done with his pint of mint chip, spoke through a big gooey bite. "You should have an ice cream party."

"That's not a bad idea," I agreed.

Carey pursed her lips and looked at the two of us like we were simpletons.

"What?" I asked defensively.

She explained that while feeding at-risk kids ice cream might be a nice treat, it wouldn't do anything for them and wouldn't teach them anything. Her idea was to bring them to a homeless shelter in Skid Row and ask them to wash clothes and serve meals for an evening. After that, she figured she could bring in a speaker who had once lived in the same shelter or a similar one.

Francis and I just sat and listened to her as she continued.

Carey wanted the speaker to talk about the positive impact of education and the negative impact of crime and drug use. "Somebody has to tell them the harsh truth," she asserted.

Her words grew more passionate with each passing thought. "We need to show them a strong example and teach them that unless they refuse to play victim and unless *they* take full control of their lives, they could all end up in a shelter too—and that's unacceptable! I think the best thing we can do is to teach them the power of serving others. Show them that someone always has it worse than them. Show them that they have the power to help others. If we teach them that lesson, then they will see that they also have the power to help themselves. They are not victims. They are powerful little humans."

Francis and I were speechless, and a moment passed in contemplative silence before my roommate decided to lighten the mood. "And *then* you give them an ice cream party?"

Carey chuckled. "Yes, and *then* I give them lots and lots of ice cream!"

"I think the chancellor will like that plan," I offered sincerely.

She was still excited. "But this can't be just a onetime thing! We need to develop a program so we can reach more and more kids."

I spent the rest of the night in silent awe of Carey. I had a number of conflicting emotions going on inside of me. But when I saw her in moments like this—when she was in charge and doing her part to change the world—I could only be in awe. She was like the sun, making everything around her brighter.

Eventually, Dylan showed up sans Naomi; and the four of us sat around, telling silly stories and laughing wildly about everything and nothing. Not only had Carey put me in a great mood, but she had the same effect on both Dylan and Francis. The night was both effortless and enjoyable, to say the least.

I couldn't get Todd's golf club analogy out of my mind, and I almost brought it up but realized it would require way too much explanation to make any sense, so I kept it all to myself.

I had an early morning the next day, so I had to turn in at a reasonable hour. Carey followed me into my room. She noticed the phone lying in lifeless pieces on my desk. "What happened here?"

"Nothing."

It was late, and each of us had things to do in the morning. We both understood that she would spend the night, but she set boundaries before we even kissed. "I want to spend time with you like this, but I'm not ready to . . ." She trailed off. I could tell she was a little nervous to say the words and maybe a little nervous to be there at all.

I knew what she meant, and I had no problem with it. I didn't see the need to move so fast—and anyway, she was not ready. I was thankful to have her with me in my bed, to have her wrapping her arms around me and kissing me deeply. With every touch and every soft sound that she made, I knew she was real. This was no dream. Carey was a real woman, and she was lying with me, affecting me and responding to my effect on her. She was reserving parts of herself, and that was her choice. Still, I saw her underlying passion was honest and obvious and animal and real.

Perhaps, in time, we would choose to explore this innocent ritual further. But for now, this moment—this urgent passionate moment— was perfect. She was comfortable and safe, and I was comfortable and safe. Waves of contentment surrounded our bodies as the endorphins buried in the most basic parts of our brains were released and crawled deliberately across every inch of our bare skin, jumping from body to body and back again in unpredictable and exhilarating patterns. To evoke that kind of passion from another person is a rare and wonderful thing. I felt my own similar feelings stirring from within. I understood that all of it was real.

"Jeff . . . Jeff . . ." Carey was gently tapping my shoulder. I blinked awake. She was crouching over me. She was already dressed. The room was dark, and no light crept in through the windows.

I smiled, turning to face her. "Hey."

"I'm going to take off. I have to get ready for class."

"Yeah, no problem. I need to get to the pool anyway." I shuddered to think about it. I had to open the pool at six and stay there for ninety minutes, and then I had to run to my political science class all the way across campus. I hated my new Wednesday morning schedule, but at least my new responsibilities were helping me pay off my swelling credit card debt.

There was a momentary pause. "I'll see you tonight?"

"What's tonight?" I asked.

"The play."

"Oh yeah, of course. Do you still want to get dinner first?"

We decided that I would walk over and we would go into Westwood a little early and grab a bite.

# Chapter 57

Wednesday on campus was nice. The days were growing a little colder, but my mind was warming up. I had a date with Carey that night, and where Wednesday had become a source of anxiety for the past few weeks, I was feeling good on this day. I entered poetry class expecting to sit alone in the last row. I knew Dara was not coming, and for the first time, I didn't care.

I knew something was up when Anson walked in with Can, flashed me a shitty smile, and pointed at me. He went to his usual seat and set his bag down, all the while looking at me and smiling. "Dude, I had no idea . . . no idea . . ."

I didn't know what he was talking about, and I searched Can's face for some answer or indication. She rolled her eyes as if to say "He's an ass."

Anson slipped past two seats back to my row and extended his hand. "I just want to shake your hand and congratulate you." His words were full of sarcasm.

I didn't take his hand. "What?"

He gave me a creepy smile. "I saw Dara on Saturday night."

"What are you talking about?"

"I saw her at her club. She looked even better than I imagined." His creepy smile grew wicked. "I wanted to congratulate you. She was the girl from your poem, right?"

Can spoke up. "Anson, leave it alone. Why do you always have to be such a jerk?"

"What are you talking about?" I asked.

"Wait . . . You don't know, do you?"

"God! Just shut up already!" Can called out again.

My mind started putting a few pieces together. "Don't know what?"

"Your Russian girlfriend, she's a stripper!" Anson laughed. "You really didn't know? She's like the queen of that place. I couldn't even get next to her. I had a crispy dollar bill waiting for her."

I waved him away. Something like anger surged through me. "Dude, fuck off!"

Anson was a punk, and punks liked to stir shit up. But the minute he saw I was getting upset, he threw his hands up and backed away to his seat in full retreat. Of course, he kept the shitty look on his face. He sat and turned to Can. "He doesn't know."

She turned her back to him. "You're an ass."

I sat there, enraged and incensed. I wanted to be mad at Anson. I might have even thought I was mad at Dara. However, time has offered me a bit of wisdom. I now understand that I was painfully frustrated, in that moment, by my unchecked naïveté.

My truest source of irritation stemmed from the fact that I was so far in over my head. I didn't understand how any of these pieces could fit together. How was my beautiful friend taking a poetry class by day and taking her clothes off for money at night? I had a skewed and naïve perception. To that point, I'd had this one-dimensional notion of a stripper as some faceless occupant of the underworld who danced on seedy stages in smoke-filled rooms. I did not know that they could be college girls who read great books by candlelight and ate salads from Montecito Pizza Kitchen.

I sat there stewing in my seat for a couple of minutes until I couldn't take the swirling and confounding thoughts any longer. I had to escape. I picked up my things and walked out of class. I didn't bother to look back. But I was sure I heard Anson, in a voice just barely loud enough to hear, calling "Aww!" in mock consolation.

# Chapter 58

Just when I thought the day couldn't get any worse, I noticed the envelope on the door, which had become an unmoved fixture in our lives, now tilted at the opposite angle. A ten-digit phone number was written messily across the back. The letter inside had been removed.

I figured there was no time like the present, so I let myself into the apartment and called the number straightaway on the phone closest to the door. I waited only two rings before a gruff voice answered. "What?"

I was annoyed and didn't hide it. "You left your phone number on my door."

"That was a cute letter," the voice admitted.

"So does that work?"

"Yeah, that works. Are they still on schedule?"

"Yes, I called them yesterday to check in. Everything is on schedule. Do you want me to bring it to you when it's done?"

"No, just park it outside your place when it's done. We'll get it."

That was much easier for me. "Fine."

He thought for a moment. "What's the name of the shop? I want to check on the progress myself."

I repeated my sentiment from the letter. "I'd prefer not to bring anyone else into this."

His voice was calm. "I prefer not to come down there and beat it out of you."

"You're really tough for an errand boy." I just didn't care at that point. "Do you deliver groceries too?"

He laughed. "You're funny, I'll give you that. Give me the name of the shop. I won't ask you this nicely again."

I told him the name of the shop. I heard him whispering it back to himself stiffly as he wrote the words down. I figured this small task might have been a little more taxing for him than most.

"Can you tell me something?" I asked.

"What?" Now he was annoyed.

My voice shook ever so slightly. I didn't know why. "You know the girl from that night?"

He laughed. "What about her?"

I felt like a fool for asking, but I had to know. "Does she really work at a strip club?"

He laughed again. "Good luck on your finals, college boy." His tone was one of condescension.

About half an hour later, the phone rang again. Matt from the auto body shop called to tell me he thought my father had just called and asked about the car. He figured he should call me right away because he remembered, when I'd first come in, I'd been trying to hide everything from my dad. That was the story I had told him anyway.

I told the mechanic that everything was fine and I appreciated that he was looking out for me. He confided, "I've crashed my dad's car a few times, so I know the feeling."

I wondered to myself if a berserk Belarusian woman had ever thrown an oversized paving stone through the back window of his dad's car, but I didn't ask.

# Chapter 59

I picked up Carey at the ΔΔΓ house as planned. She was dressed up for the occasion, which I appreciated. She wore a red sleeveless A-line dress that hit her at midthigh. She added just a little mascara, which made her unique eyes even more pronounced. I was not used to seeing her in makeup and dolled up like this, but I thought she looked good.

"I like that dress," I complimented her.

"You sure? You don't think it looks weird?"

I wanted to encourage this behavior. "No, it looks great."

"I'm just not used to dressing up. It's Naomi's. She insisted that I wear it tonight."

"Well, tell her I said it looks nice."

She pulled a black-and-red wrap around her shoulders, and she was ready to go. She looked ready for a casual dinner in the village and for a more formal night at the theater. I was impressed. We walked down into Westwood from sorority row and passed the Village Playhouse. The awning proudly announced "Opening Night!"

"I'm excited," Carey admitted.

The play was called *And If I Don't Want To?* It was by Berkeley Spanos. We had almost two hours to kill before the posted start time.

"Where should we eat?" I asked.

"I wasn't sure if I could walk in these heels," Carey said, thinking out loud. "But I think I'm okay now."

She wanted to go to an Italian restaurant farther down Westwood Boulevard. She led the way, and I followed willingly. The restaurant was nice, and we were seated in a corner table with a view of the entire dining room.

The waiter showed up and asked if we would like to start with a glass of wine. Carey looked at me, and her eyes widened. Neither of us was twenty-one, but I quickly I asked, "Can we get two glasses of the house red?" This was something I had heard my dad say at many other Italian restaurants when ordering a glass for my mom and himself.

The waiter said, "Very good. I'll be back in a minute to take your orders."

Carey whispered, "What if they ask for ID?"

"Then we probably get kicked out? I don't know."

She was good with that answer. "Okay."

The ruse worked, and we were never bothered about our IDs. In fact, we each had a second glass with our entrée. The second glass was even more delicious than the first.

Dinner was nice, and I laid down my credit card when the check came. The total, after tip, was nearly $90. I would need to sit in a lifeguard stand for five hours to pay for this. I had a 6:00 a.m. shift the next morning for three hours. That would barely even cover the wine!

On a more positive note, this dinner had been the first time in my life I had ever paid for a meal with a credit card. I won't lie—I loved the feeling, and I could see how that could get you into a lot of trouble. With every swipe of my card, I would be digging myself a little deeper into the ever-growing hole of debt that I would eventually have to climb out of someday.

I left the restaurant with all my cash still in my pocket, two bowls of vino in my belly, and the Look on my arm. Aside from some silly nagging thoughts bubbling up in the back of my mind, life was good.

Carey and I got to the theater with plenty of time and observed a large group of theatergoers mingling in the external courtyard. The crowd comprised an older demographic. From my quick inventory, I reasoned that we were probably the only people younger than forty in the immediate crowd. There were tables and some light refreshments set up for the guests. I observed a network of heat lamps evenly spaced, which seemed to provide comfort against the cool night air.

"Your names?" the friendly woman asked as we passed a makeshift check-in station leading to the Playhouse courtyard. She was ready with a printed list of guests on a stapled stack of three pages.

"Is this for the play tonight? We have printed tickets. Will that work?" I asked.

"This is for the opening night reception, for members," the woman explained. To stay warm, she wore a red fleece headband, which framed her kind face. She had deep, but earnest, wrinkles at the corners of her eyes and around her mouth, which were accentuated by her easy smile.

"Uh-oh," Carey worried aloud. "I doubt we're on there."

"I'm sorry," the woman said, smiling apologetically. "You can wait in the lobby, and the doors will open in about thirty minutes."

We started to walk away, and I wondered if we could leverage Nathan's name. I turned back to the friendly woman. "Hey."

"Yes?"

"Not sure if this will matter, but we're guests of . . ." I turned to Carey. "What's Nathan's last name?"

Carey looked at me suspiciously. "Acker, but I don't think we should—"

"Nathan Acker?" the woman questioned, her face lighting up.

Carey responded instinctively, "Yeah, he gave us his tickets."

She was genuinely excited to discuss the man. "How do you know Nathan?"

"I read scripts for him and work for him at PETS," Carey said, a little unsure of herself.

"You're a PETS volunteer?" The woman's smile brightened even more. She excused herself for just a moment to greet two other members, an older man and a woman, and allowed them passage into the reception area. She then turned her attention back to us. "I was a PETS volunteer! I worked with Nathan for four years, when he was just getting started."

"Are you Millie?" Carey asked, barely holding back her excitement.

The woman was surprised to learn that Carey knew her name. "How did you know?"

"Nathan talks about you all the time!" Carey gushed. "I feel like I know you."

"Aww . . ." Millie was touched. "Can I give you a hug?" She stepped from around the table, and they hugged. "I don't know why I'm crying."

"No, don't do that. Now I'm going to cry, and I'm wearing makeup," Carey joked. "I only wear it once a year, and I always end up crying."

She and Millie both laughed at this. They stood and chatted for a moment, their conversation getting deep very quickly and revealing the nature of their bond. Delivering supplies for PETS was an emotionally draining task and forced the volunteers to face disease and death on a regular basis. The job was not just about delivering dog food—it was about restoring dignity as well. I marveled at their instant connection.

Millie led us into the reception area. There were a few people she wanted Carey to meet, including some of the board members and donors who helped keep PETS funded and moving forward. Every single person we met praised Nathan and the amount of time and personal resources he had put into the nonprofit. Because of her work with the organization, Carey became an instant celebrity among the attendees, and she handled her elevated status with the simplicity and grace you would have expected from her.

She recognized a friend from the PETS office, whom she greeted as Birk. It turned out that Birk was short for Berkeley Spanos, the author of tonight's play. I also found it amusing that almost every woman who greeted Carey said, "Oh my god, you're gorgeous! Let me introduce you to my grandson. He's a . . ." A doctor or a lawyer or a successful actor— the list went on.

Carey always turned to me and swooningly told them, "Sorry, I'm already dating a rock star."

The most impressive thing about Carey was the ease with which she commanded the room. It was easy to get fooled by her softer side. For the most part, she seemed to be the quiet one who let her friends do all the talking. But after having spent last weekend with her during the PETS delivery rounds, I understood from firsthand experience how assertive and in control she could be.

On this night, the subject of nonprofits was in the air, and it gave her the idea to start approaching a few of the power players in the room.

Millie provided a little guidance about who she could talk to, and Carey took it from there. She was so disarming. She would start her pitch with something simple like "Can I tell you about a project I am working on with the chancellor?"

She didn't need to specify *which* chancellor because, as luck would have it, the Village Playhouse had been owned by UCLA for the past two years. The university's chancellor was already involved with this theater, and most of the high rollers in that reception knew him personally. I saw Carey give her sales pitch to no less than three people. They were all impressed with this whip-smart coed who was running an initiative to get UCLA sororities active in improving the future lives of the disadvantaged youth in the city of Los Angeles.

She got two "maybes" and one definite commitment, on the spot, for funding. It was incredible. She closed the conversation by saying, "I'm going to call the chancellor tomorrow and tell him that you're joining the team, Mr. Goldblatt."

The man exchanged a look with his wife and said, "Does she remind you of anyone?"

His wife smiled and directed her response to Carey, saying, "You're doing great, honey. Don't ever let up."

The man finally replied to Carey's comment. "Please do that. Call him tomorrow and tell him Goldblatt's on board."

The house began blinking the courtyard lights, and everyone took the cue to finish their drinks and make their way inside to find their seat.

I took Carey's hand. We had not held hands prior to that point. I don't know why I did it—I just had to.

# Chapter 60

*And If I Don't Want To?* was a complex and poignant play following the life of three siblings who were raised in a small Texas town by a military father and a church-choir-coordinating mother. The story followed a twenty-year swath of time leading up to the untimely passing of the siblings' father, which forced them all to come back home and confront old and unresolved demons.

I had not seen many plays up to that point in my life, and I didn't know much about theater, but I thought the story was powerful and important. I was happy that I had gotten to meet the playwright. That added an extra level of depth for me. Overall, I was filled with the sense that life was short and you needed to live for yourself.

Leaving the theater was a significantly less social event than entering. All the interesting people who were so happy to meet us before the show were now tired, and their only concern was remembering where they'd parked their cars. Carey and I made our way out of the theater and into the cold night air. We exchanged a few parting smiles with some of our new friends and walked uninterrupted out to the street. We turned right in the direction of Hilgard Avenue.

I shared my opinions about the play with her, and we agreed on most of it. She had enjoyed it very much and received a similar message about how important it was to live life for yourself and not for anyone else. We both felt lucky to have shared such a great experience. I mused aloud about what we could get Nathan as a thank-you gift, but we couldn't think of anything good. We agreed we would give it some thought over the next couple of days.

We got to Carey's door around eleven, but we were both tired from our nocturnal activities the night before and from getting up early that morning. Add to that, I had to be at the pool at 6:00 a.m. the following day. We tried to set a time for our next date. But with study groups, work schedules, and volunteering, there wasn't much free time for either of us. She said she had full days of PETS deliveries on both Saturday and Sunday, and on Saturday night, she was hosting a kickoff meeting with her newly assembled team for the Chancellor's Initiative. She figured using the chancellor's name would help lock down his support. Despite all her excitement and Goldblatt's recent commitment, the university's involvement in the project was still up in the air.

"Sorry, Jeff. Maybe I can bring some ice cream after work next Tuesday."

I had an idea. "Hey, can I join you on Saturday and help you with PETS?"

Carey's face lit up. "Are you serious?"

"Yeah, I think it's important work, and I want to spend time with you," I explained. "Is that okay, or would I be getting in the way?"

"No! I can use the help, and so can Nathan. This is a perfect thank-you for the tickets!" She was elated. "I can also pick up a couple more deliveries now that I have some more muscle." She winked.

"Well, I don't want to brag, but that Oro's Gym picture says it all."

Carey and I shared a sweet good night kiss, and I set off on foot back to my apartment. I knew I shouldn't have, but I stayed on the Westwood streets during the walk home and drifted a little farther south so that I would pass right in front of the Gayley Gardens apartment complex. I glanced up at the front staircase and looped around to Weyburn Place so that I might also get a view of the back balcony as I ascended the sloped alleyway.

# Chapter 61

I went to class, studied, and sat in the lifeguard tower for several hours on Thursday and Friday. A couple of my coworkers were willing to give up their shifts, and I logged over twenty hours for the week, which was great for my bottom line.

Friday night was a bit of a dud. After a few uninspired rounds of drinks at Harrington's, I decided that I was tired and slipped out through a side door to head back to my apartment. I knew I would be busy the next day schlepping forty-pound bags of dog food up apartment stairwells, and I wanted to be well rested.

The night's sleep served me well. I woke up, and the room was already bright. I heard the phone in the living room ringing and remembered that my own phone had been decommissioned. I needed to get a new one. I heard someone padding down the hall to my doorway, and a light knocking came at my door.

"Jeff." It was Espy's voice.

"Come in."

She poked her head in, her red streaks framing her face. "Phone, for you."

"Thanks," I said, stretching and yawning.

Espy closed the door, and I rolled out of bed and threw on jeans and a T-shirt. By the time I made it out into the living room, Espy was curled in a ball on the couch, reading a huge math textbook. No paper, no pencil—just the book.

"Nerd!" I called as I walked by her.

"Cracka!" she retorted without looking up.

I laughed. "When did you start answering our phone?"

"I wanted to let the boys sleep. They had a late night."

Carey had told me the day before that she was planning to pick me up in the morning and we would get coffee and head over to PETS to load up her car.

I picked up the phone and started speaking without saying hello. "Let me guess, you're coming to get me right now, and you wanted to make sure I was up—"

"Jeff," a Belarusian accent replied.

My expression froze. I looked at Espy, and she turned quickly, trying to mask the fact that she had been spying on me. She exhaled sharply and stood, making a straight "zip the lip" motion across her mouth, which I took to mean she wouldn't tell anyone about the call. She walked down the hall, and I heard a door open and close behind her.

I returned to the call. "Hey . . . What's up?"

She sounded distressed. "Can you meet today?"

"Sure. When?"

"This morning?"

"This morning is a little tough," I began explaining. "Do you think you could—"

"Jeff, is it possible? Could you come over now?" She waited for my response, but I remained silent. Dara asked again, sounding desperate. "Please, Jeff. I know I haven't been the best friend, but could you do this for me please? I really need a friend right now."

I could have turned my back on her, and that probably would have been the end of this story. But I couldn't do that. I'll admit—I wanted to see her and smell her and sit close to her and all those things. But more than that, I was responding to the genuine distress I heard in her voice. She was hurting over something and asking me for help. I couldn't let her down.

The last time I had seen her was the night that I'd pulled her out of that horrible man's bathroom. She'd been angry and nearly broken and had stormed off before I could even talk to her. I'd wondered about her since that moment. I'd heard from Anson that she had been taking her clothes off onstage for men, and I wondered if she was okay. I knew that if I could just see her and help her, she would be better, and she would love the way that I made her feel. Maybe she would love me too. I had to go to her and try to help her.

Unfortunately, going to see Dara that morning meant that I would have to back out of my commitment with Carey and PETS. I thought quickly and invented a plausible story about having misread my work schedule. I called Carey immediately, and one of her sorority sisters picked up. She reported that Carey had already left for the day to do her volunteer work. I assumed that meant she was already on the way to my place. I thanked the voice on the other end of the phone and figured I would see Carey at my front door in short order.

I showered quickly and got ready. I even put on my work clothes to help sell the lie I was prepared to tell. All the while, I listened for the doorbell to sound, but no sound came. I then waited by the door for a short while, but Carey didn't show up. I called her house again, and the same friendly girl answered. I told her to relay the message about my new shift at work and to please relay that I was very sorry.

I still had a funny feeling, so I cracked open the yellow pages, searching for a PETS listing. I saw the name and recognized the related address from our visit to see Nathan the prior weekend. I called the number and got the answering machine. I was relieved that I didn't have to lie directly to him. "Nathan, this is Jeff. I'm supposed to be with Carey today, but I'm getting called into work. I tried to call her, but she already left for the day. Can you please tell her about my schedule change? And can you tell her I'm sorry too?"

I wasn't proud of my actions, but I felt like I had covered my bases. I left the apartment and walked briskly to Dara's, hoping that I would *not* see Carey driving by. Still wearing my lifeguard clothes, I was prepared to tell her that I was on my way to work. I hoped she wouldn't realize that I was walking in the wrong direction.

I felt odd walking down my own street while trying to remain hidden from view. I wondered if this was the shame that drug users felt when they were going out of their way to lie and manipulate for a fix. Was I addicted to Dara? Was I that pathetic? Was I really trying to avoid contact with Carey? I thought back to the night at the theater and how brightly Carey had shone. I felt like maybe I was the shriveled carcass of a dead animal that couldn't withstand the brilliance of the sun.

I came upon Dara's balcony and observed the half-open door. The now-familiar Beethoven sonata fluttered down to me. I wondered if Dara was the moon, and I was more suited to worship her blue hues of nocturnal indifference.

# Chapter 62

Dara was waiting for me with the front door ajar. I peeked in casually and noticed that the ashtray had been replaced and the floor beneath the patio chairs had been mopped clean. She let me in and hugged me. I couldn't remember another time when she had greeted me this way. Her scent was familiar and affected me physically. I could feel myself relaxing. I was relieved to see her apartment exactly as I had remembered it in real life and not from my crazy dream. The vibrant colors and mismatch of patterns felt like a comfortable home to which I had been hoping to return.

"Thank you for coming," she said softly. She had a bruise on her left jawline, which she had partially covered with concealer. I scanned the whole of her and saw more bruising on her right wrist and knuckles. I felt horrible. I wondered if she had gone back to see her old boyfriend. That was what I had assumed. But in truth, I had no idea where she snuck off to during her prolonged silences. I realized that as hard as those times were for me to go without seeing her, she was probably suffering far worse during those periods.

I looked at the bruises on her wrist and then back to her jawline. I was horrified and stood there awkwardly, stuck between wanting to say something and not knowing what to say. I felt like these marks were at the core of why she asked me to come over. Dara caught me looking at her bruises and turned away.

"I just made coffee. Do you want a cup?"

We took our coffee out on the balcony. The air was chilly, and she brought out a couple of blankets.

"This is nice," she said, staring vacantly into the distance. Sitting quietly side by side, we enjoyed ten full minutes of silence broken up only by the sounds of polite sipping.

On more than one occasion, I almost asked her, "Do you want to talk about it?" But I never said it. I said nothing at all.

In time, Dara finally spoke under her breath. "You're a good man."

I didn't know much, but I understood the role I was playing for her in that moment. I was the exact opposite of whatever nasty element had angrily placed those bruises on her body. I was the soft landing for her now that she had been thrown to the ground. I thought back to the ebb and flow of our relationship and the random pattern of phone calls I had received from her; and I wondered if I could match up every single one of those calls to a similar traumatic event that had forced her to come running back to a safer, kinder, gentler guy.

I didn't like this role. In fact, I hated it. But I loved sitting next to her.

"I'm cold. Do you want to go inside?" she asked.

"Sure."

I sat on her sofa while she pushed play on the CD changer, and a rush of classical music filled the room. She took her typical position away from me on the soft cushions and stared absently at the table.

"Jeff, I need to talk to someone."

"Go ahead," I encouraged her. I knew from the sound of her voice that something was wrong. "What's on your mind?"

"I'm lost." Her eyes were still cast down. "I don't know what I am doing anymore."

I was stunned at what she was saying. I felt so bad for her. "You can talk to me."

I heard a catch in the back of her throat before she began to speak. "I came here to find my father."

It took me a moment to understand her meaning. "To LA?"

"Yeah." Dara took a deep breath. "Life in Belarus was difficult for me. My father didn't even know about me. My mother was very young and naïve, and she tried to get pregnant because she thought he would save her, but he left before they knew." She exhaled deeply.

She was opening up to me, and I wanted to offer something helpful. I did my best. "Couldn't she look for him?"

She covered her face momentarily in shame. "It sounds bad, I know. She was so poor and uneducated, but she was very beautiful." Dara spoke of her mother's beauty with reverence. "From what I can tell, he was a visiting professor at the university. He was working for the state university to help set up the new arts and culture college. I don't know everything. This is only what my aunt told me."

I was quiet. "I don't know what to say . . ."

"My mother worked in the university. She cleaned the offices at night. That's where they met. They dated in secret."

"How did they . . . ? Did he speak Belarusian?"

"I don't know, but I am sure he knew some Russian. I have a letter he wrote to my mother." Dara got up and went to the kitchen table to

324

retrieve a piece of paper. She showed me a yellowing sheet of paper marked with a handwritten note. "Here, this is it."

I held the page gently. I couldn't understand the writing. Based on her comments, I assumed it had been written in Russian.

Dara translated the words from memory. "My flower, I will never forget our time together. I've learned that I must return to America for the new school year. I promise to come back to you, and we will be together again very soon. You will fill my every thought until we meet again."

She pointed to the first line of the letter. "He called her his flower because her name is Romashka. This is an important flower in Belarus. You know it?"

She looked at me expectantly, but I had no I idea what flower it could have been. She continued, "You know this . . . for healing and for tea."

"Chamomile?" I guessed.

"Yes, chamomile. My mother is named for this flower, and my father called her his flower."

There was so much for me to sift through. I didn't even know where to start. "Why do you think he's here, in Los Angeles?"

"My aunt told me. My mother would never speak of him. For my entire life, she would never tell me his name or anything. My aunt told me everything she knew. She believes he was a professor of literature at UCLA."

"Do you have any other details? Was he tall? What was his hair color? Eye color? Anything?"

I saw a tear run down her left cheek. She wiped it away quickly and steeled her expression. "No, and besides, none of them will speak with me anymore."

"Why not?"

"My mother was only sixteen when she got pregnant," Dara continued. "And her parents had died several years before. She had no other options but to move in with her sister and my uncle. They couldn't afford living with another adult and a new baby. They already had three children."

Pregnant at sixteen? I found it strange that Dara could speak so highly of her father knowing that he had gotten a sixteen-year-old cleaning girl pregnant. But of course I couldn't say that. I could only manage a slight vocalization in response to her mother's circumstance. "Oh . . ."

Dara got all choked up. "My mother worked nights, and . . ." Tears began falling from her eyes. "My uncle was a bad man. I am thankful that those children were always kind to me. I cannot imagine how it would have been if they didn't protect me."

More tears fell. "He was bad to my mother and to me, but we had no other options."

"I'm so sorry."

She collected herself. "At first, my aunt was kind, and she tried to protect me too. But as I grew up and my uncle took more and more interest in me, she began to resent me. She blamed my mother and me for the things he did. That was just easier for her. She said I was trying to trap him like my mother had tried to trap the American. I tried running away." Dara looked at me, imploring me to believe her. "I did."

"I believe you."

"But everywhere I ran to," she continued, "I found the same bad men. *Everywhere*." She stared vacantly ahead. "When I turned seventeen, I'd had enough. I moved here to find my father."

"I had no idea, Dara."

Tears fell from both of her eyes. "And now I'm lost."

"Dara, I'm so sorry."

She sat back against the back of the sofa. "It's okay. I just needed to tell someone."

I stood and retrieved a box of tissues from the counter in the kitchen. She received it and offered a soft "Thank you" in return. She pulled out a tissue and blotted the tears from her eyes.

"Can you try to reach out to your mother? I'm sure she misses you."

"My mother stopped talking." Dara looked at me. "She hasn't said a word for five years, maybe longer. My aunt put her in a hospital years ago. She was happy to get rid of her."

The story was getting more and more heartbreaking at every turn. There was nothing I could say. I felt like there might still be a chance for her to meet her father. I wanted to remain quiet, but the silence made me uncomfortable, so I offered, "So you came to UCLA to meet your father. Is he a professor here? Do you have any idea who he could be?"

"No," she said flatly, cutting off my attempt to construct a happy ending. "And I'm not even enrolled in this school."

"How . . . ? What about . . . ?"

"I got my curiosity from him, I guess. I've always been interested in stories."

I tried to make sense of it. "But you're *not* a student?"

"No."

We sat in silence for another long period of time. Finally, she said, "I came here, and I learned the same thing as in Belarus: everywhere you go, there are always bad men." Dara turned to me and smiled a little.

327

"This is why I am happy to meet you. You are a good man. I always know when I see a good man."

I got up to sit closer to her.

"No, stay over there."

I searched for something constructive to say. "Dara, there are *a lot* more good men than you think."

"I used to think that too, but I was naïve."

"It's true—"

She cut me off. "I'm sorry, Jeff, but you are naïve about so much."

Dara knew I hated when she called me naïve, and I didn't know it then, but I realize now that she only said those words to me as a way to regain her bearing. In all our time together, she had always been the wise and world-weary soul, and I'd been the wide-eyed child. Dara had just confided in me, and she felt exposed. Calling me naïve was only her subconscious attempt to reclaim her position over me. I shouldn't have been so bothered by it, but I was.

I did know, however, that that moment wasn't the right time to concern myself with her rough edges. So despite seeing a light shade of red, I let it go. I tried to encourage her, saying, "You need to interact with men in other places. You'll see what I mean."

"You mean like college campuses?" She smirked, dismissing me. "The boys from college, they can be as bad as any others."

"Yeah, but . . ." I wasn't sure why I felt the need to make the point. "There are some places that are much worse than others." I was, of course, referring to the information Anson had given me.

She laughed to herself. "The men you meet in bad places always go home to good places. So for me, I think it is all the same."

328

I didn't even know what I was saying. "Yeah. But, Dara, some places bring the worst out in people."

She eyed me suspiciously. "Okay . . . Some places bring out the worst in people."

"It's true," I insisted.

The suspicious look in her eye only intensified. "Why are you saying this to me now?"

"Well . . ."

"'Well' what?" She was getting annoyed.

"Well, if you work at these bad places, then you're going to see the worst in people."

Dara narrowed her eyes at me. "What do you *think* you know about my work?"

I shrank physically at her change in demeanor. "Nothing."

"Tell me." She had raised her voice a little. "Tell me what you *think* you know about me."

"I don't know." My voice got smaller, and I couldn't look at her. "I don't think you deserve to end up with those bruises all over you." I was trying to be honest with her and tell her to expect more because she deserved more. I was trying to help, but her expression darkened further, and I was sure my comments had struck a nerve. The *wrong* nerve.

"You don't understand anything!"

"I'm not trying to upset you."

"Well then, what are you trying to do?"

"Nothing. I just think you deserve better."

"Why don't you just leave!"

"Dara, I'm sorry. Why are you getting mad at me? I'm trying to help."

She looked as though she was about to say something sharp in response, but she stopped herself. "Just go."

"Dara . . ."

"Please! Just go."

# Chapter 63

I returned to my apartment about two hours after I had snuck out. I was ashamed to say that I snuck out of my own apartment, but that was what it felt like. The visit to Dara's had been unsuccessful and deflating. I felt emotionally drained from the story she had told me, and I felt like a jerk based on how badly I had upset her. I thought I was helping and giving her good advice, but it was clear that she didn't want to be given a lecture on how to choose friends. She'd only wanted to tell me her story, and I should have just listened.

The apartment had already woken up. Francis, Dylan, and Espy were in the kitchen, making a monstrosity of an omelet. They heard me enter. Dylan poked his head into the living room. "Jeff, you missed Carey. She came by about an hour ago. She said you guys were supposed to do some volunteer work together."

"Yeah, I was at the pool. I thought I had to work, but I got the schedule mixed up." I played up the disappointment in my voice.

Espy, apparently, had not betrayed my trust because nobody said anything about Dara's phone call. Dylan accepted my story at face value and suspected nothing else.

I thought about Dara and her story obsessively for several hours and realized, as I sat in my apartment, that she had been the victim of evil deeds. I didn't understand the extent of those deeds, but I knew that her uncle had ripped a hole in her, and it was possible she would never recover from that. I wanted to see her, and I wondered if she wanted me to go back to her and try to save her.

I tried to study. I tried to read. I tried to watch TV. I tried anything and everything. But I felt an emptiness inside. I felt sick. I had completely obliterated the moment with Dara, and in the process, I might have caused her to turn away from the one person she thought could help her.

At some point, my mind opened just enough to acknowledge that I had completely flaked on Carey and Nathan. I hadn't even given myself a chance to think through how much damage that was going to do to that relationship. After a couple of hours, I called Carey's phone and PETS, and I got answering machines in both instances. I did not bother to leave additional messages. They both had already heard from me that morning, and besides, I didn't have the energy. On some level, I was happy I didn't have to heave bags of dog food up apartment steps and face the PETS customers. I was not sure I was in the right mental state to manage the emotional toll.

I didn't hear back from Carey until about a quarter after seven. I apologized for flaking on her, and she seemed to take it well, but some of the warmth was missing from her voice. I sensed a certain tone coming from her, and I guess I wasn't too surprised. She spoke to me on the phone only long enough to check in and tell me she was going to eat and then head to her meeting for the Chancellor's Initiative.

I was trying to gauge how mad she was and asked if she still thought she would come by on Tuesday. She laughed a little and said, "Maybe, I don't know. I wish I was more spiteful."

"Are you really that angry at me?"

"I don't know," she confessed. "Give me a day. I'll tell you tomorrow."

I was disappointed to have upset Carey. But if I was being honest, the slight sting from her call receded quickly, and all that remained were the extreme emotions I felt about Dara and her story and how badly I had managed my time with her that morning. I tried to think about why she was finally sharing her story with me.

At one point, she'd mentioned that she just wanted to tell somebody, but I was unsure what that would do for her. She had been severely scarred, right? What was her confession going to fix? Maybe I was overthinking it. Maybe there was enough value in expressing feelings and revealing secrets. Maybe she just needed a confidant. The thing was I didn't want to be *just* her confidant.

# Chapter 64

I must have called Dara six or seven times between Saturday and Tuesday night. I cringe to think about it. That was an embarrassing number of calls. I left a couple of messages as well but heard nothing back from her. I took comfort in the notion that I wasn't just calling her as an infatuated boy. I was also replaying her story in my mind, and I was genuinely concerned that she needed to confide in me and that I could help her through whatever she was dealing with.

By contrast, I had not called Carey at all since the less-than-stellar phone conversation on Saturday night. I finally heard from her on Tuesday. The ringing phone was still warm in my hand from having just called Dara, and I picked up excitedly, hoping that it was the beautiful Belarusian girl breaking her silence and finally returning my call.

The tone of my voice said it all when I heard that it was only Carey. "Oh . . . hey."

"What's going on?" She was cheerful, but there seemed to be a slight strain in her voice.

"Not much. What are you up to?"

"Just at work right now. On a break. I haven't spoken to you in a few days."

"I know. It's been a while." I tried to sound friendly, but I knew I sounded like I was pouting about something.

"It has. How have you been?"

"Good. How about you?"

"Good. Just really busy."

"Um . . ." I searched for what to say next. "How's the Chancellor's Initiative going?"

"Good. The team met this weekend. We're trying to get a follow-up meeting with someone in his office."

"That's cool."

We shared a momentary awkward silence.

"So . . . I hate to do this, but I think I'm going to have to go back on our plans for tonight."

I had no idea what plans she was talking about, but I didn't want to tell her that. "Oh? What's up?"

"I know that I said I'd stop by tonight, but I don't think I can."

"That's okay," I said sincerely. "I know how busy you are."

"I just . . . I don't want you to think I'm trying to get you back for this weekend." She offered a pause for me to respond. I said nothing. "I promise I'm not doing that, okay?"

"Carey, come on. I know you wouldn't do that."

"Okay, because I didn't think our last conversation went that well, and I felt bad about that."

"It's okay, really."

"You sure?"

"I'm sure," I laughed it off. "Let's not talk about it."

It dawned on me that even though Carey hadn't done anything wrong, she *liked* me, and she could sense that I was being distant and losing interest. That kind of relationship dynamic will often compel a person to do desperate things. Not the least of which is to apologize for nothing. I felt like Carey was wandering into that space, and I didn't want her to do that. I was being distant, but it wasn't because of anything she had done or said. In truth, she had done everything right. I just didn't *feel* it with her.

"Do you think you'll be free tomorrow night?" she asked.

"I think so. Why? What's up?"

"You think I can stop by?" Her voice had regained a little playfulness. "I have something for you."

"You do?" I tried to match the lightness in her voice. "What is it?"

"I can't tell you. It's a surprise. For the big weekend."

*Big weekend? What is she talking about?* I remained quiet because I didn't want to say anything that would reveal I had forgotten something "big" and possibly hurt her feelings. She eventually added more context for me.

"I think this might be the best surprise you'll get all year, and it will probably be the best party we've ever thrown." She was referring, of course, to her sorority party. But I had completely forgotten about it.

I didn't want to go to that party anymore. I didn't want to spend the night getting forced into a contrived intimate setting with Carey. But backing out of it for any reason at all would hurt her, *and* I suspected it would embarrass her in front of her sorority sisters. I didn't want to do that either, so I knew I had to stick it out.

"Oh, one more thing." Carey sounded like she was remembering something. "You think you can ask Dylan and Francis to be there tomorrow night? I need to talk to them too, if they're around."

"Sure, no problem."

A moment later, she had to excuse herself to get back to work. I hung the phone up and sank into my couch.

I had been thinking about Dara and leaving her messages for the last four days, and when the phone finally *had* rung, it was Carey. Within five minutes of her call, we had confirmed plans to see each other two more times within the next week.

By contrast, I had no plans to see Dara. I couldn't even get her to call me back. Something told me that my story line with Dara, misguided and pathetic though it might have been, had run its course. I was never going to get that next phone call. If I wanted to see her, I was going to have to take a little more initiative. I stood up, walked out my front door, and went straight to her apartment.

I heard music coming from her balcony as I walked up the stairs and knocked on her door.

"Just a second, I'm coming!"

She answered the door. She was dressed in a delicate lavender satin dress with spaghetti straps and a plunging neckline. In all my time with her, I had never seen her show so much cleavage. Her hair was up, with tiny strands framing her face like she had worn it to see the string quartet with me at Schoenberg. Her makeup was thicker and in darker shades than I was used to. This changed her look significantly. But without a doubt, the most striking thing for me was the diamonds. She wore a thick diamond necklace with matching earrings and a bracelet. Dara was already a perfect 10, but like this, her beauty became otherworldly.

Both of our jaws dropped.

She looked past me, searching the vicinity for someone else, I presumed. "Jeff, what are you doing here?"

"Where are you going?"

"That's none of your concern!" she snapped. "Why are you here? You need to leave."

I started my prepared speech. I thought it might be my only chance to give it. "I just came by to apologize for Saturday—"

"Don't worry about that. I never should have told you those things." Her words remained hard. "That was my mistake."

"No, you should have told me all of that, and I should have just lis—"

She cut me off. "It doesn't matter, Jeff. Don't think about it. It's *over*." She hissed the last two words.

"What's over? Our argument or us?"

She shook her head a little. "There was no argument, and there *is no us*."

Dara hit those last three words deliberately so there could have been no misunderstanding of their meaning. I stood at the door, speechless.

She still had one nail to drive into me before she closed the door in my face. "Go cry somewhere else, Jeff. You can't be here right now."

Her words were harsh. I had backed her into a corner. She was worried that whoever was supposed to be at the door instead of me was about to show up, and that apparently had filled her with fear or maybe anxiety. The cruel words she'd hurled at me were only her best attempt to get me to leave.

It worked. I went home and fell like a stone into my bed.

I reached up to press play on the CD player on my end table and advanced to the ninth track. The clear and crystalline guitar plucks introduced "Mayonaise" by the Smashing Pumpkins. The night before, I had inserted the album *Siamese Dream* into the player and listened through it a few times on a loop, swearing I could hear a battle of opposites raging between the soaring, distorted guitar and the subtler, more ethereal melodies. I saw some strange parallel to my own life at that moment.

# Chapter 65

I barely slept on Tuesday night, and Wednesday morning was brutal. I had that crazy ninety-minute shift at the pool, and then I had to zip over to my American politics class. Only twenty people were even showing up to class at that point.

It was on this morning when I first had the idea to turn in, for my final project, a single sheet of paper with only the following written: "I am putting as much effort into this paper as you put into creating a supportive and dynamic learning environment."

I went straight to poetry class nearly an hour early and entered the empty classroom. I sat in the first seat by the door. I wasn't going to stay—I only needed to see Anson and ask him a question. Sitting in the empty room, I put my head down on the desk and closed my eyes. I was startled by the opening door. It was Opeyemi himself.

He was pleased to see me. "My star pupil!"

"I didn't take you for a bullshitter, Ope."

He turned his head to a three-quarter angle and regarded me from the corner of his eye. "Why do you call me this?"

"Your *star* pupil? Ha!"

"You are Jeff Newcastle, are you not?"

"How did you know that?"

"You are the only person from outside the major who applied for this class." A mischievous gleam caught his eye. "You went to all that trouble to get into this class, and then you ran out last week."

"I was having a bad day."

"As I predicted, you were chasing after the last wisps of smoke, were you not?"

"You're referring to my poem?"

"I am referring to the flame." He stood fully upright and recited the following from memory:

*You may have gone*
*But the part of you that only appears*
*In candlelight*
*Is with me still*
*Makes love to me still*
*Hides within me*
*Still*

I was stunned that he remembered a verse of my poem.

"Now," he continued, turning professorial, "may I request that if you do not plan to stay, will you please leave before class starts?"

"But I just—"

Opeyemi continued, "I do not believe you will stay in my class today, nor do I believe you will ever find your way back to it. I'm sorry." He turned and walked toward his desk, which was tucked in the far corner of the room.

"Professor?" I called.

He turned to face me. "Yes?"

"Your book *I Cry Bomjt.* I've searched all over . . . I cannot find this word anywhere. What does it mean?"

"Keep searching. You will find it soon."

I placed my head back down the desk momentarily and was startled again by the opening door. The first few students started filing their way into the classroom. Somehow, in the confusion, Opeyemi slipped out. I could no longer see him at his desk in the front of the room. I took his request to heart and decided that it would be best if I waited outside. I only had one bit of unfinished business, and then I needed to leave. I couldn't stay in class.

No sooner had I set foot into the hallway than I saw Anson standing in a group with Can and a few others on the far end of the hall. I approached the group and walked right up to him.

"Hey, I need to talk to you."

He was startled. "What?"

"Alone," I insisted.

He smirked and exchanged a questioning glance with his small cluster of friends. "Okay."

We took a few steps to the side until I reasoned we were out of earshot. "What's the name of the place?"

He looked smugly at me. "What place?"

"Where did you see her?"

"Still chasing that last puff of smoke?"

I grabbed him by the lapels of his nauseatingly stylish gasoline attendant jacket and slammed him against a wall. I had intended to push him only slightly to get his attention, but he fell heavily against the flat surface. I saw a momentary flash of genuine fear cross his face and took a small sense of satisfaction from this. He had lorded his unaccounted-for alpha status over the class for the entire quarter. He was arrogant and brash, and in the silly little circle of pretend intellectuals that filled his world, he was able to brandish his wit and biting humor to keep them all at bay.

It felt *good* to have reached in and rattled his cage a little bit. I hoped the news would spread among his peer group so that one of the other monkeys would rise up in short order and challenge his dominance. But I still liked his poem.

The contact his body made with the wall was solid and produced a much-louder noise than I would have expected. We now had the attention of almost everyone in the space around us. He noticed the watchful stares and offered a calculated smile in the direction of his friends. His look conveyed a sense of control and confidence, as if to say "Look at this crazy person." I caught sight of Can out of the corner of my eye, and she offered no discernible reaction to the skirmish.

Anson smiled at me and put his hands up in surrender. "Hey, easy, Jeff! I was just making a joke. She's at Porcelain."

Porcelain was a well-known gentleman's club located in a less-than-desirable section of Los Angeles near the downtown. Though I had never seen one, I was given to understand that the gyrating females who danced on their stages were affectionately referred to as "dolls." The term was almost legendary among college students, who often used it as an archetype of sorts. For instance, if you wanted to call a woman beautiful, you might say she looks like one of "*the* Porcelain dolls," not to be confused with looking like "*a* porcelain doll."

343

I released the arrogant jerk from my grip and walked straight out the hallway and into the bright day beyond the door.

# Chapter 66

Don't worry. I saw it. I knew I was keyed up and about ready to snap. I walked home slowly from campus and talked myself down as best as possible. I knew Carey was coming over that night with a surprise. I knew I had to act civilly to her and my roommates. I knew all of that. I just needed to catch my breath.

Francis was exiting the apartment just as I was hitting the first step of our front stoop.

"Hey," he said, pulling the door shut behind him.

"Hey, Francey, where're you going?"

"Wooden. I'm meeting a few friends for basketball, and then I thought I would work out."

That sounded like a great idea. Some physical exertion was probably exactly what I needed to clear my mind. "Can you wait up for a minute? I'll head over with you."

I got changed quickly, and Francis and I started the short hike back onto campus. I was already starting to feel more centered.

"So," he suggested, "this is the big weekend?"

"I don't know. I don't see what the big deal is about these stupid sorority parties. I feel like they're trying to make it feel like prom, but—"

"No," he corrected. "Aren't you supposed to pick up the car this weekend?"

"Oh . . ." I had missed his meaning. "Yeah, you're right. I guess that's pretty big too. I'll be happy when all of that is over and done with."

"You worried about that at all?" I sensed his concern was genuine.

"To be honest, I'm not. They just want the car. They want nothing to do with me."

We played ball for almost two hours and won five straight games until finally getting destroyed by a team of five Asian guys who were all under five foot nine. I don't believe they missed a shot for the entire game. If you've ever played a pickup game of basketball, you can imagine how it feels to just get run right off the court like that.

Francis and I took advantage of the break in the action and headed over to the gym to push some weights around. Francis was significantly better built and stronger than I was, so I was laughably embarrassed by how we had to keep switching the plates out when we were taking alternate turns on the bench press. Fortunately for me, my roommate was not the kind of guy who would ever make a comment about such things, so that limited my humiliation to a minimum.

Around about four in the afternoon, we'd had enough and decided to head out to Westwood and grab some Mexico Fresh before going home. My finances were running on fumes, but I could always make room in my budget for one more burrito.

We both had to laugh when we entered the restaurant and recognized Yuri standing at the counter with his hands on his hips, gazing up at the overhead menu. He stood mesmerized, unmoving, with his head tilted up. We watched him holding his position for quite some time while the woman behind the counter tried unsuccessfully to get his attention.

"Sir . . . sir . . . sir . . . Can I take your order?"

"Yuri!" we called, walking up from behind him.

"Can we help you pick something?" I asked.

Yuri broke his trance and looked at us. His serious expression gave way to a wide smile. "Hey, guys!"

In my nonscientific estimation, he was extremely high. "What are you doing, man?" I chuckled, "Staring at the menu?"

"Have you ever realized that every item on this menu is a mix of the same five ingredients assembled in different ways?"

"I hadn't realized that." I glanced at the menu. "Is that true?"

The woman behind the counter spoke aloud. "He's been standing there for about five minutes."

I could only laugh. "So what do you want to eat?"

He smiled again. "I want something with a tortilla, meat, beans, cheese, and lettuce."

Francis approached the counter. "You can get him a chicken burrito."

"I'm supposed to get something for Todd as well," Yuri informed.

"Two of those please," Francis corrected the order.

"With extra chips and guac on the side," Yuri amended.

"I'm going to have to charge for that," the woman said, pressing some buttons on the register.

"Nothing's free in this world," Yuri said, staring blankly at her.

I was happy to be out on this adventure with Francis. I'd needed some exercise and comedic relief. I was still out of it but was feeling a little better.

We successfully piloted our way through the dinner orders. Yuri took his food in a to-go bag, and Francis and I found a table. Before walking out into the street, Yuri told us, "We're having people over on Friday night. Come by if you can."

# Chapter 67

To my surprise, Carey, Naomi, and Keisha were already at the apartment sitting with Dylan when Francis and I, smelling like the weight room and burritos, burst through the front door. I noticed they were all drinking Naomi's diet sodas and resting them dutifully on our Oro's Gym coasters.

I saw Carey first. I smiled and said, "Hey." I was happy to see her but felt no electricity.

She returned the smile with a tiny wave. "Hey."

"Francis?" Dylan appeared excited and started the larger discussion. "What are you doing this Saturday night?"

Francis glanced at Keisha. I could tell he was wondering if she was planning to ask him to join her at the ΔΔΓ event. He answered tentatively, "I'll probably be with Espy. Why?"

Dylan continued, "Is it definite? Do you have set plans?"

"No, nothing definite," Francis replied, coming clean. "But I'm sure I'll be with her."

"Can you get out of it?" Dylan asked.

"I guess I could, but why?"

Dylan smiled and turned to Keisha. "Tell them."

She smiled. "Well . . . It's a little late notice, but I wanted to add a live band on Saturday. I wasn't sure that I could, but I just got clearance from the venue yesterday. We thought it would be awesome if Dutch Candy could play."

I now understood what Keisha had meant last week when she hinted that she might have an upcoming gig for us. She was overseeing the planning for this party, and she'd probably had it in mind to ask us to play. I was thrilled with the idea and immediately felt a boost in my mental well-being. I thought back and realized that the last time I had felt good—like *really* good—in the last several weeks was when I'd been onstage playing our silly little thirty-minute show at BBX.

That was also the moment when I'd finally *seen* Carey—or should I say, the Look—for the first time. Maybe this was exactly what I needed to help me reset my mind and my emotions. I would be attending the party with Carey as my date, and there was a good likelihood that she would once again find herself at the side of the stage, swaying with the music and making it near impossible for me to take my eyes off her.

Francis was emphatically supportive of playing the show as well, but more than anything, I suspected he just wanted to get dressed up in his rock star gear. Ever the dutiful boyfriend, he asked if Espy could come, suggesting that she could help us set up. Before he could make a strong case, the girls stated that they were happy to let her come to the party as a guest and said that the two of them were free to attend as a couple when we weren't playing.

By way of caution, Keisha explained that the venue had a sound system that we could plug into, but she'd been warned by their events coordinator that it was not an ideal setup for a live band.

I noticed at that point that Dylan had already pulled out a notebook and began scratching out notes.

"Can we pull this off?" I asked him, kind of as an aside, but also for the benefit of everyone else to hear.

"Easy." He shrugged. "No problem. We need to free up Saturday for setup, but this will be pretty simple."

Keisha smiled at his confidence. "You think you can fill two one-hour slots? I told them you could play sets at eight and ten."

With Dylan's encouragement, we had already prepared more than enough to fill the time. He spoke up without removing his eyes from his notes. "I'm sure we can."

"Yay!" Keisha couldn't hide her excitement. "Okay, one more condition . . ."

She paused, and we waited for whatever was coming next. "You have to promise to close with the same song as at BBX."

"No problem," I offered.

I saw the wheels in Dylan's head turning. He was still looking at his notes. "I think we should add a couple of different songs. We should probably rehearse tonight," he suggested to the entire room.

The mood was both light and excited. "So was this a good surprise? Did you have any idea?" Carey asked me in front of everyone.

"This was an excellent surprise," I conceded.

Our visitors quickly got the message that we had a lot of work to do and offered to leave so we could plan and rehearse. I did not go out of my way to walk Carey out to her car, but I sensed she was lingering and waiting for me to approach her separately. I was still feeling conflicted. Although the last several hours had been good for me and the news of our next show was a strong shot in the arm, I wanted to try to collect my thoughts a little more before having a conversation with her. I figured I could call her later and talk to her then.

Almost as soon as the visitors departed, Dylan brought out a new stack of papers from his room. Then he handed out copies to Francis and me.

# Chapter 68

I knew it was a bad idea to be there, and I felt guilty, but I just had to see her. I had to see her and understand what this part of her life was all about. I had to learn for myself if there was anything I could do to help her. I would have helped if I could.

I was early by "denizens of the night" standards, and I sat all by myself in the dimly lit room, pressed up against the stage. The first lilting notes from a synthesizer, set up to sound like an organ, pulsed out of the speakers. I recognized the eerie tune as "Numb" by Portishead. I didn't understand the song at all. I'd found the music to be melancholic, bordering on unnerving. I wondered if in this room, under these new circumstances, I would uncover any new artistry in the melody and lyrics.

Dara entered from behind a black curtain at the back of the stage. She wore the same satin dress from our last meeting at the door when she had told me to go cry somewhere else. The lights played on her dress and washed her completely in blue, and she became the moon.

She saw me. There was no one else to see. Holding my gaze, she walked to a pole in the middle of the stage and leaned her back against it. She swayed from side to side and twisted around the brass stanchion, holding sickly sexual eye contact with me. This made me deeply uncomfortable. She was much closer to me; and I saw many more bruises on her arms, legs, neck, and face. She closed her eyes, tilted her head back, and rocked side to side.

The song ended softly with a haunting declaration—"a lady of war" repeated two times and punctuated finally by two heartbeat bass notes. Propped up against the pole, Dara was still fully dressed, although her spaghetti straps had tumbled off her shoulders and her dress had fallen slightly to reveal much more of her cleavage. She woke from her trance and peeked back over to me before lowering herself to her knees. Her face was now level with my own, and she slowly crawled to me. Her movements were both feline and unafraid.

"I did not expect to see you here," she purred. I didn't recognize her mannerisms. She was like another woman now speaking to me.

"I was j-just going to leave," I stammered.

"Sweet boy." She half closed her eyes and stared at me. The image of Carey came to mind. "I do not want you to leave, but if you stay, you know you need to pay me."

She swept up a couple of loose bills from the floor around her. I had been so entranced by her that I had not seen any of the money prior to that moment. The stage was covered in bills of every denomination. She held them up before dropping them and letting them fall in a flutter around her. "How do you think I can afford all those expensive things?"

I reached in my wallet and panicked. I had no money at all. I searched all the other pockets on my jeans and jacket before finally locating a bundle of tissues. I splayed them into a wilted fan as one might do with dollar bills and placed them on the stage in front of her. "Here, take these. It's all I have."

She stared at me, but she could barely say anything back to me. When she finally spoke, I heard her whisper maybe to herself or maybe to me, "Is this all I'm worth?" I heard it, but I had no idea how she could say it or even think it.

Dara stood and began pulling off her dress just as I was jarred awake by the sound of my alarm clock.

# Chapter 69

By Friday afternoon, we were already in great shape for the show. Dylan had stopped by the ΔΔΓ house on Thursday morning and located everything we would need and more. He relayed in amazement that their storage room was overflowing with all sorts of electronics equipment, including several sets of portable speakers, many amplifiers, and an array of high-quality microphones. He'd even found a mini soundboard that was still brand-new in the box.

He set everything that we would need off to the side and tagged it as "Reserved for Saturday." Keisha assured him that nobody would use it or move it between that time and Saturday afternoon.

At Dylan's urging, we added five new songs to our total set list: three originals that we had worked on quite a bit already, a reprise of "What's Gone Wrong" by the Untouchables because Espy requested it, and a punk cover of "Bette Davis Eyes" as a tribute to Carey.

Francis and I were quite touched and appreciative that Dylan had included those songs in the show. We encouraged him to add a song for Naomi, and he said it was all right and that he'd rather do something nice for us. Francis caught on well before I did and asked, "Hey, you already picked out all the songs. Were those all for Naomi in the first place?"

Dylan's smile told us everything we needed to know.

We practiced through both sets about three times, and it was totally clicking for us. We had planned to spend the whole night tweaking and obsessing over the show, but around seven, we decided that we were more than ready and needed only to relax and let the magic just happen onstage the next night.

We were packing up our things to get ready for the next day when Francis insisted, "Jeff, you have to do that thing again to open and close the show: 'If we're Dutch Candy, then why are *you* so fucking sweet?'" He hit all the appropriate inflections. "We need to make that our thing."

Dylan jumped in, "Oh yeah, I was going to remind you about that too!"

I was glad they liked the tagline. That was just something I had made up on the spot, but I appreciated that it was gaining some groundswell. I was curious to see if anyone would pick up on it tomorrow. I realized that we would be playing two sets and thought that the repetition could help.

We were all set and ready to go. Well, *almost* . . . I explained to them that I had spoken with the body shop and Matt was still expecting to deliver the car at some point the next day. My plan was to ride my bike to the shop and drive the car back here as instructed by the goons. Dylan and Francis both knew I had to take care of all that before I could do anything else. We all assumed I would get everything done by a reasonable time anyway.

The only business ahead of us was dinner and how we would spend our newly open Friday night.

# Chapter 70

Espy was already on her way over to the apartment, and with our opportunity for a guys-only night shot down, Dylan said he would probably call Naomi and see what she was up to. He poked his head out of his room with the phone to his ear. "Jeff, you want Naomi to bring Carey?"

"No, that's okay."

He regarded me curiously. "You sure?"

"I'm sure."

Dylan retreated into his room, continuing his conversation with Naomi, while Francis retreated to the hall bathroom to shower and get ready for his evening. I was left alone in the living room, trying with all my mental strength not to think about Dara and wonder where she was at that very moment.

Espy turned up on our stoop after about thirty minutes. She was wearing fuzzy pajama bottoms and a fleece pullover jacket with a pink backpack slung across her shoulder. She was greeted at the door by Francis, who was wearing plaid pajama pants and a long-sleeved thermal shirt. He announced that they were going to watch a couple of movies and order a pizza, and he said that Dylan and I were both welcome to join them. Espy pulled out VHS tapes of *The Breakfast Club*, *Sixteen Candles*, and *Pretty in Pink*.

"Are you going to watch all of those tonight?" I asked, surprised.

"As many as we can." Espy was a woman on a mission. "Can you believe Francey's never seen any of these?"

Dylan had heard Espy and came out of his room. "Hey, Espy! What's going on out here?"

"A John Hughes marathon," I answered for her.

"Feel free to join us," Espy said with her most convincing voice, trying to recruit a large slumber party.

"I don't think we'll watch the whole marathon, but Naomi's coming over. We'll join you for one of them."

"Fun! Yay!" Espy was pleased by the news. "Jeff, how about Carey? You want to call her?"

"Yeah, Jeff . . . You want to call Carey?" Dylan spoke with thinly veiled sarcasm.

I wasn't sure what he was getting at, but I nipped it in the bud. "I can't. I already have plans to head over to Y&T's. I'll throw in for some pizza, though, if you guys are planning to order it soon."

I thought about Todd's golf club analogy at that moment. Here was another perfect example of when I needed to look at where I was on the course. I was being asked to join an '80s movie party. From Todd's perspective, I needed to ask what the appropriate club for that specific hole was. Or if I was decoding his metaphor, I should have asked who the perfect guest to join me under a comfortable and fuzzy blanket was. Should I have called the girl in the satin dress and diamonds? Or the girl in the jeans and T-shirt?

Naomi arrived only moments after the pizza deliveryman. We paused *The Breakfast Club* just as Judd Nelson's Bender was asking Molly Ringwald's Claire if she was a virgin. We took a minute to grab paper plates full of pizza and drinks. Naomi reminded us to use coasters. As we were settled in to continue the movie, she eyed me harshly and asked, "Are you watching this?"

"Yeah," I answered, trying to understand why that would offend her.

"Why didn't you want me to bring Carey? She's just at the house by herself. I'm sure she'd want to see this."

Francis had not yet pushed play to resume the movie, and everyone was curled up in their seat around the TV, diverting their attention to the wildly more entertaining exchange that was developing between Naomi and me.

"When Dylo asked me, I didn't know we were going to watch this."

"Well, when you found out, why didn't you call her?"

"Because . . ." I searched for what to say. "I have other plans tonight, and I'm heading out after I eat."

"Well then, why haven't you called her all week?" she pressed.

"What? I have."

"That's not what she says. She says you flaked on Saturday, and then you haven't called her since then."

I was getting annoyed. "I spoke with her on the phone, and I saw her this week. So I don't know what you're talking about."

"I don't know, Jeff . . ." Naomi looked at me sideways. "She seems to think you're ignoring her."

I lost my cool a little. "Well, that's not true. And anyway, it's got nothing to do with you. You should mind your own business."

Espy turned to Francis, giving him an uncomfortable look. Francis's expression didn't change at all. He remained focused on the frozen screen, chewing a bite of pizza.

Dylan had heard enough. "Okay, Nay, you made your point. You're a good friend, and you're sticking up for Carey. But Jeff just told you he has other plans tonight. You have to leave it alone."

"Okay, fine." She threw her hands up and appeared to be backing away from the confrontation. But she tacked on one more question: "So what *are* your plans tonight?"

Fortunately, I had an honest answer. "I'm heading over to Y&T's. I know you hate going over there, so I assumed Carey would hate it too."

Naomi chortled, "She probably doesn't hate it as much as you think."

"Is that really necessary?" Dylan asked his girlfriend sharply, shooting her a disgusted look.

We all sat in silence for a moment. The tension was growing, and I didn't want to deal with it. I realized if Naomi and I were in the room together, that dynamic would remain. So I got up, avoiding the urge to declare something dramatic like "Fuck this shit," and went to my room without saying a word. I had to get out of there anyway and walk over to see Todd and Yuri. I had a better plan for tonight.

Actually, it was a horrible plan. But I had to try it.

# Chapter 71

There was no sound coming from behind the door at Y&T's, but I knocked anyway, wondering if they were all in the Chill Room or some other part of the enormous apartment. In a moment, Todd showed up in shorts and a T-shirt—not the manner of attire you would expect to find him in, were he hosting guests.

"Jeff, what's up?" He noticed the puzzled look on my face. "Were you expecting someone else?"

"Sorry, man," I said, copping to the mistake right away. "I saw Yuri a couple of days ago in Westwood, and I thought he said you were having people over tonight."

Yuri poked his head around the door. "Hey, Jeff! I thought I heard you out there."

We sat on the couch in the front room with the original *Star Wars* playing in the background. The sound was turned all the way down so we could talk. Todd got up to get us drinks, and I asked Yuri about our meeting at Mexico Fresh. He had completely forgotten about it, but as soon as I reminded him, it all came flooding back. He remembered saying something about Friday night. Apparently, at that point, he and Todd had only discussed having a party but ultimately decided against it. More vivid than that memory, he also recalled his revelation about the five common ingredients in all Mexican food. "Sorry, dude, I was pretty out of it."

Todd walked in with three drinks. "I remember you coming home and talking about the Mexican food ingredients. Here . . ." He offered a glass containing a dark liquid poured over ice to both of us.

"What's this?" Yuri asked.

"Jack and Coke. Don't worry, I put extra soda in yours." Todd understood that his roommate wasn't a big drinker.

"My dad would smack this out of my hand if he saw me drinking it," I muttered before tilting the glass to my lips.

"Is he strict? No drinking?" Todd asked, taking a sip from his own glass.

"What?" It took me a moment to understand his question. "Oh no. He wouldn't care if I drank. He would just hate to think I was pouring soda into whiskey."

"He's a purist?" Todd admired.

"I like that," Yuri stated. He raised a glass for a toast. "To old man Newcastle!"

We toasted to my dad.

"So," Todd said, starting a new topic, "what's the latest on your love triangle? I think the last we spoke was at golf last week, right?"

"It's pretty much the same. Maybe a little worse."

"Worse?"

"Why worse?" Yuri asked.

"I don't know. I understand the golf club analogy, Todd. You're right—

one of the girls fits my life right now, and one of them doesn't."

I saw a look of pride cross Todd's face at my mention of his advice.

"But . . . ?" Yuri asked, anticipating there was more that I needed to tell them.

"But," I began, "I can't get this other woman out of my mind. That's why I came over tonight. I wanted to run an idea by you guys."

Both Todd and Yuri leaned forward. I had their complete attention. Yuri spoke. "What is it?"

"You remember how the last time I came here, Todd, you said I should go to a strip club to get my mind off Dara?"

"I don't remember that, but it sounds like something I'd say," Todd confessed.

"Well, I learned something about Dara this week, and it's given me one of the worst ideas I've ever had."

Todd smiled. "I already love it."

I told them about my interactions with Anson and how I had learned that Dara was working at Porcelain. Based on their expressions, I knew I had caught them both by surprise; and they sat in rapt silence, hanging on my every word. I told them that Dara had reached out to me, but that we had gotten in a small fight. Of course, I left out a lot of the details regarding her life back in Belarus and the bruises I had observed on her. I tried to tell them the whole story in such a way where I was worried about her, adding that I thought I should go see her at work. I wasn't sure my logic made much sense, but I sold it to them anyway.

"So what do you think, guys?" I asked. "I'm not even sure she's working tonight, but I thought maybe we could go and just check it out."

"It's a horrible idea!" Yuri blurted.

"What?" Todd balked at the caution. "He wants to go. He has questions, and there's only one place where he's going to get any answers."

"You can't be serious! You really think this is a good idea?"

"I'm not sure," Todd stated honestly. "But if we limit ourselves to only good ideas, we'd never do anything fun or interesting *or* exciting."

"Damn you! Damn you and your logic! Okay, I'm in," Yuri acquiesced.

"Wait . . . So you both think this is a bad idea?" I needed some clarification.

"It's not that it's a bad idea," Todd explained. "It's just a *questionable* idea. It's a risk, but sometimes you have to take a risk."

The boys changed quickly, and we piled into Todd's SUV. I was aware that neither of them thought this was a good idea, but truth be told, I was not sure anyone could have talked me out of going to Porcelain. I wasn't trying to make a good decision at that point. Rather, I was on a suicide mission of sorts, and I needed only a one-way ticket. Once I got to the club and saw Dara and what her world looked like for myself, then—and only then—would I worry about my next decision.

I felt like I was shedding a skin on that night.

# Chapter 72

Todd parked illegally in front of an ATM in Westwood. He and I exited the SUV to get cash.

"How much should I get?" I asked.

"How much were you planning?" he asked.

"I don't know, $100?" I offered, completely unsure of my answer.

"Maybe get $200," he suggested.

When we got back in the car, Todd reached across and handed a wad of $100 bills to Yuri.

"Thank you, sir."

He then reached back and handed me three more brand-new $100 bills. "Here, now you have an even $500. Just in case."

I balked, saying, "Todd, I can't take that."

"Sure you can. This way, we can all get into the same rooms and stay together. Take it. Spend it. You can give back whatever you don't use."

I had no idea what he meant about getting into the same rooms. I tucked the money into my pocket. That was the most money I had ever held all at one time. I wondered how I was ever going to pay him back.

Porcelain was a long way from Westwood. We hopped onto the 405 south down to the 10 east and rode that all the way out past the 110, almost to the 5. I wasn't familiar with this part of town. We followed a series of large billboards promoting Porcelain and promising a night with the "most beautiful girls in the world."

Todd handed the woman at the front door a $100 bill and said, "For the three of us."

She handed him back a $20 bill and twenty singles. Todd peeled off maybe five of the singles and handed them back to the woman. I couldn't understand why. I assumed it was a tip. She didn't say thank you. We all walked in.

The club was overwhelming. Topless females were visible from the moment we walked in, and instinctively, I looked straight to my shoes. Todd seemed to be looking past all the undressed women and searching the club for something specific. "There." He pointed. "Follow me."

He took us to a cluster of red vinyl chairs huddled around a cocktail table in the far corner of the room. From where we were sitting, we could see the two largest stages of the four that populated the expansive complex of different sections and levels that arbitrarily divided the club. On the stage closest to us, a beautiful brunette with a flawless body was lazily working her way around a brass pole in rhythm with the pulsating bass line of "Closer" by Nine Inch Nails.

I felt mildly nauseated. The general tenor of the room was one of troubled girls who had no choice but to be bad because they were either born that way or perhaps born perfectly fine but found some tragic occasion to become broken. I wondered why this was the prevailing tone. Would men ever come to a place where women dressed in pink jumpsuits and danced to the Go-Go's?

A woman with her breasts comically and prominently popping out over a lacy black push-up bra approached our table with a round tray tucked under her arm. The upper rim of her left areola was visible. She offered a quick smile that displayed zero warmth and asked in a flat tone, "Can I get you all some drinks?"

"Three light beers," Todd requested with his trademark smile, holding three fingers in the air. "And can we all get singles too?"

He exchanged a look with Yuri and me. "What you think, a hundred each?" Yuri nodded, and Todd turned back to the waitress. "Three hundred, can we do that?"

She smiled faintly. "Sure."

I saw Todd and Yuri both digging into their pockets and producing matching portraits of Ben Franklin. I followed their lead and handed a third bill over to our group's presumed leader. I wondered why Todd had gone to the trouble of giving us money if we were just going to hand it back to him so he could request singles, but I didn't question the ritual. I figured if I was being gifted a few hundred dollars and my only price to pay was a small bit of theater, I could hardly claim it as an imposition.

"I hope you don't mind light beer," he said as the woman walked away, revealing a wedgie that made me uncomfortable just looking at it. I wondered how she could spend an entire evening like that without going crazy. "I always order light beer when I come to a place like this because I know exactly what I am drinking, and I can control how much I consume. There's also a much-lower chance that anyone slips anything into it."

I shuddered to myself. Where were we? Depressing music, unhappy workers, atomic wedgies, poisoned drinks—what was this place? And why did Dara work here? And then I thought about the several hundred dollars in our pockets *and* the expectation we had that we would spend every last dime. I realized that for some people, if you wanted to get to the gold, you needed to dig through a lot of dirt.

Yuri spoke up. "The women here are beautiful. Have you ever been here before?" He directed the question to Todd.

"No, it's my first time."

Two gorgeous women appeared out of nowhere, both blonde and both wearing string bikinis. They were smiling brightly, almost beaming. "Hey, guys!" the taller one said. "Can we join you?"

Todd spoke up for all of us. "Hey, ladies. Actually . . . Sorry to do this, but we *just* sat down and put in our drink order. Would you mind if we spent a couple of minutes catching up and getting settled in? We'll be here a while. Maybe you can come back and hang out with us a little later?"

"You promise?" the taller blonde asked.

"I would like nothing more," Todd responded playfully.

The young women ambled away. I followed their path a short distance across the floor to two more average-looking guys seated in chairs identical to our own. The friendly blonde duo exchanged a few words as well as a few giggles with the seated patrons. In short order, they found themselves sitting comfortably on the laps of their new friends, continuing their conversation in earnest and laughing along the way.

Our server returned with our three drinks next to a large stack of money all propped up on a tray. I had never seen such a thing before. She doled out the drinks as well as three separate stacks of our rubber-banded dollar bills. Neither Todd nor Yuri bothered to count their stack to ensure that there were a hundred. Rather, they each peeled off three or four bills and handed them back to our server. I did the same.

A couple of tables away, I noticed one of the bikinied blondes was standing and leading her male counterpart away from his chair and around the corner of a wall and out of sight. The other woman remained seated on the other man's lap, even though the adjacent chair had been freed up.

"So," I said to my tablemates, almost whispering, "how do we find Dara?"

Todd laughed. "Look around. You sure you still want to find her?"

I was a little offended but didn't show it. "I'm sure," I said, mostly to myself.

The time at Porcelain was surreal. We were approached several times by different women. Sometimes they were alone, and sometimes they were in groups of two and sometimes groups of three. Todd successfully fended off the first few waves by repeating a polite variation of the first "salvo" he had recited for the blondes. But eventually, and without warning, he accepted an offer for companionship and allowed a nice young woman to join him on his lap. Yuri followed suit, and I found myself eavesdropping on their conversations as an uncomfortable fifth wheel.

I excused myself to use the bathroom. I didn't need to go, but I did need to walk around and try to make sense of what I was seeing. I was glad to have made it this long and felt slightly more comfortable than when I had first sat down. I had to admit that observing Todd speak to the women was helpful. He spoke to them naturally, as if he had known them for years. Only a few days ago, I'd realized that the women working at this club were probably the same girls that I saw every day in class or at the supermarket. Todd's straightforward approach to striking up conversation seemed to cement that fact for me. I realized I could just as easily have met one of these girls at a party as in one of the uncomfortable vinyl chairs crowding almost every corner of this room.

After making my unnecessary trip to the bathroom and paying a $1 tip to the attendant for handing me a mint I didn't want and a paper towel, which he had obviously removed from the empty wall-mounted dispenser, I walked over to the bar. I figured I could kill a little more time by ordering a beer. The woman behind the bar was dressed in her normal clothes.

"A light beer please."

She went to work retrieving the bottle from an undercounter refrigerator. She popped the cap and placed the drink in front of me on a square napkin. "That'll be $5."

I handed her seven singles and turned, leaning my back against the bar and surveying the large expanse of stages, tables, chairs, and people. "Let's Go to Bed" by the Cure was playing loudly through the overhead speaker.

"You know, I can get that for you next time." The server from my section startled me a bit with her words.

I couldn't *not* stare at the outer rim of her nipple. I didn't know what she wanted me to say. "Okay. Next time."

"That's kind of how I make my money." She stared at me. The moment was uncomfortable. I realized she had just put in a drink order for another table, so she wouldn't be going anywhere for a couple of moments. "If everyone here got their own drinks, what would I do exactly?"

I was at a loss. "Sorry."

She wouldn't leave it alone. "I usually get about $2 or $3 every time I bring somebody a drink, and if I didn't deliver any drinks, then I wouldn't make any money." She stared at me again.

I reached in my pocket and pulled out two singles. "I'm sorry. I'll make sure I let you get the next one."

She snatched the $2 from my hand. She didn't even say thank you. The bartender had finished placing the drink order in front of her, and she assembled the glasses and bottles in a tight cluster on a round tray. She spoke to me over her shoulder. "Management much prefers that you sit at a table. They don't like the guests to stand at the bar."

"Hey." I stopped her with my voice. "Can I ask you a question?"

"What? I'm busy."

"Do you know all of the girls that work here?"

"You mean the dancers?"

"Yeah."

"Do you know a dancer named Dara? She's got blonde hair. She's tall, very pretty."

She laughed at me. "You just described half the girls that work here, but I don't know any dancers named Dara."

She turned to walk away.

"Are you sure? She's from Belarus. Do you know of any dancers from Belarus?"

"Where the fuck is Belarus? Look, I need to deliver these drinks."

"She's from Russia," I offered as an alternative.

With her free hand, she pointed to the stage. "Her? She's from Russia."

I looked to the main stage and saw a pretty girl with a square jaw and hair so blonde it was almost white. She was dressed in sexy military-themed lingerie and was readying herself to dance. And by that, I mean she was squirting the brass pole in the middle of the stage with a spray bottle of Windex and wiping it down with a paper towel. I turned back to the server to tell her that the dancer was not the girl I had asked about, but she had already scurried off in the direction of whatever table she was currently serving.

A disembodied voice announced through the club's fuzzy PA system, "Gentlemen, please give a warm Porcelain welcome to the lovely Anastasia, now dancing on the main stage!"

By that point in the night, I had determined that each dancer was given two full songs to perform onstage. In the first song, they remained mostly upright, dancing around the pole and teasing the audience. During this appetizer course, they disrobed—but only partially. During the second song, the entrée, the dancer removed her clothes completely and typically danced on the floor, spending most of her time gyrating, pulsing, and thrusting. Yeah, I *guess* it was sexy, but it seemed a bit overdone to me.

The men closest to the stage typically adopted one of two identities: either they were giddy and dancing along with the music, or they were very serious and staring intensely at the fully exposed dancer. Sadly, of the two personas, I found I was more of the latter. But it wasn't quite as creepy from three rows back—I swear.

After a short visit backstage, Anastasia reemerged in white lingerie to start working the clientele. I wanted to speak with her, so I casually glanced in her direction. Within moments, she was standing over me, smiling.

# Chapter 73

"Did you like the show?" Her accent was different from Dara's. I guess I should not have been so surprised.

"I did."

Her voice was warm, and her eyes were cold. "May I join you?"

"Yeah. But can you sit there?" I pointed to the unoccupied chair at my left.

There were no other empty chairs in the vicinity.

"Where else would I sit?" she questioned.

"On my lap."

"You don't want me to sit on your lap?" She laughed. "Do you know where you are?"

I laughed nervously, not knowing what to say to that. She lowered herself onto the red vinyl seat and looked at me. We managed to share a strained silence in record time. I wondered how many other times she had run this same exact play and sat down next to an anonymous nervous kid who had no idea where he was or what he should say.

I thought back to the first time I had met Dara and how she had walked right up to me in the back of the class and asked in not so many words if the seat next to mine was taken. I realized in that moment how normal and natural it must have been for her to approach a scared little boy and assume the seat next to him.

I searched for a conversation starter and realized I still hadn't introduced myself. "I'm Jeff," I said, holding out my hand.

She shook my hand. "It's nice to meet you, Jeff. I'm Anastasia."

I tried to recall anything from Todd's effortless small talk from earlier. "Where are you from?"

She tilted her head from one side to the other. "Guess."

"Um . . . based on your name and accent, maybe Russia."

"Very good." She smiled slightly. "How about you?"

"Costa Mesa."

She knitted her brows. "Where is that?"

"You've heard of Huntington Beach?" I saw her nodding in recognition. "A little farther south from there."

"So you're from here," she concluded.

"Yeah, basically, I guess." I knew I sounded nervous.

She smiled. "You don't come to this club very often?"

I couldn't tell if she was asking me or telling me. "No, I don't really . . . come to . . . any of these clubs."

"That's okay," she said, putting my mind at ease. "You're sweet. So are you going to let me dance for you?"

"I . . . I don't . . ." I wasn't sure what to say.

"You'll like it." She smiled. "I promise."

"What do you do?"

"I dance for you. We go to a private room, and we get a lot more comfortable. You just sit down, and I dance for you. You'll love it."

"Um . . ." I tried to collect my thoughts. "I was actually just hoping I could ask you a question."

Her face flickered with annoyance and then softened a little bit. "You have a question for me?"

"I do. I'm trying to find my friend."

"Your friend? Is he here with you?" She looked out over the crowd. "It's not so big." She was referring to the size of the club, I assumed.

"No," I clarified. "She works here. You might know her. Her name's Dara."

I could tell immediately from her expression that she knew Dara, but she did her best to make me believe otherwise. "I don't know any dancers by that name, sorry."

"Are you sure? She's from Belarus. She's very pretty. Her name's Dara." I held eye contact with her. "I'm sure you know her."

"I don't. I don't know any dancers by that name."

"You do know her. I can tell. Can't you just tell me something?" I nearly begged.

"Don't you know you can't come in here and ask me questions like . . ."

"Like what?" I pressed.

"I don't know her."

She was lying, and I knew it—and she knew I knew it.

"Is she here tonight?"

The new line of questioning caught her a little off guard. She sat staring at me with a sour look, like she wanted to tell me off. "I said I don't know her, but even if I did, I wouldn't tell you about her."

"She's a good friend of mine." I wanted to keep smiling, but I was starting to get annoyed. What was with all the secrecy?

"If she's such a good friend," Anastasia reasoned, "why can't you find her?"

I shook my head in disagreement. "Don't you have any good friends?"

"What does that have to do with it?"

"Sometimes you have to go out of your way to find your friends, especially when they're lost."

She leaned completely back in her chair and eyed me suspiciously. "She's not here tonight. She was, but she's not here now. That's all I know."

"Where did she go?" I figured since she was divulging information, I would just keep asking questions.

She looked at her hands. She was shutting down. "I don't know."

"You can't tell me anything?" I was sure my face revealed my desperation. "I'm afraid she may be in trouble."

"She left. That's all I know."

"That's not all you know. I can tell."

She kept her eyes down. "Believe what you want."

I spoke softly. "I'm worried about her."

She smirked, "She . . ."

I could tell she was fighting against something. "Just say it," I said as persuasively as I could. "Is she with her boyfriend?"

Anastasia expelled a humorless laugh. "Boyfriend?" She looked at me sympathetically. "I can assure you she doesn't have any boyfriends. She has clients."

"Clients?" I was unsure what the word meant in this context.

"Regulars . . . customers that she leaves with. She's with one of them tonight." She sat up in the chair and perched her palms on the armrest, getting ready to prop herself up and leave me. "I have to go."

"Wait!" I stopped her. "Where do they go?"

"They go to church and pray." She looked at me like I was an idiot. "I think you can figure it out from here."

"Is she . . ." It should have been obvious for a while now, but it finally dawned on me. "Is she a prostitute?"

The word sounded so foreign and so obscene passing my lips. Anastasia pushed herself up off the chair and began walking off. "Good luck, Jeff. I hope you find her."

I felt sick. I honestly felt like I would throw up. I didn't want to be there any longer. I saw Todd in the distance with one girl on his lap and another on the chair where I had been sitting. Yuri was nowhere to be seen. Our server passed me, and she was carrying a bottle of cheap champagne and six champagne flutes. I stopped her and handed her a wad of about ten singles. This got her attention. She looked at the crumpled bills in her hand and then at me expectantly.

I pointed to Todd in the distance. "Do you remember where I was sitting?"

She gently lifted her tray to indicate the order. "I'm heading there now with this."

"Can you tell them that their friend Jeff already left? Tell them I caught a cab about ten minutes ago."

"Anything else?" she asked.

"No, just that. Can you tell them?" I sounded a little more impatient than I had intended, but I really did not like this woman.

She looked at the money in her hand again and then back to me. "I can do that."

# Chapter 74

I started piecing together Dara's story in the cab ride home. I was horrified by the things I had heard. It had come as a major shock when I heard that she was a stripper, and only moments ago, I learned that she was also selling her body. The woman I had put on a pedestal was a . . .

I couldn't say the word because it just wasn't true. She wasn't that word or anything else even remotely close to that. She was, in fact, a victim. She was doing the best that she could do with the life that she had been given.

What's worse was that she was in danger. I had already guessed that when I'd seen the bruises, but I *knew* it now. I knew it because I'd seen it in Anastasia's eyes when she told me that Dara had "clients." I saw it also in how sad and angry that club was. There was nothing good waiting for the dancers in that club. The men who went there had a fantasy, but when the fantasy was over, they went home. Dara had told me as much when she'd assured me that the men that she met in bad places all went back home to good places. The dancers returned to that dark place every day.

There is only so long you can sit in a dark room before your eyes adjust and your entire perspective changes. You can finally see in the dark, and worse yet, the light—if and when it returns—will hurt your eyes. I was sure there were women working at Porcelain who would disagree with me. They would claim that life in the club was fine and that, in actuality, *I* was the problem with my shallow point of view. God, I hoped they were all right. I hoped, with all my heart, that my shallow opinion was as bad as it ever got for them.

I had suspected that that night would be like shedding off my skin, and it was. From that night forward, I was no longer a naïve and scared little boy. I finally understood how much pain this world could inflict. I thought of Dara in her uncle's house, and I thought of Opeyemi sitting in prison while his son died, and I thought of the Ecuadorian woman living in unending guilt for fifty years because she couldn't save her baby girl. I realized that most people carried scars like this around, and the smiles you saw on them were just masks. I thought how wise Keisha was to capture her own series of profound masks and put them on display.

I handed the cab driver a big bill, and he peeled off my change from the wad of dollars he had tucked deeply in his front pocket. He scarcely looked at me during the exchange, and I wondered what scars he might be bearing and what mask he might be wearing.

Francis and Espy had both fallen asleep in front of the TV. I shook them awake and told them to move to Francis's bedroom before shutting off the set. I secretly wished that Naomi was still up and trying to pick a fight with me so I could scream at her "You don't know shit!"

My chance to scream at her would come soon enough. What I didn't count on was that her chance to scream at me would follow shortly thereafter.

# Chapter 75

The bike ride to the body shop was miserable. I was preoccupied and feeling depressed and anxious based on the revelations about Dara from the night before. The rain had also begun to fall with about ten minutes left in the trip. By the time I rolled up into the lot at nearly 5:00 p.m., I was completely soaked despite having stopped briefly to slip a clear plastic emergency poncho over my head. I had been forced to wait for most of the day while the repairman completed the final lingering step in the restoration process, which was to replace the weather stripping around the back window. If not for this small procedure, the car would have been done and ready for delivery a couple of days early.

I had already called Matt several times earlier in the day, and I could tell he was annoyed when he finally saw me dripping wet in the small office at the shop. "I was about to close up!" he snarled.

I deflected his comment. "It's not even five yet."

"We close between three and four on Saturdays." His frustration was evident. "I had to beg my guy to stay and complete this for you."

I thought to myself that he was the one who had estimated the timeline for the job. If making this deadline had been such an inconvenience, then why didn't he tell me so before the very last day? I kept the

382

sentiments to myself. In truth, I didn't care about what he said or thought. I just needed to get out of there, get to the ΔΔΓ party, and help everyone set up for the show. Dylan and Francis had been very understanding about my prior obligations and insisted that between them and Espy, they could get everything done in time. Still, I wanted to get there and lend a hand, if possible.

Matt swiped my credit card, and I felt a small knot tightening in my stomach. I walked around the car, and I had to admit the workmanship was near flawless. If you weren't looking closely, you wouldn't have noticed anything wrong with the car at all. The only slight imperfection that I had detected was a wrinkle in the weather stripping around the back window. I realized then that the imperfections might have been the real source of Matt's agitation, but I just accepted the work as it was and moved as quickly as possible through the paperwork so I could get back on the road and drive home. He apparently appreciated my leniency because he made a display of helping me load my bike in the back seat after laying a couple of paper floor mats all over so that I wouldn't get any dirt or grease on the upholstery.

I was tempted to take the Mercedes into Santa Monica and drive straight to the event center, but I knew that would only end in another visit from the Branson Canyon goon. I drove straight home, pulled into a convenient street parking spot, and ran into the apartment to get ready and go. I got appropriately dressed in my usual black-on-black rock star uniform, relieved not to have to wear my suit, as Carey had originally requested.

I still had a lot of Todd's money in my pocket, which I used to enlist the services of a taxicab. I stepped through the back entrance of the event center with about thirty minutes to spare before we were expected to start the show.

I was greeted by a smiling Espy. "Jeff, you made it!" She didn't know the story. She still had no idea what I had been through regarding the car.

Francis had told her that I would be late because I had a shift at the pool and that I couldn't get out of it.

She called around a corner, "Guys, Jeff's here!"

Espy shook her head back and forth to show off her new dangling jewelry. She had, as promised, picked up a pair of the *DC* lightning bolt earrings and sported them proudly as a complement to her now-legendary Dutch Candy jean jacket.

I took a deep breath and tried to calm the anxiety that had been following me around since last night and, really, for the last several days. The senseless car saga was now behind me. The familiar sight of Espy gave me perspective, and I realized for the first time that I would no longer have to deal with that insanity. All I had to do now was focus on getting through two hours of guitar strumming and singing (if you could call it that) and then try to make sense of everything else. And by that, I mean trying to make sense of the news I had received about Dara last night.

Dylan turned a corner with Francis close behind. They were dressed exactly as I'd expected. Dylan was rocking the everyman trucker hat vibe, and Francis had donned full-on peacocking rock star attire.

"Jeff!" Dylan greeted me. "You're right on time."

"Yeah, we just completed all the work," Francis said sarcastically.

"Everything's done?" I asked, feeling a little guilty.

"Locked and loaded," Dylan confirmed. "All we need to do now is start drinking and get mentally prepared to rock people's worlds!"

"Hell yeah!" Espy agreed enthusiastically.

"Is the bar open?" I asked.

"It's a cash bar," Francis informed. "But we brought a cooler."

We sat in a circle in the backstage area, drinking beer out of Francis's Styrofoam cooler. I recognized the cooler from several prior outings. Music poured in from the main room of the event center as the night's DJ began spinning records. He played mostly retro disco songs, and we wondered how well his selection would flow into our garage band brand of sped-through cover songs.

"How'd it go?" Dylan asked me as an aside in reference to the car pickup and drop-off. He didn't want to speak too loudly and call attention to the topic.

I appreciated his discretion. "It's done. All over with now."

We clicked our cans in a toast to celebrate. I was happy to have the repair behind me, but as much of an inconvenience as that entire episode had been, it was something that had tied me to Dara. She and I had never discussed it, and she probably had no idea of the trouble I'd gone to just to take care of it—to protect her. It'd all been about her, and now that it was over, she was slipping further from my life.

In light of last night's revelation, I felt like I needed to save her now more than ever. This whole thing had started with a late-night phone call. Of everyone in the world, Dara had chosen *me* to come and save her from the strange man's bathroom. She had chosen *me* to share her deepest secrets. Why couldn't I be the one to save her from her desperate and dangerous circumstances?

She'd told me she was lost. She'd used that word, "lost." She'd told me the men were bad. Did that sound like someone who wanted to sell herself? I didn't believe so. I believed she wanted a way out. I believed she was the bright and beautiful sun that needed to be rescued from the recesses of the shadowy night.

I suspected there was no other person in her world who believed in her the way that I did. I was sure her father would have felt this way; and I was sure that, deep down, Dara knew all of this. I believed that was why she had always reached out to me when the bruises covered her body. I believed that the world that she was now occupying was a world into which she'd been carelessly forced by bad luck and bad men. I believed that given the chance, she would never have chosen that lifestyle for herself.

"Jeff! Earth to Jeff!" Dylan was calling to me, and everyone else shared a chuckle. Apparently, I had been lost in thought.

"What?"

He gave a heavy sigh. "I'm going in to look for the girls. Do you want to come?"

"No, I'm gonna hang back here for a little longer and finish my beer."

"Okay, you sure?" he asked. His expression was asking so much more.

"What?"

He didn't want to say anything because Espy was sitting with us, and I was sure he didn't wish to bring up anything personal in front of her, but he had to say something. "I'm going to go get Naomi and Carey . . . ," he said expectantly. "Okay? Can you promise to be on your best behavior?"

I should have just said yes, but I felt compelled to call it like I saw it. "Are you serious? You think I'm the one who starts shit? Tell Naomi to keep her mouth shut, and everything will be fine."

Dylan's face twisted into frustration and mild anger. I had just insulted his girlfriend, after all, but he knew I was right. He bit his tongue to a degree. "Okay, did that feel good? Did you get it out of your system? I did talk to her, and she said she'll be civilized."

I didn't say anything, and Dylan left to go look for our dates. I obviously had a few unresolved emotions boiling inside me, and I felt all of it coming to the surface. I took a deep and dramatic breath to calm myself and wished that Francis and Espy had not been there to see it.

"Can you just ignore her tonight?" Francis asked.

"Her problem is that she thinks this shit even matters!" I railed. "She thinks if I don't call her friend, that's a crisis, and she feels like she needs to open her mouth as if her opinion even matters—as if any of this shit even matters!"

Everyone looked down at their beers. To her credit, Espy spoke up. From her tone, I knew she was being sincere, and I needed to listen to her. "I don't think you really want to be here tonight, Jeff." She let the statement sink in for a moment. "Something else is on your mind, am I right?"

I offered only a shrug.

She continued, "Can I suggest something?"

"Sure." I barely breathed the word.

"Just play the show. Ignore everything else. Tonight's not the right night to slam you into the middle of all this. It's just not your night, and that's okay. Play your show with your best friends, have fun, and then see how you feel."

No sooner had Espy finished speaking than a shrill and familiar voice sounded off in the background. "Hey, guys! Ready to rock and roll?" Naomi stepped in the backstage wing, her words slightly impaired by the apparent effects of a preparty. Another young woman entered the space close behind her. Naomi noticed her boyfriend was missing from the scene. "Where's Dylan?"

Neither of the young women looked like themselves. Naomi, I recognized, but I had to do a double take to be sure it was Carey. I had never seen her dressed like this before, and I suspected my expression was not lost on her.

"What are you guys wearing?" I asked.

They both wore heavy makeup and big hair teased up for maximum volume. Naomi wore fishnet stockings and a cotton miniskirt stretched across her hips. She was also wearing a red halter top, which lifted and prominently displayed her otherwise-modest bustline. Carey wore a short black denim skirt and a red bodysuit with a deep plunging neckline. The revealing top offered a dramatic view of her cleavage from every angle. Both girls balanced themselves on impossibly high heels.

"It's this stupid theme," Carey said, slouching a bit. Her body language transformed from sexy to self-conscious in a split second.

"What theme?" I asked.

"The 'pimps and hoes' theme. I told you about this . . . ," she offered meekly.

"Pimps and hoes?" I repeated. "That's the theme for tonight? You never told me that."

"I did . . ." Carey sounded like she was about to cry. "When I first asked you to come with me."

"You guys came here dressed as prostitutes?" At this point, I couldn't hide the disgust in my voice. "Is everyone in there dressed like that?"

Carey looked down. "Not everyone."

"And you thought it would be a good idea to dress up as a woman who's been forced to sell her body to make a living? You thought that was a nice thing to do?"

Naomi could only take so much before she exploded. "Fuck you, Jeff! You don't control her. Carey can dress any way she wants. You're not her dad. You're not her boss. You're not even her fucking boyfriend!"

"Why would I want to date a girl who dresses like this?"

I immediately regretted saying it. Carey, who was now crying, turned and walked out of the backstage area and into the main hall.

Espy followed her, throwing me a "What were you thinking?" face. She raced past Naomi, who decided she would rather stay and tell me off.

"Right, you'd rather date a girl that doesn't even exist!"

"What's that supposed to mean?"

"Your Russian fantasy girl who obviously doesn't give a shit about you! Probably because she knows you're a pathetic, judgmental loser!"

"You don't know anything about her! You don't know anything about me! You just talk and talk!"

Francis stood and approached Naomi. "Nay, we're not accomplishing anything here. Let's just go inside and cool off. This isn't helping."

Naomi calmed down instantly. She was like that. She could get emotional, but she was always in control on some level. "You're right, Francey. We should go inside. Let's find Dylan. I'm sorry I even wasted my time on this loser."

She took a few steps toward the main hall and turned back to me, calmly leveling what she really thought. "You know what, Jeff? You're just a silly, stupid boy."

I had nothing to say to that. She wasn't right, but she wasn't entirely wrong. "Fuck off, Naomi! You think you know what's going on, but you don't have any idea."

Dylan came walking briskly and almost bumped into the retreating pair. "Was that you guys yelling? We can hear you guys in front. You couldn't make it five minutes without killing each other?"

Naomi was still calm. "It's fine. We're done now. Did you see Carey?"

"Yeah, she's in there with Espy, bawling her eyes out," Dylan reported. "Jeff, what did you say to her?"

"Blame me all you want, but all of this is her fault," I said, pointing to Naomi. "She's the one who always starts this shit, and I know it was her idea to dress Carey up like that tonight."

"You're wrong, Jeff. Again! That was *Carey's* idea. I dressed her up for the first show, and she thought you liked it, so she wanted to look sexy tonight for you. I told her not to bother."

"Bullshit! I don't believe you. Look at how *you* got dressed."

"Damn right, I dressed like this, and I look good! I don't care what you think. I dress however I want to, and your opinion doesn't matter to me."

"Well, you're a horrible influence on Carey."

"You know what? I agree with that—because I'm the one that told her to go out with you. I thought you were perfect for her, and I hated Todd."

I was confused. "Todd? Who's Todd?"

"Your friend Todd. I hated him. He's a drug dealer and super old and perverted. He used to make her do all kinds of weird stuff. He was no good for her."

"What are you talking about?" I asked. "They never dated."

"You're so fucking clueless!" Naomi laughed at me and exchanged a look with Dylan and Francis. "Does he really *not* know?"

390

"Did Carey use to date Todd?" My voice was a little too whiny as I looked to roommates for an answer.

Naomi laughed. "She practically lived at his place this summer."

"Is that true, you guys?" I asked. I could hear how pathetic I sounded. My two best friends could only stare back at me. I could tell by their frozen expressions that everything Naomi was saying to me was true. "I don't believe you! Besides, Carey's not perverted—or whatever you said."

"You're the worst kind of guy, Jeff." Naomi's words were full of contempt and condescension. "I know you think every girl is either a whore and beneath you or a virgin and just waiting for you to teach them about the world and save them from all the other men. You're pathetic! You can't save anyone."

"All right, Naomi." Dylan turned her slightly and encouraged her to go to the main hall. "Let's take a break."

She resisted him and remained staring at me, almost enjoying it. "Anything you want to say?"

"None of that is true. None of it!" I headed for the back door and out into the parking lot.

Francis called to me as I left. "Jeff, where are you going?" He came to the back door and called again. "Come on, dude! Where are you going? It's 8:03! We should be together onstage right now!"

# Chapter 76

I walked for over an hour and a half east on Santa Monica Boulevard, then cut up and over to Wilshire, and finally north on Veteran in the direction of my apartment. With each step, I was happy to put more and more distance between myself and Naomi. She had no idea what she was talking about. I hated her, and I hated the way she could so coldly express herself with no understanding of what was true and with no remorse for being so wrong. She had no idea about the things I had seen or the things that I was going through. She had no idea about my relationship with Dara, and as much as she wanted to control my feelings for Carey, she had no say over my feelings and emotions. The world did not fit simply into her view of boy-and-girl politics.

The more I thought about it, the more I realized that she was probably lying about Carey and Todd. I had spoken to Todd on so many different occasions, and he could have told me about his relationship with Carey at any time. He'd never said anything. In fact, the advice he'd given was always encouraging me to date Carey instead of Dara. But still . . . Why would she say it if it wasn't true? And why hadn't Dylan or Francis spoken up and corrected her?

The sky had turned dark over Westwood. A fine mist-like rain was beginning to fall. I wondered who else I had left in the world. Dylan and

Francis were probably onstage for their second set by now, playing without me. I couldn't play anyway. They were better off without me. I was confident that Naomi had convinced Carey that I was an evil, judgmental asshole by now. I was never going to hang out with Yuri and Todd again. They were liars anyway.

Worst of all, Dara was floating in the sky somewhere, out of reach; and she would probably never speak with me again. The air hung thickly around me, and I got a strong desire to ride my bike out to the cliffs and stare out over the ocean. At this point, my closest friends in the world were a bench on the Santa Monica cliffs and a view of the ocean.

I turned onto my street and realized immediately that the black Mercedes was no longer parked in front of my place. My heart sank. The realization hit me hard—I had forgotten to remove my bike from the back seat. I searched the area in hopes that they might have removed it for me and left it leaning against a tree, but no such luck. For a moment, I thought that I could simply take Francis's or Dylan's bike, but I didn't need or want anything from either of them.

I didn't need anybody's help, and besides, I had something else in mind. I called a cab. I still had a pocketful of Todd's money, and I would spend it all. I would spend all his money and all my money. I would charge everything to my card, and I just didn't care anymore.

I wanted to return to the scene of the crime. I asked the driver to take me to 823 Branson Canyon. I wasn't exactly sure what I was thinking, but I knew that I wanted it. Maybe I was looking to pick a fight. Maybe I was looking to tell them all to fuck off. Maybe I just wanted to walk back into their bullshit world, the one that I had been so scared of, and take back what rightfully belonged to me. These assholes had bullied me into paying for their car, but they were not going to steal my property and watch me roll over and play dead. *Never again.*

I recognized the long winding path up the canyon roads. Several cars lined the side of the street as we neared the familiar hilltop estate. The gate was opened but partially blocked by cars. I recognized the black Mercedes farther up the driveway, parked in nearly the same position as the night Dara had sent a hunk of stone through its back window.

I paid the cab driver and started a tentative hike toward the front door. It became clear from my first footstep on the property that the home was playing host to a large party that night. Music pulsed from the enormous front door. I passed by the Mercedes and saw my bike still resting awkwardly on the paper mats draped over the back seat. I peeked at the wrinkled weather stripping on the back window and wished that the evening's light rainfall had caused it to leak water into the rear of the car. No such luck.

I tried the door handle, but the car was locked. In a sick way, I was glad. I didn't wish to simply slide my bike out and slink away, rolling without pedaling down the canyon roads onto the flat grid of city streets below.

I realized that I was there for a confrontation. I was there to show them that I was a new person. I had been through so much in the last few weeks. I had caught a glimpse into these dingy and dangerous worlds outside of my own, and as far as I could tell, they were populated only by desperate and conflicted people. I was ready to show them who I was and that I wasn't afraid. Driven by anger and an overinflated sense of self-righteousness, I walked unwaveringly to meet my provocateurs.

A beautiful woman was sitting on the ground with her back against the wall. Curled up with her knees against her chest, she had positioned herself around a corner and out of view from the front door. She dragged aggressively on a cigarette and peeked up at me as I walked by. She wore a short skirt, which had, in this seated position, hitched high up her thighs. Upon seeing me, she pulled her knees tightly together to prevent me from gawking. Exhaling sharply and staring me straight in the eye, she offered a humorless greeting. "Welcome to the party."

My response was barely audible. "Hello," I said, nodding at her as I tried to read her mind and understand what set of circumstances had wedged her so awkwardly against the baseboards of this large estate.

"Do you have a cigarette?" she asked.

"No."

"Hmph." She waved me out of her sight with mild disgust.

I entered the home as I had done before. The view of the city through the wall of windows was as impressive as on my first pass through the room so many weeks ago. The space was filled with beautiful and decadent people.

The room extended much farther than I had perceived on my initial visit. Loud music played in the background as more of the room's occupants revealed themselves to me. Most of the men had a darker and menacing look about them, whereas most of the women were younger and attractive. I recognized the smell of marijuana in the air and saw stubbed cigarettes and joints in several of the ashtrays that dotted the many surfaces throughout the space.

Tucked in the farthest recess of the room, I saw a small bag of what I assumed was cocaine resting on a glass coffee table next to two unspent lines of the white powdery substance. A group of two men and two women were sitting around the illicit offering. I overheard the female closest to me saying, "I will, I will. But I need to pace myself."

Through the wide picture window behind this group, I saw several people sitting in a hot tub on a large wooden deck perched over the hillside off the back of the house. I observed that one of the women, standing waist-deep in the water, was topless. She was dancing and shouting something into the expansive and twinkling cityscape that spread out in front of her. Several others in her group seemed to be encouraging her. More partygoers milled about on the deck, sipping drinks and barely paying attention to the spectacle.

I was not sure who I was looking for, but I planned to approach the first familiar face I saw and demand them to open the back of the Mercedes and return my bike to me. It didn't take long. A large man with a bent nose approached me and flashed me a crooked smile. This was the same thug who had broken into my apartment the morning after I had rescued Dara.

"Are you lost?" he asked calmly.

"I came here to get my bike."

He laughed. "You left your bike in the car. I thought that was a little something extra you threw in to pay for my inconvenience."

"*Your* inconvenience?"

"Yeah, *my* inconvenience," he said gravely.

"Just get the keys so I can get my bike."

"Or what?" he asked.

"I don't know." I was completely out of patience. "I don't know what I'm capable of at this point. Is it really worth a bike to find out?"

He smiled. "You have balls," he said while surveying me and trying to determine his next move. "But no, I don't think I'm going to give you the bike. I think I'm more interested to see what you do next."

At that moment, I didn't care. I didn't. I felt like I had nothing left anyway. My friends had turned their backs on me. I had lost both Dara and Carey. I had been humiliated by Todd, and I just didn't give a damn about anything anymore. I thought about picking up the large ashtray closest to me and smashing the hefty man in his crooked nose. I knew there was no way this would end well for me. But I didn't care, and at least I would finally go out on my terms. At least I would get to punch back. He thought I wasn't dangerous. He thought I was just a college boy worried about my finals. I didn't give a damn about my classes or my grades or anything. I cared only about standing my ground and claiming something as my own—even if that was just a bike or some respect.

He saw me looking at the large ashtray. "You're not getting any ideas, are you?"

"Jeff?" The tense moment was interrupted by her familiar voice. "Jeff, is that you?"

I turned to see her approaching me. She was the most beautiful woman in this room by far. She wore an outfit that was near identical to the one I had seen Carey wearing earlier that evening—a black miniskirt and a red bodysuit with an impossibly plunging neckline. Her hair was in a loose bun, and I was surprised to see that she was not wearing any shoes. I found that peculiar.

"Cammy," the man said, "did you invite him?"

*Cammy?* I thought to myself. *Why did he call her Cammy?*

"No," she drawled. "I did not." Her voice was impaired. She spoke slowly, and her face was frozen in an overpronounced ecstatic smile. "I did not invite him." She looked at the large man. "What's he doing here?"

"I was just asking him the same thing."

"I told you why I came here. I want my bike."

"You came here for your bike?" Dara was not in her right mind, and she presumably had no idea about the car or the bike or any of it.

The large man grabbed my upper arm with his powerful hand. "I was just about to get rid of him."

397

I shook my arm free and backed up a step. The movement was aggressive, and a few others in the general area noticed the slight skirmish breaking out.

Dara stepped between us. She was high on something and was hardly affected by the heightening tension. "Oh, stop it," she said, laughing a little. "He's harmless. Let me talk to him." She slapped the large man on the arm and walked me away from him with her arms wrapped around me.

I hated that she had called me "harmless," but I loved the feel of her arms wrapped around me. She walked me as far as the staircase. This was the same staircase I had climbed on my first trip to this place to retrieve her from the bathroom one floor above us.

"I didn't know you would be here," I said.

"Why are *you* here?" she asked, slurring. "I'm supposed to be here. You are not supposed to be here." There was an honesty in her words, which I assumed was fueled in part by her straightforward demeanor, but mostly by whatever drugs she had consumed. "I think you should go."

"They took my bike."

"Who took your bike?"

"Whoever lives here, Dara."

"No . . . That's not true." Her eyes were half-closed, and she gave me a look. "Nobody here wants your bike. Why are you really here? Is it because of me?"

"That is why I'm *really* here—because of my bike. I had no idea you'd be here."

"Hmm . . . You surprised me." She was deep in thought despite her

398

altered state. "Are you sure you didn't come here for me?"

I thought about what she was asking me. I hadn't gone there *for* her, but I had gone there *because* of her. Everything I'd done for the last couple of days was because of her. I wasn't sure how to say it, and I wasn't sure she would even hear me if I did say it. I was speaking to her through a fog of induced confusion. "I came here for my bike, Dara. That's all."

She frowned. "You can't call me that."

"Cammy?" I asked. "I heard him call you Cammy. Is that your name when you're here?"

She grinned and giggled. "When I'm onstage, you call me Cammy, okay? Can you do that?"

"No," I responded honestly. "I won't call you Dara while I'm here, but I won't ever call you Cammy."

She smiled and closed her eyes. "You love me, don't you?" She waited only briefly for a reply that I was too afraid to give. "You know you shouldn't."

"Why don't we just leave? Let me take you home."

"What?" Her eyes opened. "And ruin this good buzz? You need to lighten up sometimes, Jeff."

I realized there was nothing left for me here. "Look, can I just get my bike? Tell the guy who lives here to open his car, and I'll just ride it home. I don't want to be here any more than they want me here."

"He didn't steal your bike, Jeff. You're making things up." She leaned into me with her eyes closed and whispered, "This is another one of your dreams."

"It's not! I had his car fixed after you threw the stone through the back window. He made me fix it, and I left my bike in the back."

"What are you talking about? The car's right outside." She was trying to understand, slurring her words more. "You aren't making any sense."

"You smashed up his car!" I was getting angry. "He found me and said I had to fix the car or . . . or . . . I don't know what he was going to do. So I fixed it."

"It's not possible. Mike . . . ," she slurred. "How could he even know who you are?"

"You gave him my number that night I came to save you."

"You didn't save me." Her words were sad. "I know you want to, but you can't." She looked at me, and I saw a moment of lucidity in her eyes. "Wait here."

She turned, walked up the stairs, and disappeared. Abiding her instructions, I did not follow. I did not wish to follow. She seemed more than comfortable ascending the flight of steps, and I did not wish to understand why she was so comfortable returning to the same place where she had been so miserable before. I couldn't bear to have seen the same mess of pillows and blankets that I had seen on the floor during my last visit.

I turned completely to face the room. My vision had gone blurry, and I saw the expansive chamber through a bluish haze. The sharp corners of the room became rounded, and the fine details of the people's faces grew fuzzy and undefined. I felt nauseated and wanted only to be out of this room and on my bike, riding on the darkened streets with the cool air on my face. I heard a rising tide of voices and laughter. I sensed insincerity and nervousness in every utterance and sound.

An ominous tune picked up on the stereo speakers. A gravelly voice that I couldn't place at the time, but have since learned was Nick Cave's, filled the room with the first verse to "Red Right Hand."

The same attractive woman I had seen sitting against the wall when I walked up to the front door was now in the house, wandering aimlessly. She approached me and came more clearly into focus. She was considerably less disheveled than I remembered from our brief exchange outside. Her skirt had been pulled back down to her knees, and she smiled warmly. "Do you have any cigarettes?"

"I'm sorry, I don't."

Once again, she waved me off before walking in another direction.

I heard voices approaching from the stairs above me. I turned and recognized him immediately. Walking behind Dara, he was in a silk robe cinched at the waist with his ample belly hanging over the tightly tied sash. He was the same man who had greeted me from his enormous darkened doorway on my last trip up this very same hill. He was as soft and underwhelming as I remembered, but his eyes remained hardened.

In his high voice, he spoke gregariously, but dismissively. "Cammy told me you have a small problem you came here to solve."

Dara continued to the landing and stood facing me, and her friend remained a couple of steps above us. I saw his eyes peeking over my shoulder. He shook his head ever so slightly at whoever was behind me. I turned to see that the same goon who had grabbed me by the arm was about ten feet away. He walked toward us, looking for instructions from his boss.

"I told him about the bike . . ." Dara could barely get the words out. She was completely out of it.

"Yeah, you can take your bike back. We had a good laugh about that." He looked over to the goon. "But I'm not going to steal some kid's bike."

Dara laughed. "I told him about the bike . . ." She said it again to no one in particular.

"Honestly, I don't appreciate you coming here uninvited. I don't want you to come back, and you're not going to like what happens if you do. But I understand that was a pretty shitty thing that we did about the car. I was angry, and I shouldn't have done that to you. Here, take this."

He reached into the pocket of his robe and pulled out a stack of $100 bills. He counted a few off, and then losing interest, he simply pinched off about half the stack. "What was it, about five grand?"

He looked at me, and all I could do was stare at him, outmatched and infuriated. He picked up on my irritation and reasoned with me. "Hey, look, this is a onetime offer." He extended the money. "Take it . . . It's for the car. I know you paid for it. Take it and get out of my fucking sight."

He flipped the keys to the large man behind me. "Open the car for him, give him his bike, and get him the fuck out of here." He walked back up the stairs. "Cammy, get your ass up here. It's time for my bath."

Dara looked vacantly in my direction. I saw the cosmos swirling in her blue eyes as they shone in the dim light. She stepped toward me and leaned over to kiss me on the cheek before whispering, "Maybe I'll see you in the sky sometime."

She turned and walked up the stairs. I stood there and marveled as she climbed higher and higher and ascended still higher.

"Come on, let's go get your bike." The large man walked out the front door, expecting me to follow, and I did. He had already let the air out of his chest. I sensed he now felt sorry for me. I hated him for this. I liked him much better when he feared that I might try to put an ashtray through the bridge of his nose.

*What the hell just happened?* Why hadn't I said anything? The man had walked down from on high, called me a kid, placed $5,000 in my hand, and then disappeared. In the entire exchange, I had not uttered a single word.

As for Dara, I wasn't even sure where she was. She'd numbed herself to the horrible reality of her life. I thought that maybe where Cammy would make a sharp turn at the top of the stairs and draw a hot bath for that soft man and his hard eyes, Dara would continue past the top of the stairs and ascend even farther through the roof, into the sky, and up to the heavens.

I had no idea how it was supposed to work. I only knew that I hated it. I hated all of it.

I slid my bike out of the back of the car and walked it slowly down the pea-gravel driveway. The large man didn't say anything further to me. He only turned and walked back to the waiting party inside the house. To him, I realized, my visit represented nothing of significance. A lost boy had accidentally wandered in off the street and nothing more. I was a momentary inconvenience in his considerably more interesting and troubling life.

Looking over my shoulder, I caught the familiar glimpse of the city between the hedges lining the property. I remembered back to that early morning from weeks ago. I laid my bike on the ground and went to the overlook between the hedges to get a better view of the sparkling city below. My perspective changed, and I saw myself from outside myself. I remembered the fire that had risen up in Dara on that morning, and I felt a similar fire rising in me. Something inside me snapped, and I let out a bloodcurdling scream. The moment was surreal.

I screamed again and reached into my stuffed front pocket, pulling the stack of bills out in the open night air. I threw the bundle as far off as I could into the direction of the glorious city. I watched as the green paper rectangles separated and danced in wild, unpredictable patterns toward the hillside below.

Turning and searching the path beneath my feet, I picked up a large paving stone from the walkway at the side to the drive and set off back in the direction of the house. I heaved the large stone into the back window of the Mercedes, and predictably, the alarm responded as every light on the exterior of the car began blinking. I walked back to my bike, set it upright, propped myself onto the seat, and coasted leisurely onto Branson Canyon Drive.

I glanced over my shoulder and saw the large man, followed by a few other party guests, running out of the house as I rolled away. I remember thinking, *Well, I got them back. Now we're even. Now it's over.*

Well, it *was* basically over.

# Chapter 77

I coasted to the bottom of the canyon roads until the asphalt flattened out, and then I was navigating the sparsely trafficked nighttime streets. By now, my perspective had returned. I was living once again in my own body, seeing the world through my own eyes. I planned to zigzag my way in a southerly direction until hitting Santa Monica Boulevard. I would follow that as far as it would take me toward the cliffs.

With light traffic and pedaling at an unhurried pace, I figured I could be at my favorite bench watching the moon cast a reflection on the ocean below in an hour and a half. That was good enough for me. There was nowhere else in the world where I belonged. No one else in the world wanted to see me except for the lonely moon in the sky above. She was my remaining solace.

My mind wandered and drifted as I navigated the rain-slicked streets. The drivers were careless and honked at me frequently. The image of the moon grew large and full on the road ahead of me, accompanied by a horrible, almost-unbearable banshee screaming. I weaved in just the nick of time. It was then I realized that the blinding light of the moon was the oncoming headlights of a massive truck and the terrifying sound was not of a woman wailing, but rather the frightened driver leaning on the horn to alert me of his impending and potentially fatal contact.

I don't believe I was hit by the truck. I *really* don't. The pedaling became much easier after that. I progressed quickly down Santa Monica Boulevard and was pleased to find the drivers had become noticeably more considerate and kept their distance from me. I felt, at times, as though the tires of my bike were not even touching the ground. All the pain, confusion, and frustration of the last several weeks poured out of me, like I was a bucket with a hole in the bottom. I made great time; and from my elevated vantage, at least twenty feet above the boulevard, I saw the ocean expanding on the horizon in front of me.

I progressed through the quaint little city of Santa Monica and glanced over to see a billboard advertising a performance by Francey Pants & Dylo Beats. I was thrilled. I was genuinely thrilled to think that their show had gone so well, and they were now headlining at other venues throughout the city. I'd been angry earlier, but I couldn't even remember why. I wanted those two to light up the sky, and I knew that they would. They just needed a new bassist and maybe a guitarist who could play more than a couple of chords.

I hoped Naomi knew I was sorry. I really had learned so much from her in the past year. I'd resented her at times, but she was a great influence on me and had taught me about life more than almost anyone else I had ever known.

More than anything, I wished I could find Carey and tell her that she'd looked so cute in that red bodysuit. She had a beautiful body, and why shouldn't she show it off from time to time or even every day if she wanted to?

I passed high over Ocean Avenue and saw the Ferris wheel lit up and spinning a series of magnificent circles on the pier. I continued right over PCH and the sandy strip of Santa Monica State Beach until I was finally airborne over the Pacific Ocean. The sun had begun to rise in the sky, and the view was glorious.

Up, up, up, I rose as my figure became smaller in the sky. My upward trajectory tilted out toward the ocean, and from the ground, I became a small speck in the distant sky that barreled at an incredibly high rate of speed toward the horizon. The view of the ocean was glorious. I could see the curvature of the earth. I decided I could stay here for the rest of my life.

And so I have.

# Chapter 78

I've remained suspended over the Pacific Ocean for many, many years. I see things from up here that I have never seen before. I see *The Bird Goddess* from the sculpture garden flying past me. I see Featherhead and Lucky Lack. I see the three faces of Seneca orbiting around one another. I see Professor Opeyemi's oldest son laughing as he runs through a field.

I see a few of the PETS customers, and they look great. The open sores that had covered much of their bodies have healed completely as a result of the salty air. I see little baby Carina quite frequently, although she isn't a baby anymore. She's a proud and powerful woman. She keeps her eyes always turned down toward the earth below. I know she's watching Carey and taking care of her. One day, she whispered to me in a dream that Carey had forgiven me. I was so relieved that I cried.

I even caught a glimpse of Carey once. I forget exactly how I saw her, but in one single glance, I realized how shockingly beautiful she was. I had never seen it before, but she just had this glow about her. It was breathtaking. I think about that frequently . . . How had I missed it?

I see the wise and wry Sky Rider disguised as Dylan and even as myself at times. And finally, I see the blue hues of the beautiful moon in the sky, just as she had promised me.

And I think most of all about Francis. I recall the time when he told the girl from our BBX show (whose name I forget, but she was the funny one) that his stage name was Rocket. I think sometimes that his name *is* Rocket, and I stare into the horizon for hours at a time, hoping to see him blaze a new trail in the sky and maybe stop by to say hello for a while. I still remember the last email he ever wrote to me, and I wish I could go back and respond to it. I don't believe that these hundred thousand words will ever be worth just the three words that I should have written to him back then.

I don't know why, but I woke up one day and knew that I needed to tell this story. I needed to tell this story like I needed to breathe. I wrote a little bit every day. I wrote a few words on the wings of the birds that flew past me. I repeated this ritual every day. Eventually, I had written everything down, and my story had been told. The words have all flown away in different directions, but that doesn't matter *because my story has been told*. At least I don't put them in a cage.

I think about Professor Opeyemi and the question he used to ask us in that silly poetry class: "Why do you write?" I finally know the answer. Well, kind of. The truth is you never know *why* you write. But sometimes—and I do mean *sometimes*—if you put all of the appropriate words in a reasonable order and you are thinking clearly, then you may finally understand why you have written.

And that's the best that anyone can hope for.

## ABOUT THE AUTHOR

Tom Flynn lives in the San Francisco Bay Area with his wife, daughter, and their dog Mollie. *A Girl Named Dara* is Tom's first novel.

For more information visit: tomflynnbooks.com

Made in the USA
Las Vegas, NV
30 June 2024

91688024R00226